D1624049

Me, Governor?

Me, Governor?

My Life in the Rough-and-Tumble World of New Jersey Politics

Governor Richard J. Codey
with Stephen Seplow

Rivergate Books
an imprint of
Rutgers University Press
New Brunswick, New Jersey, and London

Second printing, 2011

LIBRARY OF CONGRESS CATALOGING-IN-PUBLICATION DATA

Codey, Richard J., 1946–
Me, governor? : my life in the rough-and-tumble world of New Jersey politics /
    Richard J. Codey with Stephen Seplow.
        p.   cm.
    Includes index.
    ISBN 978-0-8135-5045-9 (hardcover : alk. paper)
    I. Codey, Richard J., 1946–   . 2. Legislators—New Jersey—Biography.
    3. New Jersey. Legislature. Senate—Biography.   4. Governors—
    New Jersey—Biography.   5. New Jersey—Politics and government—1951–
    I. Seplow, Stephen.   II. Title.
    F140.22C63A3   2011
    328.73'092—dc22
    [B]
                                                            2010040713

A British Cataloging-in-Publication record for this book is available from the
British Library.

Visit our Web site: http://rutgerspress.rutgers.edu

Manufactured in the United States of America

To Mary Jo, Kevin, and Chris—thank you for your love and support.

To Mom and Dad—thank you for your love and support . . .
and thank you for your political advice.

My father told me to take President Lyndon Johnson's advice,
which was: never take a job from a politician because if you do
he will have you by your balls and your heart and mind will follow.

I would also like to acknowledge all those people who bought
this book half hoping their names were in it and the other half
hoping their names weren't. Either way, thank you.

Contents

Acknowledgments

I would like to thank a couple of people for their shared thoughts and memories in the writing of this book.

First, I would like to thank Stephen Seplow for helping to write this book and thanks to Flip Brophy, the agent who put me together with Stephen and then sold the book.

Thanks to the staff of Rutgers University Press, especially Marlie Wasserman, Marilyn Campbell, and copyeditor Alice Calaprice.

Christine Baird, who was head librarian at the *Star-Ledger*, and Michael Panzer, supervisor of the *Philadelphia Inquirer*'s library, made their archives available, which made the research a lot easier.

I would like to thank my current and former staff for all their support and help over the years: Maureen Roehnelt, Peter Cammarano, Kathy Crotty, Paul Fader, Joseph Fiordaliso, Ken Condon, Larry DeMarzo, A.J. Sabath, Eric Shuffler, John McCormac, Jon Boguchwal, Justin Davis, Erin O'Gara-Meier, Marion Wade, Stephanie Wohlrab, Bill Flannery, Sam Spina, Carmen Benitez, P. J. Cassidy, Patrick Gillespie, Francine Berra, Pat Collins, Jack O'Connell, Butch McManus, Rich O'Malley, Mary Brooks, Karen Kominsky, Yollette Ross, and Lynda Stoller.

Thank you to the Executive Protection Unit of the NJ State Police, especially Lieutenant Michael Brennan and Sergeant Michael Roberts.

I would like to also thank my running mates, both current and former: John McKeon, Mila Jasey, Pat Dodd, Mims Hackett, Eldridge Hawkins Sr., Mildred Barry-Garvin, Nia Gill, Leroy Jones Jr., Stephanie Bush, and Harry McEnroe.

Thanks to those who worked with me in the insurance industry: Charlie Grabowsky, Rob Parisi, Sean Codey Sharon D'Alioa, and Eileen Quigley.

Also thank you to Bob Crandus, Don Kaul, and Phoebe Wood, who read the manuscript as it was being written and helped to improve it. Fran Dauth helped immensely with her editing.

And to the dozens of people in and out of New Jersey politics who shared their thoughts and memories for this book, I thank you all.

Me, Governor?

1

"McGreevey's Gay, I'm the New Governor"

I probably shouldn't admit this, but I learned that I was about to become governor of New Jersey from a reporter.

"I have a source who tells me that McGreevey is going to resign tomorrow," Brian Thompson, of WNBC-TV News in New York, told me in a late-night phone conversation, referring to New Jersey governor James E. McGreevey.

If Brian was right, the president of the State Senate would become governor and that would be me. But I knew nothing about it. "Brian," I said, "what kind of marijuana is the source smoking?"

Public officials regularly resign from office and the vacancy is filled by the next in line. Christie Whitman, another New Jersey governor, resigned in 2001 after she was named by President George W. Bush to head the Environmental Protection Agency. But seldom, barring assassination, is the pending resignation a total surprise to the person about to be promoted.

"No Dick, I'm serious," Brian said on the phone, sounding a lot more excited than usual. And he pleaded for a straight answer because he was scheduled to fly to Madison, Wisconsin, the next day to see his mother. He wouldn't go if McGreevey were resigning. "Brian," I repeated, "I know absolutely, positively nothing about this in any way, shape, or form. I was just with him maybe ten days ago at the Democratic National Convention in Boston. I had dinner with him. Sat next to him. He didn't say anything about resigning." I advised Brian to make his trip.

At that point, August 11, 2004, I had been in New Jersey politics for thirty years, and frankly I had thought more than once about running for governor. But the timing never seemed right. I had even established an exploratory committee in 1988 to study my chances and they were pretty poor. Now wasn't a good time, either. It would unscramble my life, which was very comfortable, although Mary Jo, my wife, was undergoing some health problems. Anyway, I didn't really believe it.

McGreevey was elected to the New Jersey Assembly in 1989 when he was thirty-two, and then mayor of Woodbridge two years later, and to the State Senate when he was thirty-seven. (An oddity of New Jersey politics—not the only one—is that you may hold two or more elected offices simultaneously, as long as you can get elected.) McGreevey worked at politics the way any obsessed personality works at anything—frantically and without letup. There was nothing else in his life. No parade was too small, no political breakfast too early, no dinner too far away. He didn't even need an invitation. I told him a few times after he became governor that his maniacal running around was demeaning to the office; he was like a five-year-old trying to please the adults. Like any addict, he always nodded as though he were ready to kick the habit. Then he would do it again. He called me once in late October and I heard a lot of noise in the background. "Jim," I asked, "where are you?" He was marching in the Toms River Halloween parade. So much for my advice. He was extremely thoughtful about policy, but that was overshadowed by his need to be liked by every side on every issue.

McGreevey had been governor for less than three years. It was a job, I'm guessing, that he had been scheming to get ever since he was in high school, and certainly since his days as an undergraduate at Columbia University. Scandals had ricocheted around his administration almost from the day he was inaugurated, on January 15, 2002, but none touched him and I couldn't understand why he would give up the power and the glamour he so craved.

It was only through another New Jersey quirk (since changed) that I was in line to succeed McGreevey. New Jersey had no lieutenant governor, the official who fills a gubernatorial vacancy in most states. Under our state constitution, the president of the State Senate moved up, while still heading the senate. Not exactly a textbook example of separation of powers, but that's what the N.J. constitution specified.

The next morning, after a restless night, I had things other than McGreevey on my mind. Mary Jo was scheduled for bladder surgery—not major, but it's never exactly carefree when cutting is involved. I drove her to nearby Saint Barnabas Medical Center in Livingston and stayed until she was wheeled into the operating room. I told the doctors I would be in my West Orange senate office and asked for a call when the surgery was over.

Bedlam awaited.

Pete Cammarano, my chief of staff, a short roly-poly guy with a raspy voice who always dresses like it's a last-minute thought, had been on the phone for hours and pretty well had it figured out. Brian Thompson had called Pete the night before when he couldn't get me at first, and Pete didn't take it seriously, either. But when his first call of the morning was from a reporter asking about the McGreevey-is-about-to-resign rumor, Pete knew we were in for a hectic day.

He called Bill Maer in Trenton, an old friend of his and a political pro who had done some consulting work for me. Pete asked him to drive over to the Capitol to see what he could see. This was at 8:30 in the morning and he saw something he didn't expect: nothing. The governor's office is on the first floor, pretty close to the main entrance, and there are always people hanging around, moving in and out. Today there was nobody. It was, Bill said later, "like a ghost town. No activity. No movement."

When he finally found someone he knew, he was told that the governor's people hadn't been around for more than a week. They were hanging out at Drumthwacket, the official governor's mansion in Princeton. That was enough for Bill. He called Pete and said three words: "This is real."

Pete says he was frantically calling the hospital trying to get me into the office. A lot about that day has become blurry—it kind of raced along like a roller coaster while I just held on to the rail—and if anyone mentioned that Pete was calling, I don't remember.

I do know that by the time I got back to the office there had been two telltale calls. I was told that Jamie Fox, McGreevey's dedicated chief of staff, had phoned to Kathy Crotty, then executive director of the senate Democrats, meaning she made the place run when the Democrats were in the majority. She had worked in Trenton for years and knew everyone and pretty much everything. Jamie was asking about the rules for a gubernatorial resignation. Kathy, who had heard the same rumors as everyone else, called Pete to tell him about Jamie's questions. That's when Pete decided to cancel a planned trip to Disney World with his wife and two sons. His mother-in-law took his spot on the plane. He's still unhappy about that.

The other call was from Senator Raymond Lesniak, a close adviser to McGreevey, a good friend of mine at the time and a powerful political influence in North Jersey. Lesniak, who lifts weights to keep in shape, is the kind of outgoing guy who will proudly demonstrate his fitness by asking you to feel his muscle. He told Pete he needed to talk to me. Now. "This is probably the most important phone call of my life," Pete remembers him saying.

Lesniak was with McGreevey at Drumthwacket when I reached him. "Dick, he's going to call you in fifteen minutes," Ray said. "He's going to resign on November 15 and you're going to be governor. I'll talk to you about things later on."

McGreevey called at about 1:30. "Dick," he said, "I just want you to know that at 4 o'clock I'm resigning effective November 15. I'm sure you'll do a great job. You're well prepared for it and I think you'll be good at it. We need to talk. The only thing I can tell you is this guy is crazy."

By this time, I knew he was talking about Golan Cipel, although McGreevey never uttered his name. Cipel was the reason McGreevey was resigning—the reason I was about to become governor of New Jersey, a job that had been filled by giants like Woodrow Wilson and Tom Kean, and a few midgets as well.

One of the first things I did was try to alert Brian Thompson of WNBC News, since he was the one who had given me the resignation news initially. Coincidentally, his producer, Felix Martinez, was at my office in West Orange on another story and I told Felix to get Brian to call me. It was important. Felix reached Brian after his plane landed in Madison, and Brian called immediately. Within twenty minutes or so, he was on the air via phone, the first reporter to break the story that McGreevey was resigning and I would be governor.

And I wasn't all that happy about becoming governor. In fact, I was damn unhappy. I saw my life being ruined. Politically, I had gone through some very trying years, battling some of New Jersey's most potent political bosses, and I knew there would be more of that. My father, a wonderful influence on me and my two brothers and two sisters, had died of Alzheimer's at the end of 2003, and that was extremely painful. It's hard to watch someone who was dignified and well respected go out in such an undignified way. I always tell my kids inject me with something. What is the point of my life being prolonged if it's like that? Then my mother, a kindly woman to whom we all went when we needed comfort, died just a few months later, her body overwhelmed by cancer. Just two years earlier, Mary Jo, who had fought valiantly through traumatic postpartum depression and other psychological problems, had been in a coma and near death. After coming out of the coma—the extreme side effect of some prescription medicine she was taking—and recuperating, she developed breast cancer and needed a double mastectomy. So it wasn't the best time for me to start running a state that was in serious financial trouble and about to be roiled by McGreevey's resignation.

Besides that, the things I enjoy most—going to the movies and to dinner with Mary Jo; watching my sons, Kevin and Chris, play basketball; coaching an eighth-grade basketball team; going to Seton Hall games, playing golf, and following Rutgers football—all that becomes less personal and less enjoyable when you're being scrutinized all the time, like any governor is. My privacy was about to be shattered, and I didn't like that.

It didn't take long for that change to take place. When I drove to see Mary Jo at Saint Barnabas, a horde of reporters followed, a frightening sight the first time it happens. I always had a good relationship with the press, but I learned quickly why people like Princess Diana plot so carefully to avoid the paparazzi. They can be a pain in the ass. I even called the hospital and asked them to make sure none of the reporters got in. I figured for sure one or two would try to sneak into Mary Jo's room.

On the way to the hospital, with the reporters following, I called Maureen Roehnelt, who had been my executive assistant, scheduler, office manager, and everything else since I first joined the assembly in 1973. She was all excited, and I said to her, "Maureen, you don't know what you're in for." Six weeks later—I still hadn't officially become governor, but the calls and the requests for appointments were relentless—she walked into my office, looking haggard as hell, and said, "Dick, this sucks." Maureen died on November, 22, 2006, after a three-year battle against ovarian cancer. Coincidentally, she and my mother used to have their chemotherapy treatments at the same place every Thursday.

Mary Jo was in the recovery room when I arrived. The operation was successful. But when I told her about McGreevey's resigning and my becoming governor, she said, "Where's the anesthesiologist? Tell him to put me back under."

"You went into surgery a wife, a mother, a teacher," I replied. "You came out first lady. You had an extreme makeover."

An hour later, I asked if in her wildest dreams she ever thought I'd be governor. "Richie," she said, "you're not in my wildest dreams."

Driving back to the office, I tried to reach my sons, Kevin and Chris, both of whom were working at different basketball camps. I never did get Chris, who was then captain of the Montclair Kimberley Academy basketball team, but Kevin, who was captain of the Drew University team, claims I blurted out three short sentences: "Kevin, McGreevey's gay. I'm the new governor. I'll talk to you later."

Until late that morning, I still didn't know why McGreevey was ending his career. After all, this was a guy who quietly thought of one day running for president. I assumed he was depressed over some subordinates who were under investigation and facing possible indictment. Maybe he was being dragged in. I didn't know.

But when I learned the real reason, all I could say was "holy shit!"

I didn't know it then, but McGreevey and his closest aides had been debating their way to this day for three weeks, since Friday, July 23, two days before the governor flew to Boston for the Democratic National Convention that would nominate John Kerry. He says in his book, *The Confession*, that he knew intuitively on that Friday that his resignation was inevitable. Others, like Fox and Lesniak, have said they thought originally that he could crawl safely off the ledge and survive at least until his four-year term ended.

Maybe they were right, but politically McGreevey would have needed to be as surefooted as a tightrope walker to pull it off. And he wasn't.

It was 11:15 in the morning on July 23 when Golan Cipel's lawyer, Allen Lowy, called McGreevey's general counsel, Michael DeCotiis, and delivered the threat that, although never carried out, forced McGreevey on to that ledge in the first place. Cipel, according to McGreevey, threatened to sue the governor for sexual harassment and assault unless he was paid $50 million—later reduced to $5 million and then $2 million—to go away. No evidence of assault or harassment was ever put forward, and McGreevey has always insisted that their relationship was consensual.

McGreevey met Cipel, an Israeli, while on a trade mission to that country in March 2000. Cipel was thirty-two at the time, and McGreevey says in his book, "My attraction to him was immediate and intense, and apparently reciprocal." Which right there was unfortunate, since the men met only three weeks after McGreevey became engaged to marry his second wife, Dina Matos. McGreevey invited Cipel to the United States to work in his 2001 gubernatorial campaign. McGreevey says that it was in December 2001, a month after he was elected governor, that they began their homosexual affair.

I ran into McGreevey's father, whom I'm friendly with, and he said he thought I was better suited to the job than his son. "He was too immature for the job," the elder McGreevey said. Jim is very smart and well educated—a bachelor's degree from Columbia University, a law degree from Georgetown, and a master's degree in education from Harvard. But he is immature, and he has terrible judgment. He appointed some truly greedy and dishonorable people to high office, he allowed himself to be led by party bosses who wanted to control him, and, in one of the more extreme examples of bad judgment, he named Golan Cipel his liaison for homeland security, a job for which he had no experience, at $110,000 a year. Here's how bad McGreevey's judgment was: in choosing Cipel, an Israeli citizen, he chose someone who wasn't even eligible for a U.S. security clearance.

This drove the media and senate Republicans crazy; investigations were threatened, rumors about their relationship were flying. And McGreevey, instead of trying to calm things, bragged to the *Bergen*

Record about having an Israeli helping with security. That just created more headlines, and Cipel was forced in March 2002 to resign that job. McGreevey then gave him the title of special adviser. But the snide stories persisted ("they frequently travel together," wrote the *Record*, in describing their relationship), and people kept demanding to know what Cipel did for his money. By August 2002, the situation had become politically impossible and Cipel left government altogether. Thanks to McGreevey's connections, he was given some well-paying jobs with well-connected Trenton lobbying firms, none of which lasted long. McGreevey didn't do his reputation any good by interceding with lobbyists for his lover.

I never knew Cipel, but Pete tells this story about the first time he saw him. It was at McGreevey's 2001 campaign headquarters in Woodbridge, which was a vast space with no personality. Pete had gone over there for something, and he saw this goofy-looking guy playing nervously on a motorized skateboard. "Who's that?" Pete asked one of McGreevey's assistants. "That's McGreevey's gay lover from Israel," she said. Pete was speechless.

McGreevey's people spent a lot of time in the weeks after the first call from Lowy, Cipel's lawyer, in negotiations that went nowhere, and McGreevey was getting a lot of conflicting advice. Fox and William Lawler, McGreevey's attorney, thought they should report the incident to the FBI, but McGreevey wouldn't permit it. Some thought that when negotiations dragged on, Cipel would just forget about it and disappear. Some thought McGreevey had to resign.

Lesniak, McGreevey wrote in his book, thought the governor could "get rid of this" for less than $5 million and a confidentiality agreement. Any amount, no matter how small, would have had to come from outside sources. McGreevey had worked in government his entire life, and he had no money. A testament to his own honesty. As I told Lesniak later, I don't know how he thought he could have raised millions of dollars, paid off Cipel, and kept it all secret. It was ridiculous to think so.

There had been rumors about McGreevey's sex life for years. I once told him that every time I left my house someone asked about his sexuality. "What do you want me do?" he replied. "Hold a press conference and say I'm not gay?" Now, honestly facing his homosexuality for the first time, he was about to do just the opposite. With the whole business wearing on him and McGreevey growing tired of living in the closet—especially with Cipel threatening to open the door—he decided to hold a news conference on Friday, August 13, to say he was gay.

The press conference was moved up a day when McGreevey learned the story was beginning to leak. And despite Brian Thompson's call of Wednesday night, McGreevey and his aides insist that he didn't decide to resign until that Thursday, several hours before the press conference.

Shortly after 4 P.M., McGreevey made a six-minute, 690-word statement that was televised nationally. It was the talk of the country for days. "My truth is that I am a gay American," he said, and then he apologized "because, shamefully, I engaged in an adult consensual affair with another man, which violates my bonds of matrimony." Further, he said, "Given the circumstances surrounding the affair, and its likely impact upon my family and my ability to govern, I have decided the right course of action is to resign. To facilitate a responsible transition, my resignation will be effective on November 15 of this year."

He never mentioned Cipel, and he gave only partial answers to two crucial questions: Why did he resign rather than just announce that he wouldn't seek reelection, and why was he waiting three months to actually step down.

The answer to the first, as I understand it, is he feared impeachment—that Republicans would argue that the governor had appointed his lover to a critically important post for which he was unqualified, and impeachment was warranted. Actually, the post wasn't all that critical. Cipel was the governor's liaison for homeland security, not the person in charge of homeland security—a post held by Kathy Flicker, an assistant attorney general.

Christie Whitman, the former Republican governor of New Jersey, asserted on Chris Matthews's *Hardball* show that the homosexuality was just a cover-up; that the scandals were really driving him from office. To which Matthews said, "Only in New Jersey can that be a cover-up." He should have said that only in New Jersey could a governor resign because of a homosexual affair and be succeeded by someone whose first name is Dick.

The date of the resignation was a lot more important to me. It was the difference between my being governor for a few months or for fourteen months, enough time to get something done.

Under New Jersey law, had McGreevey stepped down more than sixty days before the next scheduled election, a special gubernatorial election would have been on that ballot. The deadline was September 3, sixty days before the November 2 presidential election. If he went past September 3, I would be governor from the day he resigned until his scheduled term ended on January 17.

McGreevey made his choice for practical reasons having nothing to do with me. There was some political calculation—given the odor emanating from his resignation, an early election may have benefited the Republicans, which he didn't want. And there were a few more things he hoped to accomplish, but most important were the personal considerations. He had to take care of the basics.

McGreevey didn't tell his wife about the threatened sexual harassment suit until a few days before his press conference. Who could blame him for wanting to put that conversation off? When he did tell her about Cipel and that he might have to resign, her first question was, "Where are we going to live?" I would have thought she would have asked something else—like whom do you love?

He lived at the governor's mansion; had no other home. He also had to find a job. He had been in politics his whole life and he had no money. He had already been divorced once and was paying alimony and child support; now another divorce with more alimony and child support was likely. Lesniak, a man of substantial means from lucrative law and other businesses, was there when McGreevey spoke to Dina. McGreevey says in his book that he asked Lesniak to join him at the last minute "as my confessor." Lesniak assured them both that McGreevey didn't have to worry about a job. But still, things had to get worked out.

Sometime during that day, Pete hustled me out for a late lunch at one of my favorite places, the Essex County Country Club. News crews had descended on my house and my office, and I needed to catch my breath. I was pretty confused and I told Pete about my fears. In retrospect, I was a little melodramatic, saying something like, "My life as I know it is over."

Chris, who was then a high school sophomore, got a firsthand example that evening of how things would change. I wasn't able to reach him during the day, and when he got home about 5 P.M., he found a horde of reporters, photographers, and television cameramen on the lawn and sidewalk. There were also a few state troopers assigned there already. Chris had no idea what was going on, but he immediately feared the worst—that something had gone fatally wrong with Mary Jo's surgery. He learned I was going to be governor by asking one of the reporters what he was doing on our front lawn.

Mary Jo's life would change also. She was in my office one day during the transition period and Pete took her aside and told her that she'd need a secretary. She said, "I have one. My secretary at school is the secretary for all the teachers." No, he said, "You'll need a secretary because you're going to be first lady." She thought the whole thing was ridiculous, but he was right. She got her friend, Beth, from next door, to do it, and being first lady and secretary to the first lady became a lot more demanding than either had expected.

Intermittently during that first day, I received phone calls from, or made calls to, people who have been political advisers and friends for years. I had habitually called political friends late at night almost all my career. It was a good way to test out ideas and get information. My habit went into overdrive that day.

The next morning, in the big living room at my home, we had our first organized meeting. Donuts and coffee were served. Pete was there, as well as John McKeon, the mayor of West Orange who is also an assemblyman and a comrade in political wars; Frank Baraff, a political consultant who has worked for me for more than twenty years; Larry DeMarzo, my former chief of staff and a good friend who left his private-sector job to work in my administration; Harold Hodes, a lobbyist who was chief of staff to Brendan Byrne when he was governor in the seventies and a close friend; Brad Lawrence, a political consultant who has also worked for me for two decades; Kelly Heck, the assistant communications director for the senate who would become my press secretary; and Bill Maer. One person not there was Joe Fiordaliso, my deputy chief of staff, who was vacationing in Bermuda. "I guess you want to go home now," Joe's wife said when he learned about McGreevey. He just couldn't get there fast enough.

Between calls from Pete and his son and a few other people, Joe's cell phone bill for the afternoon was $238. Which he remembers clearly.

The agenda had one item to be dealt with immediately and one that would be a constant for a week or so: how to reassure the citizens of New Jersey. The state was suffering through serious trauma and I needed to introduce myself and let people know that New Jersey was in capable hands. The other question was how to guarantee that McGreevey held to his decision to remain in office until November 15. This was a contradiction and I realize it. On the one hand, I was saying that I was not happy about becoming governor; on the other, I was prepared to do battle to remain governor as long as possible. In the end, the chance to do what I long figured I could do was irresistible.

McGreevey was under pressure from day one to resign quickly so that his successor could be chosen in a special election. In any such election, Jon Corzine, the senior U.S. senator from New Jersey, would have been anointed by party leaders to be the Democratic candidate. New Jersey in some ways is still dominated by old politics—medieval, some would say. There are twenty-one counties, and the party leaders in some of those counties can usually dictate party policy. They don't always agree with one another. But Corzine, who had been CEO of Goldman Sachs and was worth hundreds of millions of dollars, had contributed handsomely over the years to their county organizations. They would agree on him.

Not surprisingly, most of those pushing for a special election had their own agenda. Republicans, sensing a chance to regain the governorship, were yelling that McGreevey was denying New Jersey voters the right to elect their governor. Newspapers, like the *Star-Ledger*, and political science professors, all waving the flag of good government, also argued that New Jersey voters deserved an elected governor.

By Saturday, two days after McGreevey's speech, George Norcross III and John Lynch, the two most powerful Democratic bosses in the state, joined by U.S. Representative Robert Menendez, told reporters they wanted McGreevey out immediately. It was no surprise that Norcross, who controlled the Democratic Party in South Jersey, would apply pressure to keep me from becoming governor and get someone he thought he could control. Even though Norcross in many ways helped destroy McGreevey's administration, McGreevey thanked him in the acknowledgments section of his book. I can only guess why McGreevey may have owed him.

I always resented backroom bosses like Norcross. They wield a lot of hidden power over elected officials by controlling patronage, but they never face the voters and they are not a legitimate part of government. Norcross, particularly, loves power and he has a lot of it, with dozens of South Jersey politicians owing their careers to him. Because of that, he is able to "influence who gets hired, who gets contracts and whose legislation sees the light of day," according to the *Courier-Post*, the leading South Jersey paper. Both Norcross and Lynch knew they would have a lot less influence in Trenton than they were used to if I were governor.

Menendez, a Hispanic congressman from Hudson County, had a different motive. He wanted an election because he wanted Corzine's U.S. Senate seat if Jon became governor. Kenny, the N.J. Senate majority leader at the time and the Hudson County Democratic chairman, is close to Menendez, and he joined the resign-now chorus. Kenny would not have been majority leader without my approval, but I knew he was close to Menendez and had no choice. We are good friends and I knew it was difficult for him to do it. But I also understood the pressure he was feeling. It was strictly business, not personal.

Corzine, himself, got in the act on *Meet the Press* on Sunday, saying, "There's a lot to be said about an electoral process picking a governor, as opposed to having it be this constitutional format we have."

On our side, John McKeon contacted some of his friends in the legislature to ask that they not add to the pressure on McGreevey. Bill Maer also reached out to friends in the legislature, and I called anyone—and there weren't many—who seemed shaky. Pete met with some of the unaligned party bosses, urging them to stay clear of the whole thing. Lesniak, who was supporting me and really cared about McGreevey, went to see the governor. "I was a little concerned myself that he would cave," Lesniak recalled. "I went to see him to shore him up—to reiterate my assurances that he would have nothing to worry about. He saw the concern in my face and he said, 'They can drag my body through the streets of Trenton and I am not going to resign early.' That's when I was confident that he was there to stay."

I also made a few calls to labor leaders to stay out of it. I might have done more, but I was confident that McGreevey would hold his ground because of his anger at the bosses and his terrible financial situation.

As for introducing myself to New Jersey, Brad Lawrence came to that first meeting with some talking points. They started:

> Immediate message—The people's business comes first—
> D(ick) C(odey) is ready and able to keep NJ moving forward.

We all knew that was where I had to start. And there was general agreement that I needed to hold a press conference quickly. I was a well-known insider in Trenton and in my home district, but to most of the state I was no better known than a state senator from New Mexico. I wasn't thrilled about facing the press in the middle of one of its feeding frenzies, but it was necessary. We did it in the gymnasium at the Theodore Roosevelt Middle School in West Orange, where I have coached the eighth-grade basketball team for years, even while I served as governor.

It was the biggest media audience I had ever played to—and it was a little unnerving. I knew the Trenton press corps well, and whenever I met with the press I usually knew every reporter in the room. Here, there were reporters from all over the country I didn't know, and I wasn't prepared for all the cameras and all the shouting in that tiny middle school gym. I defended McGreevey's position, saying he was "simply following the constitution." When they asked if I was thinking of running for governor, I said, "It's something, really truthfully, I'm not thinking about." Earlier in the day, I had done an interview with Tom Moran of the *Star-Ledger*, and he asked if I thought of running against Corzine. "That would be like the Rockefellers against the Waltons," I said. "And don't get me wrong, I like him." Somewhere during the press conference, I said what I really wanted to say: "The state will be in very good hands." It wasn't my best press conference, but I got out alive.

Two days later, on the 17th, Pete got a call from Jamie Fox. McGreevey wanted to talk. A gaggle of print, television, and radio reporters were hanging out in front of the governor's office, waiting for any morsel. To avoid the scrum, we went from my second-floor office to the Capitol basement and up a back stairway to the governor's office. When we got there, McGreevey, uncharacteristically, was alone, and he asked Pete politely if we could have some privacy.

McGreevey looked glum, as anyone would in his situation, but typically he tried to put the most positive spin possible on the fact that he had just resigned as governor of the ninth largest state because of a gay sex scandal.

His first words were, "Free at last, free at last, O thank God, I'm free at last." I didn't know whether he meant sexually or governmentally. But I wasn't about to ask. I figured it was none of my business. (When I saw him again for the first time after almost five years, I did ask him which he meant. "Both," he replied.)

We spoke for about forty-five minutes and the transition almost never came up. Mostly, he wanted to talk about the bosses, how they were trying to force him from office and how much he hated them. "There's no fucking way I'm going to resign earlier," he declared, kind of his own primal scream of independence. He was about as angry as I had ever seen him. He had always cooperated with them. At the beginning, he met with Norcross and Lynch almost every Friday at the governor's mansion, listening to what they wanted, seeming to take orders from them. I used to tell him, "How does that look? I think you'd be better off image-wise meeting with the president of the senate and the Speaker of the assembly. Those other guys have no government role." It wasn't that I wanted to go to Drumthwacket every Friday, but it just looked awful. Now, true to form, when he couldn't do anything for them, they were trying to screw him. And truthfully, he couldn't resign even if he wanted to. "I don't have a job," he said. "I don't have a car. No income; no place to live." He had to get those things settled.

When our meeting ended, I walked out front and answered a few questions. I said we talked about the transfer of power, which was technically accurate, and left it at that. One reporter, Jeff Whelan of the *Star-Ledger*, was smart to be waiting for me by my car. But I didn't tell him anything, either.

Nor did I say anything about a meeting earlier that morning at my home with Corzine, one of several Jon and I would have about the next gubernatorial election. In the first week after McGreevey's announcement, I played golf a few times and tried to get away from the office as much as possible—the phone calls were incessant and I just needed to escape. Psychologically, a lot of people already considered me governor, and they wanted to talk about jobs and patronage and stuff I could do nothing about. In fact, one of my first executive decisions was to change my phone number. That, at least, cut down slightly on the calls from job seekers and favor askers. I knew from the start that I didn't want an elaborate transition process. I had seen governors come and go, and I knew all those transition teams are a façade. You waste a lot of time at stupid-assed meetings, which I really didn't have to have. And you piss off people who think they should be on the transition team but don't get named. Which is surprising, because most of the reports they write sit on a shelf and never get read. I may not be the biggest brain in Trenton, but after thirty years in the legislature, I understood state government well enough to take over without a tutorial. We told the press that we were having transition meetings and meeting with people in state government. We did have every department head prepare a book explaining what he or she was doing, and we carried those books, pretending they were important for the transition. But that was mostly for show because the press would have hammered me otherwise. They had never really tried to investigate me, and now that I was governor, they felt obliged to look for something—anything. Especially since they never wrote about the McGreevey mess.

McGreevey had a lot of good people, and even though I replaced some, I didn't see any reason for a wholesale cleansing. Besides, I was guaranteed only fourteen months in the governor's office, and it would have been hard to get qualified people for such a brief period. I'm not sure why, but there are twenty-two members of the governor's cabinet in New Jersey and only fifteen in the U.S. president's. I met with everyone in the McGreevey cabinet who wanted to stay. They were usually pretty quick meetings. Typical was the session I had with Devon Brown, the head of Corrections.

> *Me:* Commissioner, how you doing?
>
> *Brown:* Good to see you, Senator (or Governor, whatever he called me).
>
> *Me:* Listen, this will be short and to the point. If you think you need more time, tell me. Here's the skinny. You can stay on, but if there's a riot, you're fired. Do you think there's something you need to ask about now?
>
> *Brown:* No. I get it.
>
> *Me:* Okay, Commissioner, have a good day.

Well, damned if there wasn't a little riot at one of the prisons. At least, in my ignorance, I thought it was a riot. But I learned something. There's a state law that defines a prison riot by the number of inmates who participate or the number of officers injured. And, miraculously, Brown's final report came back one short in each category. So there was no riot and no new commissioner.

One cabinet member I did replace was Dr. Clifton Lacy, the commissioner of Health and Senior Services. I asked him if it were true, as I had heard, that he personally signed every one of the thousands of licenses dispensed annually to physicians, dentists, pharmacists, chiropractors, and who knows who else. He said yes, and I told him I thought that was a stupid waste of time for someone in the cabinet. He asked if that meant I didn't want him and I said, "Yes, that's what it means."

What really upset me about Lacy was that while serving as health commissioner, he was also negotiating to become head of the Robert Wood Johnson University Hospital in New Brunswick. "It doesn't look good," I told him. He got the Robert Wood Johnson job and then left at the end of 2006 to start an institute for terror and disaster medicine.

I also asked some of McGreevey's advisers to stay with me. One was Eric Shuffler, who, although still in his thirties, had worked for U.S. Senator Robert Torricelli (another Jersey politician forced to resign in scandal) and was then McGreevey's senior counselor. He agreed to remain after I said I would insist that he leave the office at a reasonable hour and make time for his wife and newly born son. I tried hard to make time for my family and I wanted everyone who worked for me to enjoy the same balance between work and home life. When

I became governor, I gave the people who did my scheduling a list of games my youth basketball team would be playing. "Work around it," I said. I also told them to work around the nights my sons played ball and the nights Mary Jo and I went to the movies or to dinner. Of course, there was always the understanding that if I urgently needed to be somewhere—and I meant "urgently"—that would come first.

In the interim period, McGreevey occasionally dropped by my house, sometimes to talk policy, sometimes I think because he was lonely. The last time he came with his daughter, Jacqueline, who was about two and a half at the time. Mary Jo was out and I told my son Chris that I needed him for babysitting duty. He spent a couple of hours watching *Sponge Bob* on television and he wasn't very happy with the governor-to-be. So I gave him a fifty after McGreevey left.

During the conversation, McGreevey said, a little sheepishly, that he accepted only $150,000 a year, instead of the $175,000 budgeted for the governor's salary. It was vintage McGreevey. He thought he'd get political mileage out of that, but nobody cared. He wound up only screwing himself and his family out of some much needed money. He volunteered to raise his own salary before he left so I wouldn't look greedy by taking the full amount. I said, "Don't worry. I'll take the full salary and that's that." The senate president, by the way, makes $65,000, and I could have chosen that instead of the $175,000. When a reporter asked me which one I was going to take, I said, "My mother didn't raise a dumbbell." (In truth, I took an additional $3,000 for the senate job because I would have lost a year on my pension if I didn't receive some salary.)

I thought during those conversations with McGreevey of the symmetrical political dance playing out. If I became governor because of McGreevey's poor judgment, he had become governor because of a deal I helped pull off on his behalf.

It was March 1997, and McGreevey was battling to win the Democratic gubernatorial nomination so he could run against Christie Whitman, the Republican patrician seeking reelection. On the day of the annual Senate Democratic Ball, our biggest fund-raiser every year, McGreevey called me at home in the afternoon, sounding depressed. "Dick," he said, "Tom Giblin [the Essex County Democratic chairman] told me he's going to support [U.S. Representative Rob]

Andrews for governor. And you know Hudson County is going that way, and they've convinced Tom to do that so there's no fight." Because Jersey party politics is still tightly controlled by old-fashioned county bosses, if he lost Giblin he lost Essex. And if he lost both Hudson and Essex, given the way other bosses were breaking, he was finished.

Essex is my county, and I told McGreevey, "I wouldn't worry about it. Just sit tight and I think I can help."

That night at the ball, I told McGreevey and his ally, Ray Lesniak, that I was going to tell Giblin that I was supporting McGreevey, and that I thought I could bring other Essex Democrats along. In the next few days, I spoke to a few local political leaders, including U.S. Representative Donald Payne, the only African American congressman from the state, and Sharpe James, the African American mayor of Newark who was also a state senator. James and Payne both believed that Andrews was too conservative for the black community and they came along with me.

Next, I called Giblin into my office, sat him down, and said, "Tom, here's the skinny: I'm going to support McGreevey. I've got so and so, so and so, and so and so willing to go with me. I don't want to pick a fight with you. This is not about you and me. It's about McGreevey and Andrews and who's the best candidate for us." He said he thought McGreevey was an empty suit who did nothing but attend functions, and I said he might be right but McGreevey could carry Essex. He said he'd get back to me.

Then McGreevey, Lesniak, and John Lynch came to see me. Lynch and I got along then because he was my leader and I was his assistant. He was always supportive, always helpful after he left the senate in January of 2002 and I became senate leader. In between, though, there were some problems.

Lynch was a McGreevey man in 1997 and in 2001—a relationship that changed by the time he tried to force him out so Corzine could become governor. Anyway, Lynch said if I could get McGreevey the organization's support in Essex, "we'll make a deal with you."

I said: "How far are you willing to go?"

Lynch said, "Dick, I'm looking to step down. I would support you for minority leader and so would Jim and Ray. You'd have the votes to be minority leader. And if we win the majority [which happened in 2003] you'd be possible for the senate president." I figured at the time that he would go back on his word in a second and connive to make someone else president if he thought he would benefit. But that didn't happen. Lesniak at the time promised to support me for whatever leadership job I aspired to, and he kept his word when Lynch and Norcross were trying to keep me from becoming governor. But that would not always be true in later years, when Norcross and Lesniak would become allies against me.

I said, "All right, but what can we do for Giblin?" Lynch suggested making him party chairman, a deal Giblin accepted a few days later. The Essex organization, as promised, threw its support to McGreevey. He won the primary and, in typical Jersey fashion, Lynch and Lesniak, almost certainly acting for McGreevey, had lunch with Giblin the next day and tried to dissuade him from taking the chairmanship. He says that they were as sympathetic as school guidance counselors, explaining that it was for his own good, that he'd probably hate the fundraising and dealing with the outsized egos who contributed big dollars to the party. I don't know whom they wanted to install as chairman, but Giblin told them he'd give the job a shot and they didn't get their chance.

McGreevey ran a terrific campaign and lost to heavily favored Whitman by one point. That set him up to get elected in 2001. But had he not won the primary in 1997 and come so close to defeating Whitman, he would not have been a candidate in 2001, when he did win. Which means he never would have been able to resign and I would never have succeeded him. So if you think about it, that deal in 1997 made us both governor. Which is a pretty good deal.

While we didn't have any formal transition teams, obviously I knew that in fourteen months there were only a limited number of issues we could really attack. The most pressing priorities were strengthening ethics and restoring confidence in government, getting control of the gluttonously unbalanced budget, and, my passion, improving mental health and health generally. This included some initiative on stem cell research. I put together groups to think about all of these things, and they were ready to go as soon as I became governor. I also got important help and advice from some of McGreevey's people, particularly Jamie Fox, who had a fundamental belief in the importance of government. But I pretty much knew what I wanted to get done, and we made progress on every item.

Which isn't to say I didn't worry about it. I'd wake up every night, thinking I had to do this or that, and write little notes to myself. Then, I'd walk to the door and put my notes there so I wouldn't forget them in the morning. Sometimes I would repeat this ritual three or four times a night. And Mary Jo was nervous about becoming first lady. I remember once, when the timing for the McGreevey resignation was still uncertain, she told me, "Richie, I was up at four o'clock in the morning worrying whether you're going to be the governor." I told her I was and she said something like "ugh."

As serious as this was for me, and for New Jersey, David Letterman managed to have a lot of fun with it. A few days before I was sworn in, he played a mock political commercial that showed McGreevey at a microphone, as though resigning, and me with my hand raised, as though taking the oath of office. Then a voice-over intoned:

> Governor Jim McGreevey is stepping down and senate president Richard Codey will be the acting governor through January 2006. Don't worry, New Jersey, Richard Codey loves to have sex with women. That's right. Your new governor is so busy getting his freak on with hot chicks that he won't have time to govern. The man is a heterosexual love machine. Oh yeah.
>
> A message from acting New Jersey governor, Richard Codey.

On the screen, meanwhile, the words "Loves to have sex with women" were scrawled across the bottom, while several shots of very sexy women were shown in provocative poses from the front and rear.

The audience howled, and I laughed myself. But my wife didn't see the humor.

Staying true to my values and keeping my sense of balance was going to be crucial to my sanity once I became governor. I wanted my swearing-in ceremony to tell the state something about who I am: another down-to-earth, middle-class guy from New Jersey with a wife and two kids, not very fancy and not very different from any other state taxpayer. For that reason, I decided to be sworn in at my home with just a few people around. There was only one reporter in my home, from the Associated Press, although many were outside. I also believed that an expensive inauguration would have been inappropriate. As I said then, "This is not necessarily a time for a big celebration."

I was to be sworn in at 6 P.M. and I asked Leonard Lance, then the Republican senate minority leader, now a congressman, to do it. I thought that would send the proper signal that government would be proceeding with harmony and some unity. Everything was on schedule until about 4 o'clock, when I realized we didn't have a Bible in the house, a fact that would have been disconcerting to my parents, not to mention my sister, Patricia, who is a nun. Patricia, incidentally, is also a lawyer, making her perhaps the only lawyer in the history of New Jersey to take a vow of poverty.

I sure as hell didn't know where to buy a Bible at that hour. Providentially, some priests who run Seton Hall Preparatory School, which is around the corner from my house, live across the street. I called the monsignor, Michael Kelly, whom I know well, and said, "Monsignor, you know I'm getting sworn in at 6 o'clock and I'd really appreciate it if you can come and say a prayer when I get sworn in. And if you don't mind, can you bring a Bible." I never doubted that he had one in his house.

The swearing-in actually took place at 6:20, and afterward I told the reporters on my lawn that "I'm looking forward to governing and bringing back calm, peace, harmony, and a sense of stability to the State of New Jersey. Coming out of the box you're going to see a different style, a different tone and a different focus as well." I took the oath on November 14, which was really a day before McGreevey's resignation became official. I was a little nervous, just like an athlete is nervous before a big game, but I was confident and ready to get started. My life changed forever, and I knew it would never be the same.

2

The Undertaker's Son

Death and Politics Go Together

I was twelve when I got my first important lesson in practical politics. Actually my first two. That's when I started directing traffic in the parking lot of Codey's Funeral Home in Orange, New Jersey, one of two funeral homes my father owned with his two brothers. The lot held about fifty cars, but if there was an overflow because some local politician, mobster, or other big shot was getting buried, we directed cars to the driveway of the house next door. If that was full, we sent them to the mammoth Saint John's Church parking lot around the corner.

But no matter how crowded it got, my father told us, "If a politician pulls up and there are no parking spaces, just find him one. If a priest pulls up or a minister, just find him a parking spot." So I learned early that there are spheres of influence, Caesar's and God's, and you have to take care of both. One other thing my father always said: "When you go into church, make sure you treat the janitor as well as the priest. He can recommend you for a funeral just as well." For me, that has translated into "every constituent is important; treat them all respectfully."

Had he wanted, my dad probably could have been a successful pol. He had a good touch with people, and he paid attention to local politics. Friends tried a few times to talk him into running for local office, but he always said no; bad for the bottom line. He figured that no matter what he did in politics he'd risk angering and losing half his potential clientele. But taking a cue from my grandfather, who was a fireman when he started the undertaker business (using the same horses to pull fire trucks and carry coffins), my father and his brothers ran the business like benevolent ward leaders. During the Depression, when families had no money, my grandfather buried their relatives without charge. Survivors remembered. Normally, an Irish funeral home like ours does Irish funerals and Italian funeral homes do Italians. But we did a lot of Italian business because grateful children of people my grandfather buried for free kept coming back. We even got some Protestant business. My father played golf with local ministers who recommended him.

Some of the Italian business did become a little shaky one morning when a hysterical Italian widow at the gravesite started screaming about wanting to jump in the grave with her dead husband. We had an old Irish guy who used to work for us—a guy we appropriately called the Ape—and my father told him to keep an eye on the lady and make sure she didn't do anything crazy. The Ape, who was hard of hearing, spoke unnaturally loudly, and he yelled back at my father, "Ah, fuck it, let the guinea drop in." That got some attention. I must say I never understood the appeal of being buried alive. The Ape, by the way, once directed a family to Portugal for a burial. The burial was in Poughkeepsie, New York, but the Ape told the confused family to go to "Portuguese."

The Ape may have lost us that Italian family, but my father did the little things that kept most customers satisfied. If you had a baby who died, he didn't charge. If you were having a party, he'd lend you the chairs you needed. I remember going to a customer to drop off some chairs. I got to the house, asked where to put them, opened the closet, and found ten other Codey chairs already there. He'd also lend you a limousine if someone in your family was getting married. My brother Robert used one of those limousines for his first date with the girl who would become his wife. When they drove away, all the neighbors called, wanting to know who died.

The family joke about my father was that if you wanted to find him at the beach you just had to look for the guy with a jacket and tie. Though, actually, that was one of the few places he didn't wear a tie. The tennis court, where he excelled, and the golf course were about the only others. He sometimes wore a tie to the track, which he and my mother loved, and he even napped wearing a tie. If some business walked in, he just slipped his jacket on and he was ready to meet. He often said any "boob"—calling someone a "boob" was about as judgmental as he got—can think about the obvious things; it's worrying about the small details that makes for success.

Possibly because of my father, possibly because an uncle on my mother's side was a city commissioner and later a local postmaster appointed by a congressman, I started reading the political news at a pretty early age. And, of course, there was the overriding influence of President John F. Kennedy when he ran in 1960. I was in an Irish grammar school run by Irish brothers. Kennedy was all you heard out of their mouths. There's no telling how many kids of my generation—and not just Irish kids—went into politics because of Kennedy. I even had a mock newspaper hanging in the bedroom I shared with my brother Donald with the headline: "Codey Wins in Landslide."

I was born on November 27, 1946—the day before Thanksgiving—and before I got into politics, which I did by the time I was seventeen, I had a terrific childhood, dominated by family, church, and sports. And, of course, dead bodies. The family was really two separate groups. My brother Donald is two years older than I, and brother Robert, two years younger. Then there was a leap to my sisters, Patricia, nine years younger, and Colleen, thirteen years younger. All except Donald were born in Orange. He was born in Missouri, where my father was an embalming instructor in the army. My father liked to brag that he spent World War II defending Missouri and you better believe there was never any trouble there.

One funny thing about the Codey boys, we all look alike: thinning light hair, oblong, almost pumpkin-shaped faces, and slight Elmer Fuddish features. Sounds pretty ugly when written that way, but we're really not too bad. We all found women to marry us. Robert, by the way, was born on July 4, 1949, and my mother was born on Saint Patrick's Day. In our neighborhood, her parade was always more important. And true to her Irish heritage, my mother was fanatical about Notre Dame football. Once fall came and you could smell leaves burning, you couldn't budge her from the television with a derrick if Notre Dame was on. She knew statistics, she knew strategy, she knew Irish football.

We lived in a cramped apartment on the third floor of the funeral home on High Street, a middle-class neighborhood, 80 percent Irish and Italian and about 20 percent African American. There was even a small Jewish synagogue on the block, but no Jews. They had all moved out by then, although some came back for Saturday services. Today, the neighborhood is almost all African American and Hispanic. The family still owns Codey's Funeral Home, although others run it, and business isn't nearly as good. Ask me what I remember most about my early years and I think of two things: heat and sports. The worst time was the middle of August, any August, when we were indoors. That's when the heat really got to us. In an Irish funeral home, the hours from 2 to 5 p.m. and 7 to 10 are sacred, reserved for wakes. Mourners have enough problems without hearing trucks rumbling by outside or kids playing loud music or romping around in their third-floor apartment. That meant all the windows and the door leading from the apartment had to be closed. No television and no music. And in our early days there was no air conditioning. When it was 90 degrees outside it must have been 115 inside. There was little to do but sweat—quietly.

With seven people in the family, there had to be military precision for everyone to use the one bathroom and get out on time. That often meant taking showers the night before, but even then, if someone got diarrhea two people could be late. My father, who had only a high school education and expected more from the rest of us, used to say we lived in the apartment so he could save money for our education—an area in which I'm sure I disappointed him. As a student, I was average. As a class clown, I was on the dean's list.

Saint John's Church provided one-stop shopping for the neighborhood: along with the church, there was an elementary school and a cemetery. By owning the funeral home, my father was kind of God's middleman. Like most Irish Catholic kids in the neighborhood, we just assumed Saint John's was our school. It was also our church, a soaring stone structure built in the 1860s with stone dug from a local quarry. Its steeple, rising high above the city, is the first sight you see driving into Orange. Inside, there are majestic stained-glass windows and vast religious paintings on the walls. The church is twenty-six rows deep, and when I was a kid they were filled for every

Mass. The congregation now is largely Hispanic and elderly white, and it's not as crowded. We ate Campbell's soup and fish sticks or tuna fish every Friday night (I don't know if my parents ever found out, but I confess to sneaking an occasional Friday night hot dog) and fasted until taking Communion on Sunday morning. So for us, the church was a singularly important building. We never missed Sunday Mass; my brothers and I were altar boys, my father belonged to the Holy Name Society and was an usher at the 10:30 Mass. One of us had to shine his shoes every Saturday night so he looked right. Even when we became adults, he wanted to know if we were going to church.

I always figured religion is personal and I don't discuss it much. I attend Mass now on a hit-and-miss basis, although I never made a conscious decision not to attend regularly. I say it interfered with political breakfasts, especially in the fund-raising seasons of spring and fall, but I know that's something of a cop-out. A lot of politicians manage to do both. And it's not that I'm not religious. I still say a prayer every night before bed. But it's not the focal part of life that it was for my parents. You might say I'm a practicing Catholic, but I've missed so many practices it's hard for me to get off the bench. Kevin and Chris didn't go to Catholic school. Mary Jo had a third-grade teacher in Catholic school who psychologically and physically abused her and she doesn't believe in Catholic schools. And none of them are religious. But without trying to sound holier than thou, I think there is a religious base to the issues I have fought hardest for, such as improved health care, especially mental health. At least Joe Delaney, my friend since childhood, a fellow altar boy at Saint John's and still a daily communicant, says he believes I was influenced by the religious education we received—love people and do some good with your life. But Joe always looks for the best in people.

In any case, school was always a lot less solemn for me than church. After fifth grade the boys and girls were separated, the girls to be taught by nuns, the boys by the La Salle Brothers. The Institute of the Brothers of Christian Schools was founded about three hundred years ago by Saint John Baptiste de La Salle with the mission of providing a Christian and humane education to the young, particularly the poor. In those three hundred years, the order learned how to be organized and how to be strict. Report cards were issued every Friday—a gold card was the best, then pink, blue, and white. White meant you failed four or more subjects. Your parents signed the cards and they had to be returned on Monday. I can remember more than once handing over blue or white cards to my father with my stomach churning. My father, a man of about five foot, ten inches and not particularly demonstrative, would take off his belt and threaten a beating. But unlike my older brother Donald, I never remember him using it on me. Robert says he got a white card once and he was scared as hell worrying about Dad's reaction. "I handed the card to him and he didn't say a word," Robert said. "I think he thought 'I could really destroy this kid.' He just made a face and walked away." Robert still shakes a little when he tells that story. For comfort at moments like those we would go to our mom, a saintly lady and a great nurturer. But a lousy cook. The joke about her was if you wanted to hide her Christmas present, put it in the oven. She'd never find it.

The only beatings I remember as a kid were the occasional smacks across the backside from the brothers. When you did something wrong, or if they just thought you did something wrong, you got called to the front of the room, you bent over and the brother whacked you with a two by four. The first time I got hit, I took my finger and I put some saliva on it. I put it next to my ass and then made believe the finger was sizzling from the heat of the blow. The brother, not amused, just said, "Bend over again." I assumed that was part of being an Irish kid. Almost everyone I knew got whacked by the brothers at one time or another. And I knew they must have been doing it for our own good because if any of us ever told our parents, which we didn't, we knew whose side they would take. Which was a good political lesson on the value of credibility.

From Saint John's, I went to Our Lady of the Valley High School until my father and the priests agreed that my clowning might be better appreciated elsewhere. Throwing frogs around a biology class with some friends was my final act as a student at the Valley.

From there, I entered Orange High School, the first public school I ever attended. But when I didn't do well academically, my father sent me to Oratory High School in Summit, a school of last resort for some of us. Although that was never acknowledged. My brother Donald says that I started building my political base by going to so many high schools and meeting so many new people. Danny DeVito graduated from Oratory a couple of years before me. There were two hundred kids in the school and only twenty lived on the grounds. He was one of them. I don't know what he did wrong, but it must have been big. I do know that Donald, also not a stellar student, was there with DeVito, and he swears that on the day before graduation DeVito locked the homeroom teacher in a closet because he and Donald and a few others wanted to leave and go to Aqueduct.

The three high schools, all beginning with the letter O, remind me of a time I spoke at Princeton University. "I almost was a student here," I said. "But I was four hundred points short on the SATs. And that was just on the math side." Then I said my father always tried to live up to his Irish heritage. "That's why the names of the three high schools I attended began with O. And if my dad had found another one in a reasonable driving distance for my senior year, I would have gone there."

When I was at Oratory my father made me contribute to the tuition. He had a minor interest in a small factory that made speaker cones for General Electric radios. It was in a converted house— another place without air conditioning. I got $1 an hour working on the machines in the summer, but it all went for tuition. By then, though, I was doing a lot more work for the funeral home and I got to keep that money—$10 for picking up a body and $7 to be a pallbearer. Fifty cents from every job went to the pallbearers' union. When I was a pallbearer or working the front door, telling people where their relative or friend was laid out, I had to wear a dark suit, white shirt, and black London Fog raincoat. Sometimes, if I was between funerals, I played ball in that costume. I looked stupid, it was uncomfortable as hell, and everyone else laughed at me. But there was nothing I could do. The good news, though, was that greeting mourners at the funeral home, when they needed sympathy and understanding, taught me a lot about dealing with people. I also learned to drive at the funeral home, parking cars in the lot.

After finally graduating from high school I went to Trenton Junior College, now Mercer County College. The school was next to the state house and I would go in there, walk up the stairs and sit in the balcony of the assembly and watch democracy in action. That was my first experience in the legislature. From Trenton I went to Fairleigh Dickinson University in Madison, but I quit a year before graduation. I was just too busy working for my dad and starting out in politics. When I finally went back and got my degree in education in 1982, I said I went to college for two terms, Johnson's and Reagan's. I studied education and worked for a while as a permanent third-grade sub at the same time I was in the legislature. I got the permanent job because when I subbed one day the principal listened in on the class, which I didn't know they could do. The kids were quiet, so they hired me.

Even beyond the funeral home, I was always pretty good at earning money as a kid. Coke bottles were valuable in a couple of ways. Empties returned to a grocery were worth three to five cents each, and I stalked the neighborhood collecting Coke bottles from trash bags. On Easter, I'd fill them with water, go to the cemetery and give them to widows to water the flowers at their husbands' gravesites. Of course, I made sure they understood I expected a little tip.

After school, I might hang out in the A&P for a couple of hours, helping shoppers carry their bags. And I once worked for a local guy who guessed weights and ages at local fairs. Customers paid him a dollar, and if he missed, the prize was a backscratcher worth about two cents. I collected the money and gave out the backscratchers.

When I got a little older, I worked as a part-time chauffeur for the very wealthy parents of the future governor Tom Kean. The guy who did limousine work for the funeral home had the Kean account, and I used to drive the Keans to the airport when they were flying off somewhere. When Governor Kean's son, Tom Jr., was elected to the State Senate, I told him that I used to chauffeur his grandparents. "I know you didn't get tipped," he said. "My grandfather didn't believe in tipping."

"No shit," I said.

Which reminds me of the time Senator Kean and I were at the same function and I told him that we had a lot in common: we were both raised in Essex County, we were both in politics, we both had ancestors who came over on a boat. "The only difference was your ancestors owned the boat," I said.

I always thought Tom Kean was a great governor and his son a very good state senator. I could care less that they are Republicans. I assume if your ancestors came on the *Mayflower*, you're a Republican.

Not surprisingly, the job that made the deepest impression was picking up dead bodies, especially after my father became county coroner. The coroner's job didn't pay, per se, but it was a very efficient referral service for funeral business, no question about it.

In the coroner's job you had to pick bodies off railroad tracks, pull them out of rivers, and perhaps recover them after crashes. By the time I finished, there wasn't any kind of death I hadn't seen—or smelled.

My first assignment was two dead bodies after an airplane crash. I went with a guy we called Walter the Ghoul, a big, strong, not-very-bright guy who worked for the county coroner. When we got to the scene the bodies were in the woods. There was nothing but charred stuff. The Ghoul said he would grab the head of the first body and instructed me to grab the legs. But you really couldn't distinguish anything. So I just grabbed what I could—and in those days you did it with bare hands, no latex gloves—and put it in the hearse. This was forty years ago and it's still a vivid memory.

My brother Donald says that he and the Ghoul went to a house once in East Orange to pick up a body that had been dead for several weeks. The deceased had owned a few cats that had nothing to eat but the dead guy. They picked up the body and left, too shaken to say a word.

Every June, sure as the Atlantic City boardwalk would get busy, I'd have to pick up a couple of bodies of kids who had gotten drunk or smoked some dope at a prom or graduation party and got killed in a car accident. This was before seat belts and I still remember one kid from Montclair whom I knew a little. He had flown out of his car and crashed head first into a tree. I've never quite gotten over that sight.

A couple of others that have stuck with me: a twelve-year-old kid had been playing in a creek when it suddenly came up real fast and he drowned. What hurt so much was that the parents were elderly, and they had this kid, their only child, late in life. They would never have another and the devastation on their faces was just searing. And then there was the man who dropped dead on Christmas Eve. My father and I picked him up, and as we carried him out past the tree, his kids were staring blankly, not quite understanding what had happened. It was snowing that night, a perfect Christmas setting—but not for those poor children.

One time, we were sent to a nursing home to pick up a body. The head nurse directed us down the hall and to the first door on the right. There were two beds with a curtain around one. We picked up the woman in the curtained area and put her on the stretcher. Which is when she woke up. We were like, "Holy shit." She sure looked dead. Before she knew what happened, we put her back in bed, pulled the curtain around and told the head nurse there must have been a mistake.

"Oh, no," she said, looking horrified. "I put the curtain around her so she wouldn't see you taking the other one out."

When you're around dead bodies all the time, you can get a little cavalier about death. Once, my father sent Donald and me to Baltimore to retrieve a body. By this time, we were a little older and, like our parents, we really enjoyed the racetrack. My uncle Eugene owned horses, and he named the first one after a daughter who was a nun. The name: Nun Better. I eventually owned a few horses myself. Anyway, we decided after picking up the body to go to Timonium racetrack in Maryland. In those days, you parked in the infield. So we parked the hearse, pulled the curtains around the body and spent three hours betting the horses. Only the corpse came out even.

Then, there was the Saint Patrick's Day—my mother's birthday—when a guy named Duke was working the day shift. My father had bought a corsage for my mother but he couldn't find it in the flower room. He asked Duke about it. "Oh, shit," he said, "I put it on the dead body." He had seen the corsage with no card attached, and assumed it was for a woman we were burying. The florist shop was closed and my father couldn't buy another one. So he just took it off the dead lady and told the family it was our mistake. I don't think my mother ever knew.

My uncle Eugene, who did the embalming for both the funeral home my father ran and the one my uncle Frank operated in Montclair, loved grilled cheese sandwiches. I would bring him sandwiches when he was doing some embalming in our basement. Without a second thought, he'd unfold the sandwich wrapping, lay the wrapping on a nearby table, and would eat while he worked on the body.

Once, at a cemetery, a priest asked me where he should stand. I pointed to some grass nearby. How was I to know the grass was fake and covering a hole? And the priest would fall in?

Mob funerals—and we did our fair share of those—were interesting because they were often held at five in the morning. That way the press didn't show up. And when any major mobsters showed up for a funeral they would never go to church for Mass. They would go to a diner for a cup of coffee with my dad and the pallbearers, always making sure to pay, and then show up at the burial.

For a time I thought funerals might be my career. I went to embalming school—the McAllister Institute of Funeral Service in New York City—the same school my brother Donald and my cousins Raymond and Eugene, Uncle Eugene's twin sons, attended. I was in the State Assembly at the time, but Raymond and Eugene had it much harder when they went. They were in embalming school during the day and law school at night, where, frankly, the workload was more strenuous than in the assembly. But they managed to get it done. Robert, by the way, did none of this. He couldn't stand the idea of dealing with death. Eventually we all went into different lines of work, and we all did pretty well.

Donald worked in the funeral home until he was almost forty, and then went into the racetrack business. He was general manager of Freehold in New Jersey, but is now retired. Robert is a retired prosecutor from the New Jersey attorney general's office. He had a nonpartisan job and served under Democrats and Republicans. My sisters Patricia and Colleen are both attorneys, Colleen with a major New York firm. Patricia is also a nun and does a lot of work for the Church. Cousin Eugene is the presiding judge in the civil division of the Essex County Superior Court. Like all judges, he is appointed by the governor for seven years. Then, if reconfirmed by the state senate, it's a lifetime appointment. And, hell, no, I did not recuse myself when he came up. Given that lawyers consistently rank him among the top three judges in the state, I think he should be on the N.J. Supreme Court. But no one appoints him because of his last name. They'd take too much political flak. Another cousin, Larry, one of Uncle Frank's sons, became president of Public Service Electric and Gas in New Jersey. He's happily retired and playing golf in South Carolina.

My cousin Raymond is the borough administrator in Madison, New Jersey. He, by the way, was inadvertently responsible for the one and only time I was ever involved in a bribe. Shortly after I was first elected to the State Assembly in 1973, Raymond decided to try his hand at politics and he ran in a mayoral primary in Orange. I was fooling around with a young lady at the time and one night she came with me to Raymond's headquarters, which couldn't have been more than fifty square feet, to address envelopes. Next to the headquarters was a Gypsy palm reader, and the young lady said she wanted her palm read when we finished at Raymond's.

I excused myself, walked next door and asked the palm reader, "How much?" She said $10. I gave her $20 and suggested what the lady's palm would probably reveal.

I learned that night why people give bribes. They work.

When we weren't picking up bodies or burying them, we were playing ball—basketball, the Codeys' favorite game—baseball, football, softball, even some golf and tennis, my dad's two sports. Sometimes, for no good reason, I'd challenge dad to a game of tennis for my salary. Not a good idea. My sisters were better tennis players than we boys. My mother bowled.

My parents bought season tickets to Seton Hall University basketball games every year, a tradition that continues. Between me and my brothers and sisters and cousins, the Codey clan has something like twenty-five seats for every home game. Even Mary Jo goes, but except for when our sons are playing she's not a big fan. Seton Hall basketball has become part of the family history. Donald was an assistant coach there for a few years in the 1970s, but he left, he says, because "Catholic schools in those days paid you in holy pictures." And my sister Colleen met her husband Ed at the Port Authority bus terminal in New York in 1993 waiting for a bus to the Meadowlands to watch Seton Hall play Saint Peter's. Seton Hall won and they were married six years later by Monsignor Robert T. Sheeran, the university's president.

It's odd that with all our devotion to the Pirates of South Orange, only one of us, Bobby, went to college there. He also graduated from

Seton Hall law school. My older son, Kevin, went to Drew, and my younger son, Chris, goes to Montclair State. But they root for Seton Hall.

When we were kids, we'd often get the bus on the corner and the train in Newark and head to Madison Square Garden for college basketball games, and occasionally we'd go to Yankee Stadium for a game. But mostly we played.

When there were no funerals, we used the parking lot as our own macadam athletic field. We played softball there, touch football, and basketball. Everybody played in the Codeys' backyard. It was a big piece of land, about seventy yards long and about half that wide, so there was a lot of room for games. For the most serious softball games, we moved to the church parking lot, which was bigger.

My father installed a basket on the side of the lot closest to the house. We'd have one-on-one tournaments like the NCAA. We did seedings, and I kept the bracket in a notebook. My brothers and I could all shoot long set shots. I used to say if the three-point play were in effect when I was a kid I could have played big-time college ball. But in truth, I was a slow Irish kid who couldn't jump worth a damn. But I was good enough to play for Orange High School. Unfortunately, every time I moved from one high school to another I was ineligible to play because of the transfer. I wound up playing for a great Police Athletic League team and had a terrific time. Everyone had a nickname then, and mine was "Bird," because I was so thin. No one but a guy nicknamed "Moose" would call me "Bird" today.

Dinner at our house was at 5:30 and we always knew when to come in by the huge, dictatorial clock atop the church. Nobody could get away with saying they didn't know the time. The rule in our family, like in a lot of families then, was that you had to eat everything on the plate. But if there were lima beans, I'd stuff them in my pocket as soon as my mother turned her back. No way I was going to eat lima beans.

We also developed our own indoor game of basketball in a shoe box. And it could get rough, like any other game when you're close in age and playing sports. We would cut out the bottom of a shoe box and tape the box to the top of a doorway. Then we'd shoot rolled-up socks off the wall on top of the entrance and into the box. The ceilings were only eight feet, so there wasn't much arc on the shots. We played in the bedroom I shared with Donald. The most conspicuous feature of the room was the dozens of college pennants hanging from the walls. That's how we learned the nicknames of college teams. How else would you know living in New Jersey that Gonzaga University in Spokane, Washington, and Drake University in Des Moines, Iowa, are both nicknamed the Bulldogs?

No matter how much time I spent playing games or reviewing box scores, I was addicted to politics. Some kids want to be firemen; I wanted to be a politician.

Frank (Pat) Dodd was my first real political mentor. A lifelong bachelor, he was handsome, charming, and an inspiringly talented ladies' man. He was also a political prodigy, elected to the assembly in 1965, when he was only twenty-seven. The Dodds lived a block from the funeral home, so even though he was about eight years older I knew who he was from the neighborhood. And when I was maybe eighteen I started hanging out in a bar he owned in Orange. Dodd's Bar was nothing fancy, but it became a hangout for young Democrats in Essex County. It's hard to imagine now, but Kennedy's Camelot legacy was still alive, President Lyndon B. Johnson was passing his Great Society legislation, and there was an idealistic sense that the world was about to be a better place. A meeting of the Essex County Young Democrats could attract five hundred people. It was the place to be. Most of the crowd around Dodd's was like me, middle class, in college and paying their own way, or starting careers, not demonstrating in the streets against the Vietnam War. But we still felt part of something important. And even though I was about the only one at Dodd's who didn't drink alcohol, I was eventually elected vice president of the Essex Young Dems. (Another place I went occasionally with friends was McGarry's, an Irish tavern in Orange. If I had just gotten paid I would buy a round for my friends and they would laugh when I ordered orange juice.) Pat Dodd used to hold regular Tuesday night meetings in the basement of the bar. We talked politics, traded ideas about issues, and looked for dates. I drove a green Mustang in those days—a great-looking flashy car—and that somehow made me seem more attractive. I paid $1,000 for the car and my father financed the rest. I put 120,000 miles on that baby, even going to Florida a couple of times, and it's still my favorite car ever. I'm a pretty conservative gray-suit dresser now, but in those days I favored navy and green plaid slacks with a blue blazer. I almost always wore a sports jacket when I got dressed, part of the habit of looking presentable at the funeral home.

In 1968, when I was twenty-one and still at Fairleigh Dickinson, I decided to run for Democratic County Committee. It was the only election I ever lost, but it was another good political lesson. I started at a serious disadvantage. I was put on the ticket with Jesse Gray, who had led rent strikes in Harlem and was running his own slate of delegates in the Democratic presidential primary. That was not a favorable association in my district, which was overwhelmingly white at the time. Then, you had to look very carefully to find my name on the ballot. It was like I was on the map—but in Alaska.

Late in the afternoon on election day, I got a limousine and picked up all the nuns from the church and drove them to the voting place. When the party leaders, who were supporting someone older, realized what I had done, they opened the machines and saw I was leading by five or six votes. They scoured the neighborhood, rounded up every stray voter they could find, and in the end I lost by four votes.

Next day, I defiantly went to the town clerk and haughtily said I wanted to protest. It was illegal, I argued, to open the machines before the election was over. The clerk, a man of long experience in Essex County politics, was very patient. "Kid," he said, "you're right. Let me give you some advice. Keep your mouth shut and next year, you'll be the choice." He was right and that was my welcome to the organization. By the time I finished my stint as a committeeman, I think I had made contact with every voter in my little district. I eventually was elected a ward leader and then party chairman in Orange. In those days, you could hardly get a government job without knowing someone in the party organization, so I started to learn about patronage and satisfying different interests.

I got my first mention in the *Star-Ledger*, the leading paper in Essex County, after my election to the county committee. The headline called me "A political pro at age 22." The story said I was "one of the youngest men to win an elective post in New Jersey," and would be coordinating Dodd's reelection campaign to Congress. It was actually to the assembly, and I really wasn't coordinating anything. Despite the mistaken view of many that the *Ledger* and I enjoyed a cozy relationship, it was not the last time the *Ledger* had an error in a story about me.

I started working informally for Dodd, traveling with him during the campaign and sometimes going with him to Trenton, where I was an "aide," doing what I could to be useful and learn about the place.

His running mate, also seeking an assembly seat, was a guy named Billy Fusco, a big gambler, and one of my duties was to get late scores for him from whatever games he was betting on. Once when I was working in Trenton for Pat, he sent me to get the bills he needed to see for the day. Somewhere along the way, I ran into Miss New Jersey and we were having lunch in the cafeteria when Pat tracked me down. I dated her once, a lot fewer times than the more powerful president of the State Senate. One time, I drove to the beach with another guy to meet Pat at his Shore house. We walked inside and he was in bed with a lobbyist for the New Jersey School Board Association. As the cliché goes, politics makes strange bedfellows.

I spent the next few years working for the Democratic Party in Essex, working for my father, and helping Dodd in the assembly. And in 1973, when Pat ran for the State Senate, he and a man named Nick Franco, another mentor who was Democratic chairman in Orange (I succeeded him when he died), encouraged me to seek Pat's seat, and both helped a lot. Franco was in the fuel oil business and he also owned a restaurant in Livingston where I hung out a little—for the waitresses, not the food. I was twenty-six. My opponent was George Minish, the son of U.S. Representative Joseph Minish.

The whole family, cousins included, got involved, making phone calls, hanging signs, stuffing envelopes, and generally working like hell. My father took out his records of every funeral arrangement he ever made for anyone in the district and called the family personally. And then he went through the phone book and made more calls. To be honest, sometimes he said he was me so voters would think they were hearing directly from the candidate.

I had the nod from the local organization, which was a big deal. The county chairman, Harry Lerner, pushed by Pat, put me on the party line because Orange didn't have any officeholders at the time. It was very ballsy of him to go against a congressman. Because of the Minish name I was still considered an underdog, but I won easily. I remember I lost West Orange, Minish's hometown, by only one hundred votes. I trounced him in Orange, my hometown. The campaign cost $10,000, which was pretty impressive, I thought.

The general election was a cakewalk. It was 1973, the year of Watergate, and it was the biggest Democratic landslide in New Jersey history. The Republicans won just fourteen of the eighty seats in the assembly. When I took the oath of office in January 1974, I was less than two months past my twenty-seventh birthday, one of the youngest people ever elected to the assembly at the time. As the youngest freshman, I was sworn in first and then had the privilege of administering the oath to the other members of the assembly. I was supposed to share that honor with Edward Hynes, a freshman from Bergen, who was also twenty-seven, but about six months older. But Hynes was in the lobby talking to some people and he couldn't be found. So they proceeded without him.

As Woody Allen says, 80 percent of success is showing up. Another political lesson I never forgot.

3

The Give-and-Take
of Politics

I hadn't been "Assemblyman Richard J. Codey" for too many years before I got a chance to participate big time in New Jersey's give-and-get political tradition. It was 1976, and Brendan Byrne, the popular Democratic governor who also happened to be from Essex County, was twisting arms and using all the political capital he could muster to get the legislature to pass the state's first general income tax.

The pressure to act was enormous. The New Jersey Supreme Court had just forced all public schools to close because the legislature had not allocated enough money to support an education bill passed the year before. The bill had been passed to comply with an earlier court holding that because of unequal property taxes, schools in wealthy districts spent so much more per student than those in poor districts that the whole system was unconstitutional. That, the court said, had to be rectified. The education bill was supposed to be the remedy. But when the legislature didn't appropriate enough to end the inequality, the court ruled no money at all could be spent on public education until the problem was solved. No money meant no schools. The proposed income tax was supposed to raise enough to close the expenditure gap and open the schoolhouse doors.

The tax was obviously needed and I favored it. The state's property taxes were already too high, murdering people on fixed incomes. And it was impossible for property taxes to go high enough in the poorer districts to meet the schools' needs. But even with the schools closed, the income tax was so controversial that Byrne agreed that it would end automatically after two years unless approved by the next legislature.

The assembly vote was going to be close; one vote either way could decide it. And I wanted something for mine. A new highway in my district, part of I-280, had no westbound exit in Orange, hurting business on Main Street, and causing some bad tie-ups. "I'd love to vote for the income tax," I told Byrne, "but I'd also love an exit in Orange." A day later, there was Alan Sagner, the state commissioner of transportation, at my front door. He just happened to come by to show me his exciting plan for a $560,000 westbound exit in Orange. I learned later it was one of many deals Byrne made to get that tax approved. Still, it took three votes over six days before we could get forty-one votes in the assembly, a bare majority. The lobbying on the floor was so intense that at one point Assemblyman Thomas Deverin, his face anguished, turned to his friend William Hamilton, the assembly majority leader, and pleaded, "You don't know what you're doing to me. Willie! Please, please, Willie! I can't." It was so painful that Assemblyman John Froude and I threatened to change our favorable votes to abstentions if the pressure persisted. The senate followed the assembly, voting 22–18 for the tax, making New Jersey the forty-third state to adopt an income tax. One newspaper, the *Herald News* of Passaic, ran an editorial listing those of us who voted for it. The headline read: "The Bad Guys."

The tax was made permanent a year later when Byrne was reelected and Democrats carried both houses. But even then, the senate passed it by only one vote.

And that's why if you're driving west on I-280 and you want to stop and look around Orange, you will get off on what the city council, in its wisdom, voted to name the Richard J. Codey exit. The sign, of course, was stolen long ago.

About five years later, I was campaigning for emergency call boxes on 280 in my area. The road was theoretically patrolled by the state police, but it was essentially ignored. This was before cell phones, so if a motorist got in trouble there was no way to call for help. Also, 280 passes through Newark, which scared the hell out of people from the suburbs. So with a reporter from the *Ledger*, I pulled over to a shoulder one afternoon to test how long we would have to wait before a trooper showed up. I never got an answer because I had to leave after an hour for an appointment, but that was long enough. After the *Ledger* story appeared, then-Governor Tom Kean called and said, "You'll get the phones, but politically in the long run it will hurt you." His point was that once the phones were installed I couldn't fight for them any longer and I'd lose an issue in the next election. But I found new issues and I never lost an election after that.

I was still single and living at home when I got to the assembly in 1974, although we moved that year from the funeral home to a huge Tudor house next door with imported marble and wood floors. The neighborhood was close enough and the neighbors good enough that my parents were able to buy the place from the Kildaires, two wealthy, never-married sisters, with a handshake. If the third-floor apartment was cramped, the house was as spacious as a ballpark. I lived at home because it was cheap and I was hardly ever there anyway.

In addition to the assembly, and the work I was still doing for my father, I was named to the Orange Housing Authority in 1974. Then in 1975, when Nick Franco died, I succeeded him as Democratic Party chairman in Orange. There were always a lot of benefits in death for me. I became ward leader when the ward leader died and city leader when the city leader died. We even made some money when we arranged the funeral for one of them.

The housing authority was great for my career. There were five commissioners and we ran the housing projects. A lot of people were trying to get into subsidized housing and I could give it to them. But the real bonanza came when we built housing for seniors, which was very much needed. In fact, there was never enough. You sold your house, you made a profit, you didn't have any more property taxes, and the rents were cheap. And it was secure because only old people lived there. It was a winner for everyone. To get in, you had to apply, which usually meant you had to know a politician. People did anything to get accepted, even change their opinions and their party. It was political nirvana. I was helping people and building a list of grateful constituents at the same time.

One thing I learned dealing with public housing: send a certified letter to a poor person and it's like sending it into outer space. They'll figure it's a bill and never open it. To deal with public housing people you've got to call on the phone.

If the housing job was terrific, being Democratic chairman of Orange sucked. Every county committee person wanted a job for himself or one of his kids, and it's not as easy as it looks to get jobs for people. (Sometimes, people I helped get into public housing decided they didn't want to be there anymore. So they also called for jobs.) Invariably, every election day, early in the morning, I'd get a call about some broken machine. "Why call me," I'd say. "I don't know how to fix the machines. Call the county." Then the party workers always bitched about not getting paid enough to get out votes. Local elections in Orange were nominally nonpartisan, so you didn't formally select candidates and run campaigns. The leader's job was to deliver big majorities for the Democrats running for county offices like county clerk, or the legislature, Congress, governor, senate, even president. In Orange, Democratic majorities came with the turf. It was the size that mattered.

But it was in the assembly that I found my career. I entered my thirty-fourth year in the legislature in 2008, the last member standing from the class of 1974. I never really made a conscious decision to stay this long. But it kept being stimulating because the scenery kept changing as I moved up from the assembly to the senate, moved into the leadership, moved into the governor's office for fourteen months, and before I knew it, I was the senior member of the legislature. I got into some interesting things, particularly mental illness, where I helped improve the lives of many patients and their families. And I really enjoy talking to constituents and trying to help them. But, truthfully, I have a lot less patience with the pettiness and the selfishness and the political deals people make to help themselves.

I had a chance in 1992 to run for Congress, but my kids were nine and five, Mary Jo had had serious problems with postpartum depression, and it wasn't a good time for me to go to Washington. Ten years earlier, I would have done it in a heartbeat. And if I had a chance to do everything over again, I'd probably try to do what Corzine did—make some real money first and then go into politics. Of course, if people could do the lives over you'd make a lot less money in the funeral business.

The legislature was a far different and less professional place when I got there. Staff and resources were minimal, almost nonexistent. My first district office was in the basement of Pat Dodd's bar; he was my mentor. My second office was a beat-up storefront on Main Street. Only two people worked there, Maureen Roehnelt, who had worked for Pat and then ran my office until she died of cancer in 2007, and Ken Condon, whom I called chief of staff (even though there was no staff), who dealt mostly with constituent requests. Ken left me in 1978 for a $7-an-hour job in the casino industry, but by the time he finished he was president of Bally's Atlantic City. Larry DeMarzo, who became a lifelong friend and adviser, succeeded Ken after he walked into the office looking for a bill he needed for a law school class at Seton Hall. Ken introduced him to me and we agreed that he seemed like a smart, knowledgeable guy who could be chief of our very small staff. I offered it to him a few days later and that was that.

Back then, we seldom saw bills before voting on them, and we had very little understanding of what we were voting for. People from the governor's office ran the caucus and pretty much dictated the agenda. Committee meetings, if the committee met at all, were usually held in secret. Now, everything is open, and professional staffs in both houses make sure everyone sees and understands proposed legislation well in advance of any vote. Lobbyists in those early days routinely gave legislators tickets for ballgames and took them to Lorenzo's, a popular Trenton restaurant, for lunch and drinks. Sometimes, the legislators never returned, and sometimes they returned too drunk to be on the floor of the New Jersey Assembly. They might be seen by kids on a school tour. So we hid them in the basement and someone else cast their votes. Everyone smoked—the bigger the cigar the better—and the Capitol was not air conditioned. As soon as it got warm, the place smelled like a backroom poker parlor in Atlantic City.

I don't mean to toot my own horn, which I'm not reluctant to do. But I knew the place better than most freshmen in 1974 because of my work with Dodd, and I had a good nose for an issue. By 1975, I was already sponsoring some legislation that was getting noticed.

I proposed one of my first bills with more than two hundred elderly Jerseyans in the gallery on what was known as Senior Citizens Day. It was to reestablish a Division of Aging to create a master plan for supplying support and services to seniors, and to answer their questions about health, housing, and other necessities. The bill became law and the division is still going strong in the Department of Health and Senior Services.

I successfully sponsored a bill, first proposed by Governor Brendan Byrne, allowing judges to sentence big-time drug pushers to life in prison. I got a lot of attention campaigning against the policy of some hospitals to distribute birth control pills to minors without parental consent. I lost my effort to legalize Sunday horse racing in the state, even though Jerseyans were driving to New York, Pennsylvania, and Delaware to bet the ponies and leave their money in those states. Eventually, though, Sunday horse racing was approved. And I went berserk—even wrote an opinion piece in the *New York Times*—over the state's Economic Development Authority's giving McDonald's a $47,000 low-interest loan to build two restaurants in New Jersey. McDonald's borrowing from New Jersey, I said, is like the Rockefellers borrowing money from the Waltons. Authority loans were supposed to help attract business that otherwise would not come to New Jersey. There are always a lot of people in New Jersey looking for a hamburger, and McDonald's would have built the two restaurants, loan or no loan. For the Authority to take credit for attracting McDonald's, I wrote in the *Times*, "is as ridiculous as for the weatherman to claim credit for a sunny day."

I also tilted at a few windmills in those assembly years. One example: I called for a constitutional amendment allowing local governments to charge for municipal services for tax-exempt properties such as churches, charities, and service organizations. Those organizations get a lot of services—fire, police, street lighting to name three—and they pay nothing. My idea was to tax only for services received, with none going to schools or county government. And the tax was to be levied only on land value, not the buildings, so as not to discourage growth and improvements. Well, it went nowhere. The churches lined up against it and no one wanted to ruffle the robes.

I also voted to decriminalize marijuana, a vote I'm not too proud of. It's not that I ever smoked the stuff. I was a young legislator, friendly with other young legislators, and I joined with them in voting for the decriminalization. But I've become convinced that marijuana leads to the use of harder drugs, and the state shouldn't be encouraging its use by making it legal. Anyway, the bill lost by 53–11, not much of a contest.

Most controversially, I sponsored a bill to reestablish capital punishment for people who kill on-duty police and firefighters. A broader bill passed both houses in 1977, but Byrne vetoed it. Capital punishment was finally restored in 1982 and stayed in effect until 2007, when for reasons explained later I led the effort to repeal it.

After a while, I began to get noticed in the press. Which was helpful politically and very good for my ego.

In October of 1977, *New Jersey Monthly*, a slick magazine with high-end advertising, included me in a list of "up and coming legislators." "At thirty, one of the most effective fighters in the legislature," the magazine said. "Rammed his death penalty bill through the lower house . . . . Demanded a state probe into the racing industry and got it. Demanded a tighter set of restrictions on lobbyists and got it."

Then, there was my favorite line: "Even if he is promoted to leadership in the future, Codey is too independent to be an administration puppet." I quoted that in a newspaper ad I bought for my reelection campaign the following month. I got 29,012 votes; the top Republican, 12,774.

A few months later, the *New York Times* wrote: "Assemblyman Richard J. Codey of Orange has shown signs of developing into a Democratic power-broker."

And by October 1979 *New Jersey Monthly* moved me up in class, from an up-and-comer to one of the ten best. They described me as "a quiet guy with the inscrutability of a mortician, which he is. He is also one of the least pretentious of the Bests . . . . Detractors say he gets impatient in committee, sometimes casting his eyes to the ceiling at a stupid comment or cutting off a fumbling speaker. Generally he has been quite fair, soliciting opinions from committee members and giving everyone a chance to speak. Inscrutable Richard Codey just has a low tolerance for fools." I campaigned on that one for years.

It was true, as *New Jersey Monthly* said, that I forced tighter restrictions for lobbyists, but it didn't take an ethical icon to know they were gaming the system and changes were necessary. Lobbyists have a legitimate function in the legislative process, making a case for their clients' interests. Sometimes, they'll even tell you something you didn't know and change your mind. Given the number of lobbyists, about 8.5 for every legislator, it must be very lucrative work. The New Jersey Legislative Manual for 2007 devoted forty-five pages to listing registered lobbyists, and only seventeen to the legislative Code of Ethics. I don't know exactly what that means, but I know that when you count salaries and expenses, more than $50 million a year is spent on lobbyists trying to influence government in New Jersey. It would probably be a lot more if we hadn't set limits, largely because of public pressure, on the money they can spend buying meals for legislators, handing out tickets to ball games, or paying for trips. All the lobbyists together now spend only about $20,000 a year entertaining legislators; as recently as the early 2000s, one guy alone, then-Assembly Speaker Jack Collins, a Republican, netted $15,207 by himself, largely on free winter trips to Florida to play golf. He didn't run for reelection after that was reported.

And to be perfectly honest, a few legislators can get pretty greedy with lobbyists. A favorite ploy is to ignore three or four phone calls from a lobbyist until he or she nervously comes by your office to ask why. "Been busy, " says the legislator, "but if you can make it to the $1,000-a-head fund-raiser I'm throwing next week, I'm sure I'll have time to talk." I can honestly say I've never pulled that stuff, but I know guys who have. Even for them, the money mostly gets access; it rarely flat-out buys a vote. And I'd be lying if I didn't say that during election season, I get on the phone and beat the bushes for money for Democratic candidates. There is also an annual Senate President's Ball meant to raise money. Getting Democrats elected was one of my jobs as senate president, and sometimes you just have to load up the coffers. Which is a lot easier when you control the agenda in the senate. Lobbyists, like everyone else, can legally contribute up to $2,600 to a candidate for a primary campaign and another $2,600 for the general election. That's $300 more than you can give a presidential candidate. And I still wish the limits were higher. I should mention that some of my best friends are lobbyists, although I think I'm as good at ignoring their pleas as anyone else's.

Anyway, lobbyists were doing some things in the 1970s that I thought should not be allowed. When things were a little slow, and money wasn't coming their way in the bundles to which they were accustomed, some would persuade friends in the legislature to introduce bills against their client's interests. They knew the bills had no chance, but they would be hired to do battle against this phantom threat and get paid handsomely for the effort when they won. A guy who represented some chemical companies was famous for this. I never heard of a legislator getting a piece of the action, but who knows? My bill forbade this charade, and if a large number of legislators were getting rich from the practice it probably would have quietly died.

The bill added a few more restrictions on lobbyists, but Byrne refused to sign the one I thought most important. It would have outlawed contingency fees for lobbyists—payment only in the case of victory. The obvious drawback to contingency fees is the overwhelming compulsion to offer a few bribes if your side is only a vote or two shy of victory. When Byrne declined to sign that part I stormed out of his office during the signing ceremony. "He said he doesn't see anything wrong with that," I yelled in disbelief to the reporters. I still don't know why he opposed it. But I'll say this for Byrne: the longer he is out of office, the better he looks and the more popular he gets in the state—and deservedly so.

A lot of other restrictions have since been adopted, and more are probably on the way. I've introduced a bill prohibiting all gift giving by lobbyists. It passed the senate, but not the assembly. But I think its time will come. The public is demanding it.

My committee on state government spent a lot of time on civil service questions near the end of my time in the assembly. But I lost one battle back then that I'm now glad I lost. New Jersey's civil service law granted "absolute preference" for military veterans—that is, any vet who passed a qualifying test for a job, regardless of score, moved automatically to the top of the list. Women's groups strongly objected on the obvious grounds that, given how few of them served in comparison to men, they were being discriminated against. I believed a better balance was to give all vets a minimum number of preference points, with disabled vets getting more. This would give them an advantage—but with limits. When we sent that bill to the full assembly we got our clock cleaned. The vote was 48–12 to retain the preferences.

I now think the assembly was right, at least for those vets who served on the front lines. They've earned the benefit.

Another proposal that got some attention would have allowed potential voters to register on election day—a process called instant registration. James Hurley, a Republican and assembly minority leader, made the most passionate argument against it. "New Jersey has had a reputation of being a corrupt state," he said. "Now we can have instant corruption—instant fraud." The senate passed the bill, but it never got out of the Democratic caucus in the assembly. Which had nothing to do with me—or the merits of the bill. Vincent Rigolosi, the Democratic chairman in Bergen County, decided the law could potentially help the Republicans and he ordered all Bergen assemblymen to oppose it. That did it in.

One thing that annoyed me when I came to the assembly was the paltry salary paid lawmakers: $10,000 a year. That's because the job was considered "part time." In reality, if you did it anywhere near the way you were elected to do it, the average guy didn't have time to get another job that would pay enough to support a family. The result was a legislature full of pretty affluent people.

I got an unexpected opportunity to fight for higher pay in June 1977, when I opened the mail one day and found a check from NBC for $10,732.80. I was flabbergasted. My only contact with NBC was several months earlier, and it was not very glorious. I was supposed to appear on an NBC program, but when I got to the New York studio they told me I had the wrong day. They sent me an expense check a few days later and that was the end of my television career for a while. But my name was still in the computer, and for some reason the computer thought it a good idea to send me check for $732.80 more than I made in Trenton. Of course, I immediately told the press, and I said I thought it disgraceful that we got paid so badly that this NBC check could have more than doubled my income.

Fortunately, I was never living on $10,000 a year. I made some extra money working for my father, and in the late 1970s I started selling insurance. Eventually, I started a brokerage business helping companies get the best deal possible on their medical insurance. I don't have any fancy house at the Jersey Shore or a home in Florida, but we're comfortable.

Anyway, I was able to use NBC's mistake as an excuse to get some publicity for raising salaries to $18,000. "Public service shouldn't be a financial sacrifice," I argued in introducing the bill. "The way it is now—with $10,000 salaries—all you have is legislators who are not truly reflective of the population because you have to be somewhat wealthy to afford to serve in the legislature." I won, giving us the first increase in a decade.

Salaries are now up to $49,000 for assemblymen and senators, and I received $65,000 when I was senate president. Legislative salaries haven't been raised in ten years and I don't see them being raised anytime soon. There's always a lot of yelling in some newspapers and among some constituents about legislators getting rich at the public's expense. I don't mind that as much as I do my fellow legislators who make demagogic speeches against any pay raises and then put the money in their pockets when the raises are approved. There's no law that says they can't give it back to the state, but they never do.

Sometimes in the assembly you help pass a bill that would embarrass you if they asked about it in a freshman political science course, but you do it anyway. Thomas Gallo, an assemblyman from Hoboken, retired at half pay in 1979 as secretary of the Board of Education. Tommy was still in the assembly, collecting his $10,000, but no one before had ever been on the state payroll while collecting a state pension. So James Bornheimer, an assemblyman from Middlesex and Gallo's drinking buddy, sponsored a bill which I and a bunch of others co-sponsored, allowing Gallo to keep his two paychecks. When Bornheimer was asked why he sponsored such a bill he 'fessed right up. "Tommy asked me to put it in for him so I did it as a favor," he said.

About the same time, Bill Perkins, an assemblyman from Jersey City, tried to reduce prostitution to a misdemeanor. His logic was simple: "You pay a girl for sex," he said. What's the difference with that and taking her out for dinner and a glass of wine and then expecting to have sex? Trouble was, no one wanted to test that reasoning on the voters in the next election.

And near the end of 1976, the committee I chaired on State Government and Federal and Interstate Relations got the assignment to write the bill that would bring casinos to New Jersey. That assignment came to define my assembly years.

I had never been in a casino, never shot craps, played blackjack, thrown a quarter in a slot machine, or bet a number at the roulette wheel. All the betting I had ever done was on the horses. William Hamilton was then Speaker, and he told me very practically, "You're single, you got a lot of time. I'm going to have your committee do the bill." He knew the process would take an enormous amount of time; no married guy could do it properly and also keep his home life happy.

Pat Dodd had something to do with my getting the chairmanship in the first place. As a compromise, he had been elected president of the senate in 1973, and I gained stature just by being his running mate and friend. To show off, I'd sometimes go over to the senate and stand on the podium with him. He'd whisper in my ear, as though we were talking policy, but really he was pointing out women he had slept with, and asking if I wanted to date any of them. He had advised me to try to make my name by taking over a committee, and my relationship with him helped me get one. Although when I first became chairman in 1976, there was no way of knowing that casinos were coming my way.

Atlantic City, with its once upscale Boardwalk, the Steel Pier, Skinny D'Amato's 500 Club with illegal gambling and featured acts like Frank Sinatra and Martin and Lewis, had been a fading resort for years. A "dowager," the newspapers said. Even Miss America was losing her popularity. Then in 1964, Democratic governor Richard Hughes and Republican political boss Hap Farley joined forces to persuade the Democratic Party to hold its national convention there. The theory was that people would see the Boardwalk on television, see the ocean, see the possibilities, and Atlantic City would be revived. The theory was wrong. What people really saw was a dying town going to hell, with hardly any good hotels and a lot of blighted neighborhoods. It would doom the old Atlantic City and start the search for something to replace it.

By 1974, Steve Perskie, an assemblyman representing Atlantic City, and Joe McGahn, the senator from the resort area, managed to get a referendum on the ballot to legalize casino gambling. Casinos would have been permitted anywhere in the state, provided the municipality approved, and they would have been state owned. It was blown out of the water. Two years later, with Perskie as the prime mover, the legislature agreed to a new ballot referendum, limiting casinos to Atlantic City under private ownership. As a tactical move, the referendum also said the proceeds would help seniors and the disabled pay property taxes, rent, and utilities. If the elderly campaigned for the referendum, its chances were greatly improved. Resorts International, betting that gambling was coming, had already bought one of the largest hotels in Atlantic City, the Chalfont-Haddon Hall, and an option on about fifty-five other acres. To back the investment, Resorts pumped a quarter of a million dollars into the "vote yes" campaign.

The referendum carried easily this time. And that's when the proposed Casino Control Act, establishing rules for licensing and regulating casinos, written by Perskie and the attorney general's office, came to my committee.

It was bill number 2366—a number many will never forget.

My goal was to produce legislation allowing the casinos to operate profitably, but with regulations so tight that the mob and other undesirables could not get in and bettors would be protected. I received quite an education along the way.

Resorts owned a casino-hotel in Paradise Island in the Bahamas, and before the hearings started, I flew down there to study their system, and to meet with Jack Davis, Resorts' president. When I came off the plane there was a guy waiting for me on the tarmac with a limousine. He was a little over six feet, 190 pounds, a full head of black hair and he went by the name of Jam Up. He was Davis's right-hand man for getting things taken care of, and he drove me right out of the airport. Jam Up did not bother with customs. When I got to my hotel room there was a basket of fruit big enough to feed North Dakota. A few minutes later, Jam Up called and asked, "Do you like the basket we left you?"

"Very nice," I said. "But I can't accept it."

He asked if he could take it home, which was fine with me, but he made me promise not to tell Davis.

I visited Davis in his office, which was in the hotel, overlooking the pool. Next to the swimming pool was another pool where the hotel kept a few dolphins. Some of the women sitting around the pool, practitioners of the world's oldest profession, were absolutely gorgeous and dressed in the skimpiest bikinis imaginable. Any skimpier, and they wouldn't have been dressed. "There's some nice talent out there," Davis noted, and I replied: "I can't disagree with you on that, Mr. Davis."

"Would you like to have some fun with the talent?" he asked.

And I, as indignantly as possible, said: "Mr. Davis, I never liked dolphins."

I didn't know it at the time, but Joel Sterns, a well-connected Trenton attorney who was doing Resorts' lobbying and legal work, had warned him not to offer me any bribes. "I told them you can't give him anything," Sterns later remembered. "It will come back to haunt you." As Sterns said, "Their business was comping. That's what the casino business is about."

In the Bahamas, paying off became as natural as tipping in an American restaurant. Hell, they couldn't get beef off the boat without paying someone. Naively, Resorts once asked to have a government representative present in the casino counting room to prevent skimming. Then they learned the government representative was skimming.

I paid for my flight, my hotel room, my meals (one of which was in the restaurant where James Bond dined in *Thunderball* and for everything else. Davis never outwardly offered anything, but I had the clear impression during my three days there that I could have had anything I asked for. Years later, Davis said the thing he remembered most about my trip was that "he wouldn't take anything. He paid for everything."

But they knew how to operate. Around 1985, Jim Crosby, the founder and chairman of Resorts, was dying of emphysema. He was in his fifties and an incurable smoker who puffed away even while on a ventilator. He was a big tennis fan and he flew to England for Wimbledon. But he could hardly breathe, and he couldn't walk from the parking area to the stadium. So Jam Up got a limousine, decorated it with the Bahamian flag, and persuaded everyone that he had the prime minister in the back seat. I'm not sure why the Brits believed the Bahamian prime minister was a white man, but they got very close to the entrance.

In addition to my trip to the Bahamas, I visited Nevada. Other members of the assembly, the senate, and a task force appointed by Governor Byrne visited casinos in Nevada, London, and Puerto Rico. Nevada was like old home week—almost everyone I met running casinos was an ex-bookmaker from New Jersey, some from my neighborhood. We took some heat for "junketeering," but in fact the trips really helped us learn about how casinos operate. When I got back, I put in my expense voucher, but the reimbursement was taking longer than usual. When I called to find out why, I learned that the auditors had some questions. I flew coach instead of first class, and so my expenses were a lot less than everyone else's who went. They wanted to know why. I think they hadn't seen a coach ticket in a long time and they were confused.

I was only thirty years old at the time, and I knew this would be an exceedingly important opportunity for me. Given the reputations of both New Jersey and the casino industry, I knew that the hearings had to be as open as possible, and people on all sides had to come away knowing they had been fairly heard. We held public hearings, calling people from all over the world to testify. Then we got a proposed bill, 2366, almost one hundred pages long, and we read through it line by line, and anyone who wanted—from Resorts, the public, a casino task force office—could ask questions and suggest changes. Then the committee voted on proposed amendments, and those we accepted were drafted into legislative language and we moved on. Overall, it took five months and a lot of patience before we were done. No one could remember anything that transparent taking place in Trenton.

Lobbyists, more comfortable out of the sun, were a little stunned. Davis, accustomed to dealing with a less than open government, was surprised. People like Perskie and Senator McGahn were not happy. They were in a hurry to get the cards dealt, to start revitalizing the crumbling city. Resorts had a hotel and was ready to start. McGahn's brother, Paddy, a guy with an outsized personality who couldn't help being a center of attraction, had headed the committee to bring gambling to Atlantic City and represented Resorts there. Resorts, which didn't miss many tricks, also hired Marvin Perskie, Steve's uncle, as another lawyer. But as Perskie later acknowledged, "Dick was right, dead right. It made the product politically bulletproof. When everyone had their say, no one could suggest the possibility that any games had been played or there were any special provisions for this lobbyist or that."

The whole process was very good for my ego. I was a kid, still without a college degree, and most of the casino big shots were a lot older and making big dollars. But I found out that I was as smart as any of them. I also should stop here to mention Wayne Bockelman, a policy wonk who was the legislative staff aide to the committee. Bockelman was the guy who actually read the bill, line by line, wrote the legal language for the amendments, and kept track of a million details. No one understood the bill better and no one could have been more helpful.

Davis was there almost every day during the hearings. If someone proposed something that he liked, he subtly nodded one way toward Sterns, his lawyer in Trenton, and if he didn't like it, he'd nod another way. Then Sterns stood and argued whichever way Davis wanted. I wasn't at the senate hearing, but I've read that a similar game of charades went on in the senate, with lawyer Paddy McGahn giving hand signals to his brother, Senator Joe McGahn.

There were hours of arguments about how to tax the casinos, where to invest the tax money, how strictly to control who could work in what capacity, which games to allow, how many hours a casino could operate each day, the rules for tipping dealers, rules on credit, rules on where alcohol could be served, how much square footage could be allotted to a casino and how much to other public spaces, such as restaurants and entertainment areas. After a while, as I said at the time, it became like a schoolyard shoving match: "Let's see who can be the toughest. I can be tougher than you." The State Commission of Investigation (SCI), which really didn't want gambling in the first place because it so feared mob infiltration, wanted regulations that probably would have made it impossible for the casinos to operate profitably. Every time we rejected one of its proposals or weakened it, the commissioners ranted about the politicians caving in. I really thought the legislation should cover just licensing and regulations and we should leave the business of casinos—hours of operation, the games allowed, etc.—up to the Casino Control Commission. But Byrne wanted those details in the bill and we wound up with more of that than I thought reasonable.

One of the big battles was over hours. The casino people wanted to stay open twenty-four hours a day, and frankly I had no problem with that. Byrne did. He was offended by the idea of people gambling through the night without taking a break to reconsider what they were doing with their money. Byrne, who could be stubborn as hell, was ready to veto a bill allowing twenty-four-hour gambling. So we compromised: the casinos could be open eighteen hours a day during the week and twenty hours on weekends and holidays. It's now twenty-four hours.

In the end, we passed what I called at the time the "finest measure of its kind in the world. It will stand the test of time. We have given law enforcement agencies every tool they need to keep organized crime out of New Jersey."

To be fair, not all law enforcement agreed. The SCI believed stronger measures were necessary to "more effectively dilute the threatened subversion of this new industry by organized crime and official corruption." And Jonathan Goldstein, then the U.S. attorney in New Jersey, was livid about the bill. "Casinos are good for the casinos and crooks and no one else," he said. He then turned down an invitation to testify before my committee, and that made me livid. "The committee asked Mr. Goldstein to testify," I said with as much sarcasm as I could generate, "but we're apparently not worthy of a response in a telegram or letter."

In addition to setting the hours, the bill also said casinos had to be part of hotels with at least 500 rooms, each room at least 325 square feet. By coincidence, that was the number of rooms at Howard Johnson's, and Howard Johnson's was owned by Perskie relatives. Nevertheless, an attorney general investigation found no problem. The hotel also had to provide public space for meetings, dining, and recreation. The space was determined by the number of rooms. The point of this was to revitalize Atlantic City as a general tourist and convention attraction and not turn it into one large casino. But 500 rooms was also something that Resorts lobbied hard for. Its hotel, the Chalfont-Haddon Hall, had more than 500 properly sized rooms and the requisite amount of open space. With some work, they could have stretched it to 750 rooms, and Senator McGahn raised eyebrows when he proposed that 750 rooms be the minimum. Byrne, who could recognize a hustle as well as anyone, said, "If somebody submits a regulation which favors 750 rooms, you've got to look and see if he represents someone holding 750 rooms." As it was, Resorts opened thirteen months earlier than anyone else and made more money than they dreamed of. The McGahn proposal might have kept competition out of the city for years.

One major provision: the casinos were to pay an 8 percent tax, to benefit the elderly and help the disabled pay their property taxes, utility fees, and other costs, plus 2 percent to be reinvested in Atlantic City or other designated areas of the state. The low tax was meant to entice more casino construction, which it did.

At my urging, all casino advertising carried the slogan, "Bet with your head; not over it."

The licensing procedure we adopted was far more stringent than Nevada's, and I'm proud to say there has never been one known incident of mob involvement in the casinos, although that cannot necessarily be said of the vendors.

There's one real interesting thing that I never understood for sure. Young assemblymen really have three different constituencies: the voters in the district, the party leader in the assembly, and the county party leader. In the 1970s, Essex County was run by a tough boss named Harry Lerner, who was eventually indicted for extortion, although the case ended in a mistrial. The only time he ever bothered me was when he said he wanted me to vote for the income tax. But during the casino hearing, he called again and said he wanted to have lunch. That was a pretty big deal. We got the pleasantries out of the way, and he said, "Young man, when do you think you'll be done writing this bill?" I gave him my best guess, and he said, "Okay," and then emphasized that he didn't want it done before some particular date. I told him not to worry, we couldn't do it that fast anyway, and he repeated: "You understand, you can't do it before then." I said, "Mr. Chairman, I understand. No problem."

I think he was a consultant to someone, claiming that he controlled me, and the longer the hearings went on, the longer he got paid. But I never knew for sure.

Because of the intense scrutiny for licensing casino employees, Resorts had not yet opened a year after the bill passed. The Chalfont had been remodeled, but the huge investment was sitting idle. The state also had a great deal at stake in getting at least one casino open for gamblers. To speed things along, Sterns came up with the idea of the Casino Control Commission granting a ninety-day temporary license. And Steve Norton, Davis's company calculator, responsible for working the numbers on everything, was playing tennis one day with Governor Byrne when he proposed the idea. Byrne went for it and signed the bill on March17, Saint Patrick's Day. Oddly, I drove with Perskie and a few other legislators to what was supposed to be a signing ceremony in Princeton, and then Byrne signed it in private at the governor's mansion. The Casino Control Commission granted the license in time for a Memorial Day opening in 1978. And then something amazing happened.

"When the doors opened," Gigi Mahon, a journalist, wrote in her book *The Company that Bought the Boardwalk*, an unflattering look at Resorts and New Jersey, "the scene was wild. People raced for the tables, pushing and maneuvering, desperate for a chance to leave their mark, in the form of a five or fifty or a thousand dollars left at the tables. The tables were jammed ten and twenty deep. You couldn't move through the aisles. The smoke was so thick; it was as if the place was on fire. The dealers were bewildered virgins, innocents in the way of gamblers." Gamblers were also unseasoned, and play was slow because rules had to be explained.

Lines of people, four and five abreast, stretched for blocks. Resorts sold tickets on the boardwalk to waiting gamblers, which got them into a disco or a theater and moved them to the head of the line for the casino.

To show how little we knew, in March 1977, just months before Resorts opened, Robert Martinez, then head of the governor's task force on casino gambling, predicted that a casino could expect to net $12 million a year on revenues of $30 million.

In actuality, Resorts won $233 million the first year, with pretax profits of about $135 million. No casino in the world had ever done business like that. At the end of February 1979, almost two years after the casino bill had been passed, the Casino Control Commission voted 5–0 to grant the permanent license. Seven weeks of hearings, declared Joseph Lordi, the commission chairman, revealed "absolutely no evidence of organized crime involvement" in Resorts. By then, Resorts was grossing $588,000 a day.

After Resorts opened, they had a "Salute to Hollywood" show with Janet Leigh and people like that. Jamie Lee Curtis, the daughter of Janet

Leigh and Tony Curtis, was also there and she and I danced. I was single at the time, but I was with two married friends and they looked very envious. They were not happy with me anyway. Not by coincidence, three hookers from the Bahamas were also at our table. I went up to Jack Davis and complained in my indignant way, "What's this shit? There are three hookers at our table." As always, he said he knew nothing about it and blamed Jam Up. My friends thought I had lost my mind.

I was also a great fan of Rodney Dangerfield. Something about his delivery and his "I get no respect" shtick made me laugh like hell. About two years after Resorts opened, we were holding hearings about raising casino taxes, and during a break I asked Davis, "How come Rodney Dangerfield never plays in your casino?" Davis said he never heard of him, and Norton said he wasn't good enough. But Davis told him, "If Codey says he's funny, we'll book him." Dangerfield got $10,000 and Norton said later, "He did a lot better than Dolly Parton." In fact, Dangerfield was the first act they made money on. I took a picture with Dangerfield and he said, "In another year that will be in an attic." I guess he thought even his photographs got no respect.

There was one additional battle with Governor Byrne, this one over the Casino Control Commission and its chairman, Joe Lordi. Both Byrne and I knew Lordi—and respected him—because he was the Essex County prosecutor for almost ten years before Byrne appointed him as the first chairman of the Casino Control Commission in 1977.

Some quick background. In early 1980, after an FBI investigation and sting operation—known as Abscam—nineteen politicians, many from New Jersey and bordering Pennsylvania, were indicted. FBI agents posed as wealthy Middle Eastern businessmen willing to pay huge bribes to politicians who could ease their path into various businesses, including the casinos. Videotapes were made of U.S. Senator Harrison Williams of New Jersey, the highest official nabbed in the scam, and others, taking money and pocketing it. One of the least known was Kenneth McDonald, a New Jersey businessman and a member of the Casino Control Commission. He was indicted for extortion, but he died of cancer in 1982 before his case was tried. There was subsequent evidence to suggest he may have been innocently lured into the scheme and never took anything. Williams bragged on the tapes that his influence with Lordi saved one casino $3 million. McDonald resigned from the commission two days after the story broke, but Lordi denied the accusation, and there was suddenly a lot of talk from Byrne and others about the need for a revamped casino commission to ensure its integrity.

Lordi was never charged with anything—Williams was just showing off—but Byrne wanted Lordi, the only full-time member, and the remaining part-time members to resign so he could appoint another commission, all full-time. I had no problem with a full-time commission or the other changes he was proposing, but I was adamant in insisting that Lordi not be removed. His reputation would automatically be destroyed if he were replaced because of Williams. "A man's integrity is not negotiable," I said, and I wouldn't budge. Neither would Byrne and it got real ugly for a while. As a headline in the *Star-Ledger* said in February 1980, "Codey Feeling the Heat from Byrne on Casino Bills."

What persuaded me 100 percent was when I went down to Lordi's house in Newark. We sat down, just the two of us at the kitchen table. He said, "I did not do what Senator Williams accused me of doing. I have done nothing wrong." That was all I needed to hear. As Patrick Breslin of the Associated Press wrote, "Codey did not want to carry the ax used to chop off the head of a political ally," meaning Lordi.

Byrne's attorney general, John Degnan, led the fight against Lordi. He was thinking about running for governor and trying to prove how tough he was. Byrne, coming close to going off the deep end, even threatened to close all the casinos if he didn't get his way by making sure licenses were not renewed. It took almost three intense months, but eventually a compromise was reached. Lordi would remain chairman of the new full-time commission for a period and then he would remain a member until his term expired on June 30, 1981. In fact, he remained chairman until that date, and I spoke at a dinner in his honor when he retired. So did Jean Byrne, the governor's wife at the time.

The Lordi battle, with its hint of scandal, attracted huge headlines for days. Lordi's appearance before my committee was even televised.

I learned then that a prosecutor with political ambitions can be a dangerous animal. I have believed since then that prosecutors should have to wait two years after leaving that job before they can run for political office. It's too easy for them to make headlines by going after prominent politicians. This is not a shot at former Republican U.S. Attorney Chris Christie, who did a great job on public corruption, prosecuting about 130 public officials, many of them Democrats, before resigning in November of 2008. He announced two months later that he would run for governor to unseat Corzine–which he did in 2009. I just don't believe Christie or anyone else should be allowed to do that. I finally introduced a bill in 2009 to bar state and county prosecutors, including the attorney general and assistant attorney general, from seeking elective office for two years after leaving their posts. We couldn't legislate about federal prosecutors, such as Christie.

At one point in the casino fights the Byrne people really angered me, accusing me of getting too close to the casino industry. As I said then, "I don't smoke and I don't drink, and when I go to Atlantic City, I go to see a show and I don't gamble. And I pay my own bills. Absolutely."

I always felt a little awkward arguing with Byrne. We lived near each other, he was a major figure in local and state politics, and he and my father played in a weekly doubles tennis match at a public course not far from our home. But that's politics. And I was a big supporter in 1981 of naming a new sports arena in the Meadowlands the Brendan Byrne Arena. I even wrote an op-ed piece in the *New York Times* about it. He deserved it for providing the leadership that converted the Meadowlands from an empty wasteland to one of the country's great sports complexes.

It was because of casino gambling that I almost lost Mary Jo. Sometime in the 1980s we were traveling to Nassau so I could attend a gaming conference. It was 6 A.M. on a winter morning (when else but winter would there be a conference in Nassau), my mother-in-law had come to babysit, a car had come to drive us to the airport, and we were walking out the front door. I remembered forgetting something and put the bags down to run upstairs for it. I came back, put the bags in the trunk, got in the front seat to talk to the driver, and off we went. At the terminal, I turned to say something to Mary Jo, but what I actually said was, "Holy shit, where's my wife?"

"Your wife was *supposed* to come?" the driver asked, a little astonished.

There were no cell phones in those days so I told him to haul ass back to the house. And being smart, I went immediately on the offensive. "How the hell did you do this?" I demanded. She said she had gone to the bathroom and we just pulled away. I thought she was in the back seat sleeping, but I never peeked in.

Luckily, there was no traffic at that hour and we made it back to Newark International in time for the flight. I don't gamble in casinos, but I know it's not a good omen to start off for a gaming conference by losing your wife.

———

The death penalty had been abolished in New Jersey thirteen years earlier, but there was about a murder a day in my district, and people, both black and white, wanted protection. I thought it just made sense that capital punishment would help deter some of these murders and save innocent lives.

By 1976, my bill called for the possible death penalty for the murder of police and firefighters and for any other murder committed willfully and with premeditation. It called for two separate trials, one to determine guilt, and one to determine punishment. A couple of weeks after I introduced it, a patient at Trenton State Psychiatric Hospital called my home and threatened to kill me unless I withdrew the bill. The police took it very seriously. When I had to go to Trenton, a trooper picked me up at home and dropped me at a remote spot where I got into another trooper's car. He then drove me to a third trooper, who drove me to the State House, where an undercover trooper stayed with me. They even followed me on all my dates, although the dates never knew. If we went to a movie, they just bought two tickets and sat nearby. It was a terrible way to live. One time in Trenton, the head of the Policemen's Benevolent Association, a big, gruff guy, told me, "Nothing to worry about." He had a gun and he had me covered. In truth, I was more scared of him than the guy in the hospital who threatened me.

I had forty-six co-sponsors, a majority of the eighty-member assembly, for the bill in 1976, and a *New York Daily News* poll showed 68 percent of New Jersey citizens favoring capital punishment. But Assemblyman William Perkins, the Judiciary Committee chairman and a staunch opponent, refused for more than a year to let it out of committee. He said he had "better things to do than sentence people to die." He noted once that I was in the funeral business and said, "I wonder whether it is the nature of Mr. Codey's business that gives this bill its urgency and makes him want its release." Good line, I had to admit. Byrne once joked that I had a conflict of interest in supporting the death penalty.

With so many co-sponsors I finally managed on October 7 to get the full assembly to order the bill released—although you usually don't like to run around a committee chairman like that. Byrne, who as a state superior court judge wrote a 1971 opinion that found New Jersey's capital punishment law unconstitutional, told a joint session of the legislature that he would sign a death penalty bill, provided it was part of an overall reform of the state's penal code. It was interesting. When he said he would sign it, there was enthusiastic applause. When he added that it had to be part of a penal code overhaul there was silence. The U.S. Supreme Court had suspended capital punishment in 1972, saying it was arbitrary and discriminatory in the way it was used. Four years later, it set down specific guidelines for making the penalty constitutional, and my bill was meticulously reworked to meet those guidelines.

After a somber three-hour-and-twelve-minute debate on November 22 (coincidentally, the thirteenth anniversary of John Kennedy's assassination), the assembly passed the capital punishment bill 58–16. We also approved broad penal reform in a companion bill. Before the senate took up the measure, I had to compromise on one major element. Senator John Russo, the bill's senate sponsor, wanted to eliminate the death sentence for accomplices to murder, which my bill allowed. With the senate vote expected to be close, I thought it prudent to give in on that. And the senate passed it with twenty-one votes, a bare majority. But Byrne, who fundamentally disagreed with capital punishment, vetoed the bill when opponents in the senate gave him an opening by not sending penal reform out of committee.

Byrne vetoed it a second time in 1978 for the same reason, but this time he really put some pressure on me. I introduced a motion that year to merge the death penalty bill with the one revising the penal code, which Byrne really wanted. One without the other, I said, "is like peanut butter without the peanuts." Just before the vote on my amendment, Robert Mulcahy, the governor's chief of staff, and Richard Coffee, the state Democratic chairman, called me into a conference and wouldn't let me out until I agreed not to lobby for my own amendment. They never threatened me that I remember; they never offered me anything. Neither was that kind of operator. As Mulcahy, who became athletic director of Rutgers University, recalls, "We just appealed to reason." Needless to say, my amendment lost. Byrne wound up signing the penal code revision and vetoing the death penalty. Capital punishment finally became law in New Jersey in 1982, when Republican governor Tom Kean signed it.

To give you an idea how adamant some people were about the legislation, one senator, Wally Shiel from Hudson County, complained that the bill didn't go far enough. How much further could we go than kill a guy?

Shiel, by the way, was also the Democratic chairman in Hudson County and a very powerful player. Once he asked me to meet him for lunch in Jersey City, the seat of Hudson County. He wanted to make a deal: If I could get the state senators from Essex County to back him for senate president, he'd get the Hudson County assemblymen to support me for house speaker. I said I thought that would be a tough sell for him, seeing that the then-speaker, Chris Jackman, was from Hudson. "If he doesn't do what I tell him, I'll break his legs," Shiel said as evenly as if he were telling me the time of day. I couldn't drive back to Essex County quick enough. And the deal never happened.

Despite Shiel's exuberance for capital punishment, there was some strenuous opposition from African American members. Ronald Owens and Eldridge Hawkins, both also from Essex, said history showed that capital punishment was used almost exclusively against blacks and Hispanics. Historically, they were right, but I didn't think that necessarily had to be true in the future. Anyway, the concerns were needless because the bill was never used against anybody. People sat on death row, but no one was ever executed. Appeals were just endless and, in truth, I don't think any governor really wanted to be the first to execute someone. I issued a moratorium against the death penalty in 2004 when I was acting governor, trying to figure out how much it cost to keep people on death row for no reason. And in 2007, as senate president, I co-sponsored the bill that made New Jersey the first state in the nation to legislatively outlaw capital punishment since the Supreme Court reinstated it in 1976. The 2007 bill passed the state senate with twenty-one votes, the bare minimum. That was the same number who voted for it in 1977.

Speaking on the senate floor in support of the repeal, I said I still believed society has a right to have the death penalty. But, I asked, "How can I argue the deterrent effect of the death penalty when we haven't had one . . . ? Don't tell someone that we're going to execute somebody when the reality is it's not going to happen—at least here in the State of New Jersey. Maybe in Texas. Maybe in other states. But it's not going to happen here in New Jersey and we have to accept that." So, unless the law is later changed, history will show that Ralph J. Hudson, electrocuted at Trenton State Prison on January 22, 1963, for murdering his wife, was the last man executed in the State of New Jersey.

I was grateful that Shiel wasn't around to threaten my legs.

And thinking of Shiel, another of my favorite Hudson characters was David Friedland, a very smart guy, but a very crooked one. Friedland was in the assembly when I got there, and then in and out of the State Senate before I arrived. He was gone because he was convicted in 1980 of extorting a kickback on a $4 million loan from the Teamsters Union pension fund, for which he was counsel. He started cooperating with authorities, wearing a wire and turning in corrupt politicians, in return for leniency. But even as he was working with the government, federal officials found evidence that he was involved in another scheme against the same pension fund, this one to defraud $20 million.

So in September 1985, weeks before he was finally to be sentenced in the first scheme, and while awaiting trial for the second, he faked a drowning death off Grand Bahama Island. It took more than two years for authorities to catch him, and then it was only because he had become too prominent running successful scuba diving shops and enjoying a flashy lifestyle in the Republic of Maldives. He even posed for a Maldives postcard. "If he had elected to become low profile, he might still be at large," the United States marshal for New Jersey said at the time. Friedland wound up spending about nine years in prison.

One other fact about my first few legislative years: I was, as far as I know, the only New Jersey assemblyman to help a couple from Philadelphia get married. They wanted the wedding in Atlantic City and they wanted it performed by a federal district judge from Pennsylvania, for whom the groom-to-be clerked. One big problem: New Jersey, for some long-forgotten reason, had a law against federal district judges performing marriages. I heard about this from the groom's parents, who lived in Essex County, and I introduced a law that allowed the judge to come to New Jersey and marry the couple. "Being a bachelor," I said, "I like to see someone else get married."

And then I saw the eyes.

4

Mary Jo

Love at First Sight

My friend Fran Fonzino was talking with two women on her stoop when I arrived. I was just back from a week in the Caribbean with a girl who was legal, but still pretty young. I was twenty-eight and she had just graduated high school. I shouldn't have done it, wouldn't do it today. But this was 1975. I met her when a friend asked me to speak to his high school class in West Orange, and she was a student who caught my eye.

Anyway, I dropped her off and drove to see Joe and Fran Fonzino. Joe and I grew up together and remained close; we still are. Fran and I became friends after they met. As I often did, I went there hoping for a good dinner.

I said hello to Fran, ogled the other women on the stoop, and went inside to wait for Fran. "Who is *that*?" I blurted out as soon as she walked in through the door.

"Which one?" she said.

"The one with the eyes," the most wonderful green eyes I had ever seen.

Turned out her name was Mary Jo Rolli; she was nineteen, she lived across the street from the Fonzinos, and she had a deal with Fran. Mary Jo studied education at Caldwell College and Fran typed her papers. In return, Mary Jo babysat for the Fonzinos' daughter, Tara.

I was infatuated immediately and it was obvious. In an unpublished autobiography called "Breaking the Silence: My Battle with Post-Partum Depression," Mary Jo wrote that she "noticed that after Fran introduced me he kept looking at me. Fran pointed to a better parking spot where his car would be more secure and he never even glanced away from me to the car. He just remarked, 'Forget about the car.'"

I asked Fran later if she could get me a date, but after a couple of days she told me it wouldn't work. "She has a boyfriend and it wouldn't be appropriate," Fran said.

"Listen," I said, thinking as quickly as I could, "we go out, I don't tell anyone. She's not engaged, so she could cheat a little." Mary Jo, who is almost without guile, wasn't really worried about any boyfriend. She just didn't want to go out with an old man like me. Especially one she figured couldn't be too interesting. Mary Jo cares as much about politics as I do mah-jongg, so when Fran told her I was an assemblyman, an office she had never thought about—maybe never heard of—she assumed I worked on an assembly line in Newark. And what kind of future was there in that?

Besides, she figured any honest twenty-eight-year-old man would be married and have a few kids. As I said, this was 1975. But I kept visiting Fran's place, always with donuts or some other little treat. Mary Jo was often there, and slowly she began to see the potential in an old man. "He seemed grounded," she recalled later. "Guys I dated in high school didn't have any ambition. They all wanted to go to California. To see the sunset." Fortunately for me, I didn't give a damn about California or its sunsets. Still don't.

It took a while, but by late summer we went on our first date, a double date, really, with Joe and Fran.

I was running for reelection in 1975 and Mary Jo reluctantly agreed to hand out some literature. But I knew she didn't have her heart in it when I asked her about a couple that was supposed to get some of her material. She said she guessed they were fine, but they weren't home. "That's surprising," I said. "They are both crippled and they are usually on the porch." Mary Jo just stammered something. She was really leaving the stuff on a table at school.

We double-dated a couple of times more with Joe and Fran, typically going to a movie and dinner. Of course, every time we did this, the Fonzinos had to get—and pay for—a different babysitter. Within a month, we were on our own and that was that.

We always looked like we were going different places. I was an assemblyman, dressed in a suit and tie, and she was a college student, dressed in shorts or jeans. Even now, she hates putting on dressy clothes. She's back in jeans as soon as she gets home from anywhere, and any jewelry she's wearing comes off before we hit the front door. We also had different interests. My two passions were—still are—sports and politics; she didn't care about either. She was studying education and that was what she cared about. But she was the pretty girl next door I always dreamed about, and there was no bullshit to her. She was not very cosmopolitan, as she says, but her looks and her honesty were seductive.

A perfect illustration is how she decided to go to Caldwell College, a small Catholic college for women. She knew about it only because she used to pass it on her way to a swimming pool she used every summer. She wanted to be a teacher and Caldwell had an education program. She never looked at another college. Later, she got her master's degree at Seton Hall, also right in the neighborhood.

She is the daughter of an Italian father, a grocer who ran a small market with his brother, and an Irish mother who was a nurse. Mary Jo, unfortunately, attended Our Lady of the Lake Catholic School in Verona, where she ran into Sister Steven Louise, a third-grade teacher who, in Mary Jo's eyes, relished shaming her students.

"One time when I didn't know my number facts, she began screaming at me and demanding that I answer the math facts," Mary Jo wrote in her autobiography. "She got me so frightened I wet my pants. . . . [Another time] I didn't know the answers because I was too shaken to think. She took my ponytail, wrapped her fist in it and slammed my head into the blackboard."

Sister Steven Louise is the reason our sons never went to Catholic school. She's also one of the reasons Mary Jo does not attend Sunday Mass, although she certainly hasn't abandoned religion. She prays often and profoundly feels that God has put her here for a purpose. But as for Catholicism, she says, "It's not like there are different degrees of Catholicism. You either pass or you fail. If you have to go to church every Sunday and not use birth control, a lot of us fail."

Anyway, we dated for five years before getting engaged. I can't say what took so long. I was living at home, no real responsibilities, comfortable as the proverbial pig in you know what. Also I had been engaged once before and that didn't work out. Most Sundays, I went to Mary Jo's place for her father's meatballs and spaghetti, and I always brought what her sister Susan calls "the same friggin' victory cake." Eventually, Mary Jo insisted that we had to get engaged if we were to keep going out. Fran drove me to New York to buy an engagement ring. Truthfully, I wouldn't know a diamond that came from a Boardwalk game in Atlantic City from one that came from a mine in South Africa. So I may have paid a little too much. What came after I gave Mary Jo the ring was completely unexpected—and prophetic.

She became seriously depressed, suddenly scared of getting married, essentially unable to function. She was teaching basic skills for first graders in Orange, a job she adored, but except for work, she could do almost nothing. She couldn't even decide whether she still wanted to get married. One day yes, one day no. This was something unknown to me and I never really figured it out. I mean, she's the one insisting we get married, and now that it's going to happen she's depressed.

For the first time in her life, she saw a psychiatrist. The doctor concluded she was afraid of leaving home because she had never accomplished her lifelong ambition of pleasing her mother. It was overwhelming to think that now she'd have to please someone else for the rest of her life.

All of this was going on as I was making my first run for the State Senate. Pat Dodd was retiring and he pretty much bequeathed the seat to me. But still, I had to run in the primary against two candidates and then in the general. I won easily, but Mary Jo played almost no part in the campaign. She couldn't do it.

Sometime during the therapy, which lasted about ten months, Mary Jo had an experience that she considered transformational, and it helped get her past the uncertainty. She had removed her engagement ring, threw it haphazardly on her messy desktop, and forgot about it. Four months later, she was in her room, lights off, and, she wrote in her autobiography, "prayed to God to help me make up my mind about marrying Richie." Her mother called her for dinner and, still in the dark, she reached out and her hand, as though being guided, landed on the ring. "That," she said later, "was like my sign from God."

We were married on November 28, 1981, two weeks after the election. We didn't even have the $60 to properly clean and preserve her wedding dress, but we were happy and her depression faded—at least for the time being.

We wanted a baby, but getting pregnant wasn't as easy as we thought it might be. It took us three years of trying, but it finally happened in January 1984. And then she prayed to God, first for a normal pregnancy and delivery, and then she promised that she would be the best mother possible and that He would never be sorry for the gift He was giving us. As I said, her faith was deep.

When Mary Jo first became pregnant I wasn't really thrilled, but then when Kevin was born on October 21 it was instant love. Not so for Mary Jo. From his first minutes in this world, her response to motherhood was gloomy and detached. It was like Seton Hall winning the NCAA championship and me not celebrating. Nobody would have predicted it. I was as excited as hell; but after nine hours of labor, when the nurse put our son in her arms she said she had no feeling. No joy. No relief. No love.

She didn't visit the nursery; she didn't want to feed the baby; she complained of pain all the time. She took the phone off the hook, refused to talk to anyone, and asked for no visitors. Friends sent gifts; she showed no interest. It was worse when she came home. Many days she wouldn't even dress or shower. We had a nurse to care for the baby, and Mary Jo stayed in bed the first week, with the covers over her head, never coming down to see Kevin. She looked awful. She was overcome with obsessive, depressive thoughts—"scary thoughts," she called them.

Here's her recollection: "I could see a glass in the sink and think, 'smash the glass and cut the baby's throat.' There were awful, aggressive thoughts like that up to fifteen times a day. Scary thoughts.

"Giving the baby a bath and washing his hair, a thought would just come into my head: 'Go ahead, cut the baby's throat. It will only take a minute. You are capable of making worse mistakes. Go ahead, make this one.'"

Mary Jo was initially too ashamed to confide any of this to her obstetrician. When she finally called him after about a week, he recommended Dr. Hilda Templeton, a psychiatrist who worked with postpartum depression. Dr. Templeton prescribed Xanax, and Mary Jo, feeling disgraced by her depression, was like an embarrassed teenager buying his first pack of Trojans when she went to get her medicine.

When after a few weeks she forced herself to go out with Kevin, she spent hours with her friend Wendy Natale, a fellow teacher who gave birth to her daughter Nicole one week before Kevin was born. Wendy had the warmth and joy that Mary Jo thought a new mother should have. She wanted Kevin to have a mother like that so she set out to give him one. If Wendy wanted to walk the malls, Mary Jo said fine. If she wanted to have pictures taken of the kids, Mary Jo had pictures taken. If Wendy wanted to enter Nicole in some kind of "most adorable" contest at Toys R Us, then that's where Mary Jo thought Kevin should be.

But then came that Friday night in January, the night she says she hit bottom, the "night I opened the microwave to see if I could fit the baby inside. This was it. I thought I had completely lost my mind." Kevin was three months old.

I kept repeating meaningless platitudes, like "hang in there; it will get better," but she knew better. That Sunday night, as desperate as she was, Mary Jo was tutoring Fran's son Michael at our house. Fran, like me, always believed the depression would just pass. Isn't that what always happened? But she was jolted when Mary Jo started mindlessly drawing pictures on her brown corduroy pants and revealing her "scary thoughts," as tears rolled down her face.

On Monday, Mary Jo called Dr. Templeton, and said she thought the only solution was suicide. That way, she couldn't hurt the baby. Talk about screaming for help. Dr. Templeton called me and said Mary Jo needed hospital care. I took Kevin to my mother's and the next morning I drove Mary Jo to the Carrier Clinic in Belle Mead, New Jersey. I was crying. I couldn't talk. Here I was, almost forty years old, my first kid is three months old and someone I love is severely depressed and going to a psychiatric hospital. Worse, she was telling me to file for a divorce and marry someone who would take good care of our baby. It was ripping my heart out, and all the time I was berating myself for not giving her the attention she needed. "You'll get better, you'll get better," I sobbed. And she said, no, she was a different person and she couldn't get better. She said she had taken good care of Kevin and now she was putting him in my care. I hugged her and said again, as defiantly as I could, "You'll get better."

After a few minutes in the Carrier waiting room, Mary Jo was summoned and I was asked me to leave. She later said that a psychiatrist asked her one question: "Did you have a plan to actually kill yourself?" She said, yes, she was going to put all her pills in some yogurt and take an overdose. "He quickly jotted something down in my chart," she wrote in her autobiography, "probably something like 'You're in.'"

There were visiting restrictions the first two weeks, but after that I drove to the hospital at least every other day. One of her roommates washed her hands a hundred times a day; they were raw, as though someone had slapped them repeatedly. I could take Mary Jo out, and we'd go for lunch, or to a movie, or to a hotel and make love. I needed the intimacy. She was going through the motions.

Mary Jo hid her illness so successfully that her sister Susan says she was shocked when their mother told her that Mary Jo was hospitalized. Even Wendy was surprised.

But she was no better when she came home a month later. The depression continued, so did the thoughts of killing Kevin. Dr. Templeton kept changing her medication, hoping to find something that worked. Psychiatric drugs are unusually patient specific. Lipitor will reduce cholesterol for almost everyone. But with psychiatric drugs, what helps one patient doesn't necessarily do a thing for the next. There's a lot of trial and error.

One night I came home and said as innocently as I could that I'd like a grilled hamburger for dinner. She always made a terrific medium rare hamburger. The stress of everything, though, was just overwhelming her. "How in God's name am I supposed to cook a hamburger on the grill with a baby?" she screamed. "Are you stupid or something?" I muttered something about hamburgers not being that complicated and walked upstairs. And one time, as I was talking on the phone with the governor, she yelled at me for ignoring Kevin. "I don't give a damn who called," she screamed. "Watch your son."

After ten months, in the summer of '85, the miasma lifted, like a storm cloud floating off. Dr. Templeton put Mary Jo on what's known as an MAO inhibitor—a strong antidepressant with potentially dangerous side effects, including stroke, unless the patient adheres to a very particular diet. In a matter of two weeks, she was back in the game, living with some energy, some joy. No more scary thoughts. I'm not sure she was all the way back to her old self, but the drug was a wonder.

Except for one thing: the medicine made her hungry all the time for the things she could eat and she ballooned to about a size 14. Not a subject I dared bring up.

Things were calm for the next couple of years. Mary Jo was teaching part time. My career was going well in the senate; I was moving up in seniority and influence. And most importantly, Mary Jo was not depressed. All was so well that we decided to have another kid. The first thing she had to do, though, was stop the MAO inhibitors; too dangerous for the fetus. Because she had trouble getting pregnant the first time, she bought one of those kits that tell you the best time to try to become pregnant. She called me at the office one day, full of energy, and said it was post time. I rushed home and smelled some wine on her breath. Neither of us ever drank, but someone told her that a little wine could loosen her up and help her conceive. I like to believe it was me, not the wine, but she got pregnant immediately.

This was September 1987. And by October, when she had been off the medication for a while, depression pounced again. Before I knew it, Mary Jo sunk back into the hell that consumed her after Kevin was born. Her enthusiasm disappeared. She became indifferent about work. By February, she was thinking again about hurting Kevin and suicide was on her mind. She ate almost nothing and lost weight even though she was pregnant. At times, I wouldn't leave the house without a friend or relative there.

Abortion was never an option for her; she wanted the baby too badly. But there were real fears about her killing herself. With medication not feasible and Mary Jo near her breaking point, Dr. Templeton recommended shock therapy. There were no guarantees, but all the evidence suggested that it wouldn't harm the baby.

The drive to Fair Oaks Hospital in Summit was brutal. I tried to make conversation; Mary Jo said only "yes" or "no." In the hospital, we were escorted to the shock therapy room which, bizarrely, was in a basement behind a hair salon. I told hospital officials that I wanted to be with Mary Jo during the treatment, but the psychiatrist tricked me into leaving the room by saying I needed to sign some papers and he jolted her while I was gone. I was livid. I found the psychiatrist, pinned him against the wall, and warned him: "Don't ever do that to me again. That's my wife, pregnant with our child, and I'm going to be with her." He took himself off the case after that.

Every treatment was the same. She would get jolted; her body would flop uncontrollably and then she would vomit on the way home. She felt useless and ungrateful for not being excited about the gift of a second child. She was supposed to have twelve treatments but we stopped them after eight because she had picked up a book written by a Fair Oaks doctor who was critical of shock therapy. It scared her. Already, there was significant loss of memory. She couldn't remember where her brother worked, and her first morning back at school she couldn't remember how to find the teacher's parking lot, or the names of her pupils. She tried to fake it for a while, but it was untenable, and in May she told her principal that she was having a difficult pregnancy and needed a leave until the following school year.

Despite all that, I thought the shock therapy did some good. She got through the pregnancy and Christopher was born on June 29, 1988—healthy and apparently unaffected by the therapy, although he does sometimes play according to his own rules. Mary Jo resumed her medicine immediately after giving birth and returned almost immediately to normal. You'd have thought she won an Olympic medal, she was so jubilant when she walked from her hospital bed to the nursery to get our baby and feed him. Just like the other new mothers. It was wonderful.

Mary Jo was in a room with three other women, two of them joyful after normal births, one despondent after a miscarriage. It broke my heart and I asked the nurse to put that woman in a private room so she could be alone with her family.

It was in 1984, when Mary Jo was suffering through her postpartum depression that, she decided, and promised God, that if she ever recovered she would tell her story publicly so others could know as much as possible about the disease and those gripped by it would know they were not alone. Mary Jo was angry even then that no one ever warned her or any new mothers that there was a monster out there—postpartum depression—and alerted them to warning signs.

By August 1993, she was ready to tell her story. Kevin was eight, Chris five, and she had told them as much as she thought they could absorb about the illness. That way they would not hear it from a stranger. She gently told Kevin that she knew she was sick because even though he had been a great baby, she was still depressed.

Kevin says that it wasn't until he was twelve or thirteen when he first really grasped that his mother once thought of putting him in the microwave to kill him. Mary Jo was driving him somewhere and, he recalls, "She was telling me how much she loved me and how much she went through to have me—all the doctors she had to see to get pregnant. And how long it took. And the struggle she had to raise me.

"As a twelve-year-old, to have your mother say she wanted to put you in a microwave—it was shocking. But it's impressive that she got through all that and was able to raise us. That was really the only discussion of it. I never discussed it with my brother and I never felt any anger for her. Although I do think that I would have had skin cancer had she put me in."

Anyway, when Mary Jo said she wanted to go public I called a *Star-Ledger* editor and told him that Mary Jo wanted to tell her story, and they sent a reporter named Joan Whitlow. Mary Jo thought she had to do it, even though she worried that school officials would not let her teach anymore and Cub Scout officials would make her give up the pack she led. That never happened, although I think she wished it had when she went to Cub Scout Camp and got lost in the woods after taking a shower.

In fact, she was stunned by the support she received. Personally, I am not comfortable with her speaking openly about the urge to put our son in the microwave. And her sister was so embarrassed that she wouldn't leave her house for a few days. But I never tried to stop her, just like she never tried to stop me from running for office.

She did a little speaking after Joan Whitlow's article appeared and she was invited, with Dr. Templeton, to establish a support group at Saint Barnabas Hospital for new mothers with postpartum depression. I was there when they announced it; a very proud moment. Mary Jo facilitated the group for a long time and it's still functioning.

But it was after I became governor that her profile soared. Just as people pay more attention to a governor than a senator, they pay more attention to a governor's wife. Even though she is never quite at ease as a public speaker—in fact, it scares the hell out of her—she sometimes accepted two or three speeches a week to mental health and women's groups. Her friend, our neighbor Beth Milton, who signed on as her secretary, organizer, and general helper when I became governor, kept track of it all. My office helped write a basic speech for her, but ultimately she hired a speechwriter, Catherine Carlozzi, who could travel with her and adapt the speeches according to the audience. But even as generous as Mary Jo is with her time, she had to refuse more invitations than she accepted.

Now that I'm no longer governor, her schedule is less hectic, but there's still a speech or two most months. And, of course, she still teaches five mornings a week. When I became governor, she asked if I thought she could continue teaching. I said I wasn't sure, and she suggested I think about finding myself a substitute first lady. That ended my doubts. She is just a passionate teacher, and after all these years, it's still fun for her to rummage around school supply stores for things she can use in class.

Wherever she speaks, and sometimes just at the movies or out for dinner, women come up to tell her how guilty they always felt for having depressive thoughts and to thank her for letting them know they are not alone. It's not unusual for me to come home and find some woman in my living room, crying, as Mary Jo tries to comfort her. Psychiatrists even ask her to talk to their patients. One woman wanted Mary Jo to take her baby until she got better. I put a stop to that one. The mother would come back and take the kid and Mary Jo's heart would be broken.

I couldn't keep track of the awards she won for her work, and neither could she. Her most important one came on April 13, 2006, when after years of advocacy, Governor Corzine signed a law requiring that new mothers be screened for postpartum depression and that pregnant women and their families be taught about the sickness. There is even a hotline that women can call when they need comfort in a hurry. Mary Jo has also testified before Congress in favor of similar legislation on a national scale. (She won a partial victory when Congress passed President Barack Obama's health care legislation, which included a provision sponsored by Senator Robert Menendez of New

Jersey that pregnant women must be taught about the illness. Disappointingly, screening didn't get through.) Once, Mary Jo testified along with Brooke Shields, another victim of postpartum depression.

When I spoke to Shields on the phone she offered to give me her cell phone number. "Miss Shields," I said, "you just made me the envy of every man in New Jersey." When Tom Cruise, the actor and proselytizer for Scientology, chastised Shields on the *Today Show* in 2005 for taking an antidepressant to treat her postpartum depression, I lashed out. "Tom Cruise knows as much about postpartum depression as I do about acting," I said. "He should stick to acting and not talk about women who need help." The headline in *People* magazine said: "Governor Defends Brooke Shields in Feud with Tom Cruise."

Mary Jo speaks out and gives speeches because she feels she must, but she hates large political galas. She feels she has little to say to the politicians and businessmen who are usually there, and she'd rather be home working on lesson plans. So I tell her which ones I think she really ought to attend, and she makes those. But I am very judicious.

Depression sometimes seems like a guerrilla army, springing up from nowhere, never defeated totally. And there was one more offensive against Mary Jo a few years before I became governor. It damn near killed her.

It started in January 2002, when, once again, she grew lethargic, didn't want to get out of bed, and felt herself slipping. By February it was worse, and Dr. Templeton, without any tests, increased her medicine dosage over the phone. Mistake.

On March 9, Kevin called and said, "Mom's fainted and the cops are here. "I got on the phone with an officer who told me that perhaps Mary Jo's blood sugar was low and he was taking her to Saint Barnabas Hospital. Good thing. She had had a minor seizure. But at the hospital, she suffered a grand mal seizure, losing consciousness and having wild muscle convulsions. When I got there, she had moved into the post-ictal, or post-seizure phase, yelling gibberish and still shaking uncontrollably. She was like the young girl in *The Exorcist* without cursing. Five people were holding her and strapping her down.

The doctor, fearful that something fatal was happening to her brain, wanted to put her in a coma to quiet her down and perform the necessary tests. I was afraid it was a tumor and demanded a CAT scan first. The wait was frightening, but the test was negative and the coma induced. Trouble was, no one could figure out what it was. It was Saturday, and no neurologist was on duty. One I knew was away. A local neurologist refused to come, saying why bother, he would be off the case by Monday anyway. I was angry enough to choke someone and I lodged a complaint with the hospital. Finally, a neurologist was tracked down at a dinner in New York and she rushed back to see Mary Jo.

She wanted to do some brain tests, but the only appropriate machine was being used on a young kid. Someone said they would get it, but I stopped them. I couldn't do that. Nothing was decided on that Saturday and the doctor said her partner would come the next day. He turned out to be the head of neurology at NYU, and he felt that the medicine prescribed by Dr. Templeton had caused a chemical disturbance and would probably work itself out of her system in a day or two. But when they started to take her off the coma-inducing medicine, her body reacted violently.

Now, we were in a life-and-death race. Every day she was in the coma reduced her chances of ever coming out by about 10 percent. She was down to about 40 percent when an anesthesiologist I knew slightly entered the case. He concluded that the medication that put her under was aggravating the serotonin level in her brain, and he slowly reduced the dosage. He said he wanted to give her two hours to see what happened, and he told me to squeeze her hand and talk to her. If the quaking resumed, though, he'd have to put her under again.

Sweat was pouring down my face. I had never been so nervous. Her body was flopping around, but less violently than a week earlier. About fifteen minutes before he was going to put her under, I said, "I love you. Do you love me?" I'm sure there were tears in my voice.

She moved her head up and down, "Yes."

The room was electric. Calm down, the doctor instructed, and squeeze her hand. About ten minutes later she was able to follow another simple command. Then the doctor gently removed the respirator. She tried to talk but couldn't; the respirator had burned her throat. Then the doctor asked for Kevin and Chris to come in, and those green eyes shone for the first time. The emergency was over.

Those few weeks took their toll on the boys. Mary Jo had collapsed in the kitchen while talking to Chris. Kevin, in the living room, heard her fall "like a ton of bricks," and Chris was screaming. Here's Kevin's recollection: "Before running in, I called 9–1–1. Then I ran into the kitchen and saw Mom. Her eyes were buried in her head. And then they came back. At the hospital, she was lying on a bed waiting for a room. She said, 'I love you guys,' and I said, 'I love you, too.' And then she had another seizure in the lobby." He says now that he dealt with it by sleeping twenty hours a day, waiting for someone to wake him up and say she was okay. "When she finally came out of it," he remembers, "it was amazing to see her—like she came back from the dead. No doubt, those were the worst two weeks of my life."

And he tells me now that it was all made more difficult because I didn't have any answers. "That scared me," he says. It scared me, too.

A few days later, she was taken from intensive care to a regular room, where therapy started. I walked with her every day as her legs started to regain a little strength. Her brain was also out of shape and it took a few days for it to start functioning properly. She had no sense at all of having been in a coma. When our friend Fran visited, Mary Jo told her that she thought I was losing my mind, that I told her she had been in the hospital for more than a week. She was incredulous when Fran stuck up for my sanity. Overall, she was in the hospital for three weeks and in a rehab facility for another week.

While she was in the coma, I stayed in the hospital pretty much full time. Monsignor Michael Kelly, the head of Seton Hall Prep, came by and prayed for her, and I cried while I watched. McGreevey came by to say hello. It was very thoughtful. He even assigned me a trooper, who drove me home every night so I could shower and change, and then he drove me back to the hospital.

At night, when the place was nearly empty, I'd walk around and I became friendly with a Jewish woman whose husband was dying. I brought McGreevey into her husband's room and he spoke Yiddish with her. He had learned just enough to make Jewish grandmothers love him. The woman's husband died about a week after Mary Jo got to the hospital. Her son acknowledged my presence at the funeral and thanked me for spending time with his mother. Sometime later, when I was governor, I received a letter from him saying how proud his mom was that there was a governor and a former governor in her husband's room before he died.

Then another family came in—half Italian, half Jewish—and the mother needed a liver transplant. I helped arrange a bed for her in a New York hospital. Her son was a rabbi and he asked if he could say a prayer for Mary Jo. I looked at him, I thought about Monsignor Kelly, and I said, "Please. One of you guys is probably right."

But all the prayers couldn't stop Mary Jo's bad luck. To guard against another seizure, she was taken off her antidepressants, which, predictably, brought back the depression. Then, a few weeks after getting out of the hospital a routine mammogram discovered breast cancer. It hardly fazed her. She was so depressed anyway that she couldn't get any lower. She cried a little when the doctor told her, but she said it was caught very early and he could almost guarantee that she would live to see her grandchildren. Because of cancer in the family and because she knew that she would be forever checking for lumps, she opted for a prophylactic double mastectomy. But she never shed another tear over it.

She was taking a light dose of chemotherapy—not enough to cause hair loss—but because of the continuing depression her doctors recommended that she discontinue the cancer treatment and renew shock therapy. This time, she underwent twelve more shock sessions. I was then co-president of the senate, and to keep people from knowing, and the press or others from showing up, we'd go to the hospital at 4:30 in the morning, check in under a fake name, and she'd get jolted. I made sure to be there for each one.

It took six months for her to function normally after that, but she got there. And in a few years she was testifying before Congress. Hard not to love her. After all the suffering she wakes up every day, never cranky and with a great, positive attitude.

One thing I'm personally proud of: I think I gave my kids a good memory of how devoted I was to Mary Jo, a lesson they can emulate later.

Gratefully, the kids were never teased about their mom's illness, even after I became governor and the story became general knowledge. "It was not an embarrassment," Kevin says. "I am proud of her. She helps a lot of people."

I also learned a lesson. The State Senate was then split 20–20, and I served as co-president with Senator John Bennett, a Republican. But some backroom guys who were political opponents were maneuvering to get a few Democrats to switch their votes to give Bennett a clear majority and the senate presidency. Nothing came of it, partially because Bennett refused to go along. But someone asked me at the time how I was holding up, and I told him, "When your wife is in the hospital and your children ask if their mother is going to die, everything else is a piece of cake."

5

Family

From day one, from the moment I first saw red-faced Kevin in the hospital, I took fatherhood very seriously. Maybe it was my age, thirty-eight, pretty old for a first-time parent, maybe my upbringing, maybe something in my genes, but I was insanely excited. I knew a lot of politicians who neglected their families, too consumed by meetings, campaigns, events, and everything else to pay attention to their offspring. No matter what I did professionally, I was determined to be different.

When the kids were small, even before Chris, the younger one, could read, I started writing them short notes about things they did or we did together. I hid them in a folder, figuring the boys would appreciate them more when they were older. Or maybe I thought they would bring back memories when I was gone. Or maybe I wanted to make sure I had a way to remember those times.

The earliest notes were written in November 1991, when Kevin was seven and Chris three. The first to Chris said, "Today, Kevin helped you put your coat on and walked you out the door to go to pre-school. I hope you two are always close. Love, Dad." I also wrote a note to Kevin the same day telling him that "I watched with great pride as you helped Chris get his coat on to go to school. I hope you always show that kind of love toward Chris."

A note to Kevin a month later reveals a lot about what bound us over the years. "Today, you finished your first Pee Wee basketball at the Boys Club in Newark," one said. "You were very proud of your trophy. You were the best dribbler there for your age. Love, Dad."

A couple of my favorite notes:

To Kevin in 1994: "Tonight, mom & I and you and Chris went to the movies together and afterwards to dinner. We do this a lot and I love to be with my family."

And in 1995, I wrote almost identical notes to both boys: "Tonight [we] went down the street to see Seton Hall Prep play. As always, we had a race down the street. These times are very special to me. I wish these feelings could just stop in time. Love, Dad."

Sports, basketball particularly, are a big deal for me and the boys. I played high school and PAL ball and I love the game. Kevin was shooting hoops in the backyard by the time he was three; same for Chris. Then they played in Little Lads leagues, Pee Wee leagues, AAU leagues, and a few more. I coached their teams from the fifth to eighth grades—and I still coach youth teams. Kevin went on to play for Montclair Kimberley Academy and Drew University. Chris played for Kimberley, but not Montclair State, where he is a student.

Which is to say, Kevin and Chris played a lot of games in a lot of places. And I don't think I missed a half dozen total. As I said earlier, even after I became governor, I gave my secretary their team schedules and the schedules for teams I coached and told her to work around them. State business occasionally had to take precedence, but not often. Politics is my career, not my life.

Incidentally, our original plan was to have three children, and I thought it would be fun to name them in alphabetical order. So Kevin's middle name is Xavier and Chris's is Yale. We stopped there because of Mary Jo's pregnancy-related setbacks, but a third would have had the middle name of Zachary or Zane. When former governor James Florio asked Mary Jo why she allowed me to do that, she replied, "I'm just glad he didn't want to start with the letter A."

In the Codey division of labor, I did sports with the boys and took care of discipline when needed. Mary Jo handled the rest—the house, the shopping, the school work, the sympathetic shoulder, and whatever else needed to be done. I don't do barbecues; I don't fix things.

Looking back, perhaps the most telling thing about that early note to Kevin is that he—and later, Chris—played in Newark, about the only white kids in the league there. From the time they were four until they were ten, for five months every Saturday I took them to the Newark Boys and Girls Club to shoot pool and play in the basketball league. Even though West Orange was fairly diverse, I thought there were important life lessons for them to learn by playing games where they'd be the only white kids. I thought it would help them to never feel out of place, no matter what the situation. Also the competition was better. They never brought the subject up and neither did I. Only one question was asked: Can you play? That's what counted, and that was a lesson I wanted to teach.

They also played a lot in mostly black East Orange, and I sometimes took them to black churches so they could see a different culture. It was also good politics, as I mentioned in one note to Kevin. The hand-clapping Baptist enthusiasm was so infectious, the kids kind of enjoyed going. Kevin was once asked the difference between the Catholic Church and an African American church. He simply replied: "An hour and a half."

Kevin was a real basketball star when he was young, and by age eight he was already spending a good part of his summers at basketball camps. This note in August 1992: "Today you finished P.J.'s camp [P. J. Carlesimo, a friend, coached Seton Hall from 1982 to 1994 before coaching in the NBA]. You loved it. 2 weeks ago you did the camp at Seton Hall Prep and loved that, too." In that same note, I mentioned that we had erected a nine-foot basket in our backyard (regulation is ten feet) and wrote, "You practice all the time." Both kids were also ball boys once in a while at Seton Hall games.

In 1993, I wrote Kevin, "You and I play one-on-one all the time. You are getting better all the time." I did the same with Chris when he was old enough, and both kids say the games ended when they started to win. I don't think that's quite accurate, but I do know they loved beating the old man. In Chris's words, "It was a big stepping-stone for us." They also claim that I cheated once they closed in on me, calling walking when they didn't walk and three-second violations, an unheard of infraction in one-on-one basketball. I don't know what they're talking about.

As ballplayers, Kevin, who was short for his age until he shot up to six foot one when he became seventeen, was always a better shooter than Chris. In fact, in his junior year of high school he was ranked as the third best shooter in the state. Trouble was he couldn't run. When he raced we didn't time him with a stopwatch; we timed him with a calendar. Chris as a kid was tenacious and would fight anybody for a rebound. He was tall as a kid, but stopped growing at five feet eleven inches, and was always stronger going to the basket. But asking him to stay after practice to work on a few things was like asking a mule to become a horse. Wasn't going to happen.

Kevin, trying to impress me when he was eight, wrote a note saying he had almost touched the rim. He wasn't tall enough to dunk the ball in a desk drawer. Even as a high school freshman in his first varsity game, he was only five feet two inches and ninety pounds. When the coach put him in, he told Kevin to shoot when he crossed the half-court line and Kevin happily obliged. He was fouled while shooting. "Hey, number 10," an opposing cheerleader yelled as he walked to the foul line. "Is that your number or your age?" I don't know if Kevin heard her, but he made all three shots.

Kids, of course, often get pigeonholed because of their size, which I think is a great opportunity to make some money. If I had another son I'd feed him just Devil Dogs and milk shakes and make him as fat as possible the year before he became eligible to try out for Little League. The minute he walked on the field the coach would take one look and undoubtedly say, "You're going to be a catcher." Then I'm going to file a class action suit with every other parent of a fat son and sue Little League International and make a heck of a lot of money.

One more basketball note to Kevin will indicate how dedicated we were: "Today was a busy day," I wrote when he was ten and a half. "We left the house at 10 A.M. to play in the national Little Lads tournament in Hamilton at 11:30 A.M. After your team [East Orange] won we drove back to Bayonne to play in a tournament there. Your team easily won. We got back in the car and drove to Hamilton to play a championship game against Puerto Rico at 5:30 P.M. Your team lost by two points. You missed two foul shots with 2 seconds to go to send the game into overtime. You played very well the whole game. You were very upset after the game driving home, but later you were ok. For me, it was a very special day alone with you. I was very proud of you. Love, Dad." That game was broadcast live in Puerto Rico. And I remember telling Kevin on the way home if he ever ran for office he should have no trouble getting the Hispanic vote. Kevin never forgot those two foul shots. Neither have I, to tell the truth. I can also tell you that that was not our only tripleheader day. Not by a long shot. Pun intended.

It wasn't only basketball. We played tennis and they took lessons. They also took golf lessons and played baseball. And when Chris was six or seven, he was a big fan of Dan Marino, the great Miami Dolphins quarterback who never won a Super Bowl. So I gave him a football and signed Marino's name. Chris was thrilled. About six years later he asked me to 'fess up, did I sign the ball. "Of course," I said. "But you were thrilled when you got it. That was the point."

But basketball was what they practiced almost every day, even if I had to bribe them. When they pleaded for a dog, I think in 1995, I said they had to practice seventy days in row. I don't know if they did that or not, but it wasn't until 1998 that I wrote to Chris: "Today we bought you and Kevin a puppy. I named him Thunder. You have been bugging me to do this for a long time. Love, Dad."

These days, Chris plays pickup games at college and Kevin plays in a men's league, but golf is his game. He and I play almost every summer weekend at the Essex County Country Club, which I joined when he started playing. Chris plays, but not as often. I used to ridicule golf as an old man's game and I didn't start playing until I was fifty-five, too late to get any good. Kevin is much better than I am with my 18 handicap. I hate losing to him, but I'm pretty proud when I see him smash a ball about a quarter of a mile down the fairway. Three guys sponsored me for club membership: county sheriff Armando Fontoura, who is Portuguese; Arthur Goldberg, the Jewish CEO of Bally's, who died shortly after that; and Nick Politan, a federal district judge in New Jersey. Put the three names together and it sounded like an immigration law firm in Newark.

In 2002, I wrote Kevin a note about "how thrilled I was" that we won the club's father–son championship. I'm sure most of that was his doing. He says now that he could have been a lot better if I had him chipping golf balls in the backyard all those years instead of shooting baskets. He might be playing on Sundays with Tiger Woods.

Many of the other notes I wrote were about routine matters of a child-parent relationship—the first day of school, taking them to school, shopping for Christmas, going to football games together, vacationing at the Shore, spending time with relatives, parent–teacher meetings. The reports were always pretty good, although Chris, as one teacher said, always wanted to be the center of attention.

One note was to Chris in 1999: "Today you were elected Hazel Ave. School president. Mom and I were very proud of you. Maybe this is the start of a political career. Love, Dad." Chris says I was ecstatic when I picked him up at school that day, beaming as though I had just won an election.

Most likely, though, if there is a future politician in the family, it's Kevin. Chris pays more attention to the daily flow of news and he is the one who appreciates what he has learned about government because of me. He's also a little more extroverted. But Kevin's the one who goes to meetings with me sometimes and says he'd like to get into politics. He now works for my insurance consulting firm and I've told him he should make some money before entering politics.

But he likes the idea of providing the help that politicians can provide. He has seen me get jobs for people or find someone a doctor when absolutely needed, and he has seen constituents come up to me during dinner to say thanks for something I've done. He has the right instincts. When he was a caddy he made sure to warn the newer kids on the job to stay away from playing poker with the older caddies. Some of them would cheat you out of every last dime. He was also kind of enamored with the perks that came with me being governor—like the chance to meet and get his picture taken with Barack Obama during the presidential campaign.

We moved in 2009 from West Orange to Roseland, a nearby community in Essex County, and when I couldn't make it to an event at the Roseland Democratic Committee he filled in and made his first political speech.

He said he was nervous as hell, but he started enjoying himself after getting a few laughs with a story about his introduction to the Roseland police before we even moved. He was stopped for driving while talking on his cell phone, which is illegal because of a law I sponsored and had passed. His audience thought that was pretty funny. I didn't when he told me.

Kevin also filled in for me a year later when I was having kidney stones removed and couldn't attend a rally of families and hospital workers protesting Governor Chris Christie's decision to close the three-hundred-bed Hagedorn Psychiatric Hospital in Hunterdon County, which treats geriatric patients. Eventually, I was able to get together with Michael Doherty, a Republican senator, to sponsor a bill that saved the facility.

Chris isn't sure, but I think he's going to be a businessman of some kind. Even when he was a little kid he figured out how to make money by selling candy in the stands during Kevin's games. And he started the *Codey Family* newspaper, 50 cents a copy. The *Star-Ledger* sold for less. The issue he's most proud of had his drawing of a toilet bowl on the front, with the story: "The toilet bowl overflowed."

So if you ask the difference between Kevin and Chris, Kevin wants to save the whales; Chris wants to make money from the whales.

One thing I never wrote about in a note—something the boys have never quite gotten over—is their walk to Munchie's in January 1996, one day after we awoke to about twenty-eight inches of snow in West Orange. Chris was eight, Kevin eleven. But as usual, I asked them to walk to Munchie's, a deli two blocks away, to get the papers and a sandwich. When they describe it, you'd think they were torture survivors in a Siberian prison, still bitching about hypothermia and frostbite. I told them it wasn't all that bad—just a little snow. And hell, I wasn't about to go out in all that snow.

I mentioned that I was the one who handled discipline. The goal there was always the same: teach them respect for authority and institutions and how to treat their fellow human beings. I always remembered when I was out to dinner with my father: if someone walked to our table to say hello, you had better get your butt up to show respect.

A couple of examples about discipline, not surprisingly, both instigated by Chris. It was a Thursday in October 2006, a school day. Chris came to my office with a friend at about 11:20 A.M. and said he wanted to cut "just one class" and go to the Yankee game. The Yankees and Tigers had been rained out in a playoff game the night before and they were to make it up that afternoon. Chris's friend had terrific tickets and Chris wanted me to sign a note saying he was sick.

I said, "Chris, I'm not going to lie and your grades can't afford it." That was it, I thought.

Next thing I knew it was 3:30 and Mary Jo was on the phone. She had just gotten home from work and had a message from a school administrator. Chris had left school, saying he was sick, and she was calling to check on him. Of course, Chris wasn't home.

After another exchange of calls, the administrator told Mary Jo that Chris had gone to the nurse, said he was vomiting, and was going home. But, the administrator said, "I understand he went to the Yankee game." The other kid's mother had given permission for her son to leave school. So when he and Chris left the building together, you didn't have to be a school principal to figure out what happened.

Mary Jo then called me and bawled me out because she thought I was holding out on her. I explained what happened and said, "Obviously, he didn't obey me and he'll have to pay the punishment." But I was also angry at the administrator for lying. She knew damn well Chris wasn't sick when she called the first time. So I called her and said she was a "sneak" and "deceptive" and told her not to call my house again. I said Chris was seventeen, that was his excuse. She had no excuse. Then I complained to the headmaster. He agreed the matter could have been handled more forthrightly.

I called Chris at the game twice and reamed his ass. That was in the sixth inning and I know he didn't enjoy the rest of the game. As he says: "I knew when I got home the shit would hit the fan. It would be volcanic." I took his car keys for two weeks for lying, and added a third week for stupidity.

"You went to into the nurse's office, told her you were sick and were throwing up," I told him. "You left the nurse's office and walked out the front door with your friend, whose mother had told the school he could go. So when you walked out of the building with him what do you think they thought? You get the extra week for not having any street smarts. Which is really upsetting. Worse than going to the Yankee game."

Chris says now he always felt a little guilty about lying to the nurse. "She was a substitute nurse and I hated to do it to her. But I really wanted to go to that game and there was no other way."

Then there was the time Chris finished his junior year, but I never saw any grades. He gave me a cock-and-bull story about not receiving them, but that would have been a first. I said to Chris and

Kevin, "Both of you go upstairs. I want the grades in my hand in five minutes." Then Kevin came down and handed me the grades. He said he saw them first and put them in a drawer and forgot about them. I got the two of them and handed out my verdict. Chris was grounded for two weeks for lying. Kevin was grounded for one, and when he asked why he was being punished at all, I said, "You get the week for thinking I'm stupid enough to swallow that story."

My mission as a parent is to provide love and discipline. The love is unquestioned. The boys sometimes question the discipline.

There was no disciplinary action on Chris's graduation day at Montclair Kimberley, when he couldn't resist one last prank. He was never an A student and he never studied as hard as he should have. But as the graduates gathered in the basement of the church in which the ceremony was held, he took a cum laude ribbon and pinned it on his gown. I didn't notice it at the time and knew nothing about it until the headmaster called the next day and asked what I thought of Chris's stunt. "Mr. Headmaster," I said, "I don't know what you're talking about. All I know is, he's got his diploma in his hand." Then he told me the story and said it was the talk of the faculty's end-of-the-year meeting. He estimated that two-thirds of the teachers thought it was great and the other third wanted to kill him.

I asked him how he felt, but he said, "I can't say."

"To be honest sir," I said, "that was a kind of 'hump you' to a few administrators."

"I can understand that," he replied.

I thought Chris had humorously proved the old adage: If you're going to do something wrong, make sure they can't get back at you.

6

Sports in My Life

There are a lot of similarities between sports and politics. In politics, you are only as good as your last vote. In sports, you are only as good as your last game. Always—as a kid, a college student, a politician—I read the papers every day. And always I turned to the sports section before I looked at page one. Unless, of course, I was on page one. I played basketball, baseball, and tennis and now golf. As for watching, if it has a ball, I'm pretty much there. I've also been known to bet a few bucks on the horses. I have team jerseys and signed balls in my office and in my den at home. I am the kind of guy for whom ESPN was invented. So here are some sports-related stories.

———

Saint Barnabas Hospital was sponsoring a charity golf event. John Daly, the highly talented but very overweight and undisciplined former PGA and British Open champ, was playing, along with Rocco Mediate, another pro; Joe Pesci, the actor; and Mikhail Baryshnikov, the ballet star whose hobby is golf.

Hospital officials invited me to a small dinner, no more than fifteen people, the night before the match, and I found myself sitting next to Daly and his wife. Daly started by telling me that he had sworn off hard liquor, limiting himself to just beer.

Here's how the conversation proceeded:

Daly: Senator, you want a beer?
Codey: I don't drink.
Daly: When did you stop?
Codey: I never drank. I just never did.

Daly: You *never* did? Do you even know how many cans of beer in a case?

Codey: No idea.

Daly: Twenty-four. Twenty-four hours in a day. I don't think that's a coincidence.

Then, Mrs. Daly looked over at me and said, "How do you like John's hair?"

"Fine," I said, a little surprised.

"I give him haircuts," she said. "John doesn't like to have his hair cut and only lets me cut his hair. But I have to promise him sex."

I looked at her, smiled a little mischievously, and thoughtfully replied: "I think I can use a little trim myself." That was not his third wife, Paulette, who was later reported to have had a long-running affair with Roger Clemens, but his fourth, Sherrie, who served a prison term in 2006 for laundering drug money and was later accused by Daly of stabbing him. Daly, by the way, is this kind of guy: he turned down a suite in the Short Hills Hilton in exchange for a spot for his bus in the country club parking lot.

Anyway, I always root for John Daly, and he almost always disappoints me. In fact, Daly can be such an undisciplined reprobate that in 2008 his swing coach, Butch Harmon, fired him as a client. "He's a tremendous talent," said Harmon, who once worked with Tiger Woods. "But the most important thing in his life is getting drunk. If he's not going to give 100 percent effort, it's a waste of my time." It takes a special guy to get fired by a person he's paying.

———

If Daly is a party animal with a challenged work ethic, Vijay Singh, who spends endless hours hitting golf balls at the practice range, is known as being colder than an Alaskan winter. In 2005, the PGA championship was scheduled at the famous Baltusrol Golf Club in Springfield, New Jersey. Singh, by winning the tournament the year before, was obliged to come to New Jersey early in the year for a press conference and a leisurely round to drum up interest. As governor, I was asked to play with him.

He was a lot friendlier than his reputation and we got along fine, chatting through our eighteen holes. He looked at me quizzically at one point and said, "My wife says the guy you replaced is gay, but he has two wives and two kids. How's that?"

"I never could explain it," I answered. We ended the day with Singh's inviting me and any guests I wanted to join him for breakfast when he returned for the tournament.

The PGA was played in August, and as the leaders, Singh included, were getting close to the end of Sunday's final round a ferocious thunderstorm forced a postponement until Monday. Singh was in a minor panic because he had checked out of the Hilton Short Hills and had nowhere to stay. I told him I thought I had enough influence to take care of it and I did. Sometimes, governor is better than long and straight off the tee. After Singh played the final three holes on Monday, he came by to say good-bye. "I just want you to know," I told him, "that I got a call from the manager of the Short Hills Mall. He said I should tell your wife he's going to miss her." He knew what I meant. The mall, across the road from the Hilton, should have a sign out outside saying "Only rich people need enter." With stores like Saks, Nordstrom, Bulgari, Neiman Marcus, and just about every other high-end retailer in the world, it supposedly takes in more dollars per square foot than any mall in the country. "What I made in the tournament," Singh complained, "my wife spent across the street." He made $131,180.

Phil Mickelson won the tournament on Monday and I was on the stand to hand out the trophy. He graciously asked my sons Chris and Kevin to join him after the ceremony, and he took some pictures with us. The boys loved it.

———

Two quick personal stories about golf. I had played a matchplay round against a guy at my club and he beat me two and one, meaning he had won two more holes than I did with only one to play. I couldn't catch him. A week later I was having lunch, and this guy's wife was at the next table. "Hey," she said, "I understand my husband played you and cleaned your cock." "Not quite," I said, as her face turned redder than a Tiger Woods Sunday shirt. Of course, she meant to say "clock."

The Essex County Country Club runs a two-day tournament every year, called the President's Cup. One year, I played out of my mind in the opening round and finished the day in first place. I didn't play as well on the second day, but because of rain a lot of my challengers dropped out. I left, sure that I had won. But a local attorney played very well and he tied me. Which put him in a panic, and he pleaded with club officials to give the cup to Codey. Can't do that, they said. Against the rules. So they had what's called a match of card, where they compare the players' scores for each hole. If one player shot better on the first hole, he wins. If they were even, they compare the second hole and they keep comparing until they get to a hole that one of the players won. I actually won the first hole and was declared the winner, much to the attorney's relief. He was seeking a judgeship and he feared that I might blackball him if he beat me. I would do no such thing, but that gives you an idea of how politics is played in New Jersey. In the end, the senator sponsoring him withdrew that sponsorship. So the attorney wound up losing both the tournament and the job.

———

One sport I like, although it's not very popular these days, is horse racing. Little is more pleasant than a sunny summer afternoon at a racetrack, watching a sleek chestnut-colored thoroughbred, weighing about 1,000 pounds, running between thirty-five and forty miles an hour on ballerina-thin legs with a few bucks on his nose.

I used to own a few horses, some of which even made some money. I loved hanging around the track, talking to trainers, jockeys, and the run-of-the-mill characters you find there. And I always enjoyed naming my horses. But when I wanted to name one Seton Hall, university officials had some misgivings, concerned perhaps that horse racing was inconsistent with the school's Catholic tradition. So I named him Seat 'N' Haul. I actually used the N letter a lot in naming horses. There was Ham 'N' Egger, See More 'N' Do Less, Nickel 'N 'Dimer, and Snoop 'N' Scoop, a horse I bred myself. I had a sire I used to compare to a politician; he'd screw anyone in sight.

When Snoop was preparing for his first race, my trainer, J. W. Thompson, told me the horse was running into shape but would need one race to be truly fit. A friend of mine, another trainer, touted me on his horse, a Jersey-bred filly named Open Mind going off at 10 or 11–1. You feel funny betting against your own horse, but I took the advice and made some nice money. Open Mind went on to win a Breeder's Cup race, which is about as good as it gets. Snoop, as we thought, turned out to be pretty good, winning about $125,000, a fine career, but he was no Open Mind, which won twelve races and $1.8 million.

If I caught a betting break with Open Mind, I paid with another horse—a New York–bred animal named New Point. Thompson trained and based him at Monmouth Park. His plan was to give the horse a good workout in a cheap race at Monmouth and then ship him to New York for a maiden race—a race for horses seeking their first victory. If the winner happened to be New York bred there would be a bonus, bringing the winner's purse to $25,000—a good day's pay even for a Trenton lobbyist. Thompson instructed the jockey at Monmouth to go easy—no whips. It was just a workout. The jockey, who didn't speak much English, misunderstood and rode as hard as he could. Much to my disgust, New Point won his first race. The winner's share was all of $4,000. For that, I lost the chance to run him in New York and I hadn't bet five cents on him.

"Next time," I yelled angrily at Thompson, "give him instructions in Spanish."

Kevin loved Scoop. We once went to watch him run in the ninth race of the day. I told Kevin before the race, "If he wins, I'll take you to Toys R Us." He won and I did. Kevin was one happy kid. Of the two, though, Chris was more enchanted with the track. When he was about to turn five, I wrote him a note saying, "Today, you asked mom to have your fifth birthday party at the racetrack and have dad buy the kids the paper so they can pick the horses."

He still goes occasionally, and he does pretty well, but I've made clear that you can't beat the horses by betting on them. Sometimes, though, I worry that he liked the track too much. Here's an example of why: One night after Mary Jo and I had seen a movie we called and asked him to join us for dinner. When he sat down, Mary Jo was in the bathroom, but he was all excited.

"Dad," he said, "did you see the sign outside?"

"No, what did it say?"

"Tuesday night, entries $9.99."

"Chris, you son of a b," I laughed, "you're spending too much time at the racetrack. It doesn't say *entries*; it says *entrees*. That means meals. With all the money I spent on high school for you, you're lucky your mother's in the bathroom. Otherwise she'd hit you with her lasagna. "

Kevin, on the other hand, gave up the track long ago. He had made $35 dollars for six hours' work as a caddie when he was a freshman in high school and then lost it all on one bet. That ended his handicapping career.

One other track story. I ran into a guy one day and he said the piss catcher job had opened up at the Meadowlands and he was interested. Could I help him? He then called my office to discuss it, and my staff, of course, thought it was a joke. Piss catcher is the rather inelegant title for the guy who catches a horse's urine so it can be tested for drugs. The line for the job is never very long at the unemployment office and I was able to help the guy.

Which reminded me of the story about a piss catcher who was fired at Suffolk Downs in Boston. He got nervous when he had a horse that was unable to pee after a race, so he pissed in the cup himself. His career ended when the tests came back positive for alcohol and nicotine.

Anyway, my devotion to the sport of kings is what got me interested in straightening out some systemic problems at New Jersey's five racetracks when I was in the assembly. (There are only three now, so obviously all the problems didn't get fixed.) Garden State burned down, was rebuilt, went broke, and is now a shopping center. And the Atlantic City Race Course is down to about two weeks a year of live racing, although there is year-round simulcasting of out-of-town races for bettors. Casinos were just too much competition. The remaining tracks are Monmouth, Freehold, and the Meadowlands.

Race-fixing scandals were exposed in the mid-1970s at Garden State and Atlantic City, and several jockeys and trainers were convicted and jailed. As chairman of the assembly's State Government Committee, I led an investigation into racing, and the committee produced what I thought was a pretty high-level report and list of recommendations. A lot of the scandal involved big-odds bets, such as the exacta (the bettor has to pick the first two finishers in order) and trifecta (the bettor has to pick the first three finishers in order). Jockeys and trainers were taking bribes to keep their horses out of the payoff positions. They were also placing bets on other horses. We recommended that in trifecta and exacta races, jockeys and trainers be allowed to bet only on their horse to win. Nothing fancier. We also recommended that two jockeys should be selected at random (but not told) and be videotaped in every race. Officials could then review the tape to guarantee that jockeys did all they could to get their horses home first. There were a bunch of other proposals, some designed to stop cheating, and some designed just to give the $2 bettor a better break at the track. They didn't all pass, but some did.

"I have rarely seen any politician show the slightest intelligence or savvy about racing matters (except where they affect revenue) but the Codey Report is brilliant in its proposals," wrote Steve Klessel, the horse racing writer for the *Philadelphia Daily News*.

I also fought successfully to reduce the taxes paid by tracks. I thought the tracks would bring in more fans, be more prosperous, and, ultimately, be a greater benefit to the state if the tax money went into larger pari-mutuel pools for bettors and more lucrative purses for owners. Larger purses attract better horses, making the racing more interesting. There were too many slow horses running in Jersey, and they were running too often. Which meant they were being drugged.

Some reporters at the time wondered if I had my own conflicts in investigating horse racing, and seeking bigger purses, but I didn't think so. There was no way I could help my horses win a race.

———

My real sport is basketball, as a player, a coach, and a spectator. After falling in love with the game playing in our parking lot, I played high school ball and had hoped to play at Fairleigh Dickinson. Unfortunately, FDU's coach at the time, Bill Raftery, who later coached at Seton Hall and then became best known as a television commentator, saw things differently.

As I saw it, I could shoot as well as anyone on the team from twenty feet and beyond. I have long believed that I could have played for a Division 3 school if the three-point play had been in effect when I was in college. Which isn't to say I didn't have my shortcomings. I was about the slowest guy on the court and my vertical leap was about an inch and a half. As a friend once said of me, "He might have been pretty good, but it took him more than ten seconds to get across the ten-second line."

"Don't let him tell you he could play basketball," Raftery once told the *Star-Ledger*. "At Fairleigh Dickinson, we were a struggling team and I cut him." Anyway, I kept playing in one league or another until I was about forty, and broke my ankle for the third time—twice playing basketball and once, the last time, playing tennis. I figured someone was giving me a sign, and I decided to restrict myself to playing golf. Before my career ended, I played a lot in a league at a Jewish community center. When I showed up for my first game, there was a Christian referee and he asked me what I was doing there. "I belong," I told him. "You don't have to be Jewish."

"Okay," he said, "but if you go to the foul line, I don't think you should make the sign of the cross."

I never stopped being competitive. In 2005, when I was governor, I went to Cliffside Park Middle School to honor Chris Keethe, a student whose suggestion that all homes be required to have fire extinguishers became a law that I signed. The ceremony was in the school gym and I issued a challenge: If the school's best shooter could beat me in a free-throw shooting contest he'd get my governor's watch. One kid who said he was "used to pressure," took me up on it. Not wanting to take any chances, I asked a group of girls to stand under the basket and jump around when he shot. He missed both, and I hit two. "Nothing but net," I bragged. I still gave the watch to Chris Keethe.

Even more gratifying was the night, also in 2005, that I went to watch Chris's Montclair Kimberley team play against Solomon Schechter Day School. I won the $1 Schechter raffle—and no, I don't think it was rigged—for the right to take a half court shot during half time. Sink it and it was worth two tickets to a Nets game. Well, with four hundred anxious people staring silently in the stands, I bent my knees deep (or as deep as I still can) aimed, and heaved. Again, nothing but net. The place went wild. I high-fived Mary Jo, I chest-bumped a Schechter player, and I smiled for days. I have season tickets to the Nets, so I gave the tickets to someone who usually can't afford to go. The school gave the tape to ESPN and some other news outlets, and people started thinking I could shoot like Michael Jordan.

That wasn't true, but don't tell me Raftery couldn't have used me at Fairleigh Dickinson.

————

A great joy for years has been coaching youth basketball, where, some would say, I may get a little too competitive. When I coach the kids I want to win as much as any pro coach. I'm proud to say we have had great success over the years, with a lot of the boys going on to play in high school and college.

But the kids and their parents will tell you I'm not great at hiding my emotions. Chris, in fact, used to keep score of my temperament at each game on what he called his mad-o-meter, which went from one to ten. I never got close to a one, but sometimes he'd rate me eight or nine and I'd argue for a five or six.

Here's what some parents and kids said when asked about my demeanor. Susan Rowek, whose son, Andrew, is Kevin's age and played for me for years: "He's animated but he's into it. It was funny to watch. They'd be twenty points ahead and he was still not happy. He was unhappy about something once and he was running on the sidelines on his knees, flipping his tie up in the air and yelling at the refs. He'll deny that but my husband and I saw it." (She's right; I deny it.)

And her son Andrew: "He scared the living daylights out of me. He'd stand on the sideline in a suit and tie and he'd start yelling, 'Tighten up the defense; think about what you're doing.' You didn't want him to get off the bench and throw the clipboard. It was pure love. I played for Seton Hall Prep, but going in I had a knowledge of basic principles because he instilled them in us from the fourth grade. I wouldn't have played at such a high level if it wasn't for him."

Eric Roehnelt, who went on to play for Glen Ridge High School and for one season at Muhlenberg College: "He used to call me after games and critique the game I played and that was good. I still shoot free throws the way he taught me. And he introduced me to coaches who would yell at you. Which was good, because I got screamed at on all levels."

Chris always told his teammates when he played for me how lucky they were. "You put up with him only on the court," he'd say. "I live with him twenty-four hours a day."

The first game I ever coached was against a team from Short Hills, one of the wealthiest communities in the state with a fabulous school system. I walked up to their coach and told him, "You know, you should let us win." He asked why, and I told him, "Because in fifteen years, all my players will be working for your players."

In the late 1990s I was coaching a game in Bayonne against a team from Staten Island; the score was tied and a championship was at stake. They shot and missed with a few seconds left, and in the scrum for the rebound they fouled my center, a poor foul shooter. Their coaches were yelling at the refs and there was a lot of commotion. I waved Kevin, a very good foul shooter, and the center to the bench. "When you go underneath, don't foul if Kevin misses the foul shots," I instructed the center. He looked a little perplexed and reminded me that he got fouled. "Let's make believe," I said, and Kevin made both shots. Later, a ref asked if I switched foul shooters. "Guilty," I said. "I positively did."

"It makes me feel good," he said, "to know there's a state senator in Trenton with a brain."

In my first year of coaching, we were in the semifinals of a tournament and the game was on a Sunday night. I got a call from my center, the second-best player on the team, who said, "Coach, I can't play tonight. I've got to be at church." After cursing to myself, I said okay and hung up. Then I called the other coach and told him there was a science fair in the gym we were supposed to play in and we couldn't get in. And he very nicely agreed to reschedule for the next night.

ESPN did a story on me when as governor I persuaded the legislature to approve the first law in the country to test high school athletes for steroid use. They put a mike on me during one of my games, and when I got the kids in a huddle we tried out a new cheer. I yelled, "One, two, three," and they shouted: "Democrats."

One kid who played for me, Ralph Jones, knew Chris in fifth grade, which is how I learned about him. He was always big for his age, but he never played the game before he showed up for his first practice. He was wearing brown loafers because he didn't own sneakers. From that beginning, Ralph went on to play at Seton Hall Prep and Rutgers–Newark, and I still call him every once in a while just to see how he's doing.

I've had wealthy kids and poor kids; black, white, and Hispanic, and one of my rules is that if a kid can't get to a game, I will pick him up or ask someone to do it. No player suffers because for whatever reason his family can't get him to a game.

I don't want to sound too holy here, but I see myself as more than a coach, but as someone they can rely on for as long as I'm alive. I've paid to send about a half dozen of them to private high schools; I've paid to send more than that to basketball camps, and I can't tell you how many college letters of recommendation I've signed for them— and their girlfriends.

If I made sure every kid would be able to get to every game, I also decreed that if I'm driving there is no pop music on the radio. I'd ask them current affairs questions, usually for $5 each. After 9/11, we were driving to a game—it was a fifty-minute ride—and I said, "Okay, for $25, which country invaded Afghanistan in the 1990s and was defeated?" My son said Pakistan. Another kid said Haiti. Finally, a kid says Russia and I handed him the $25. We won the game and when we stopped for pizza on the way home I asked him how he knew the answer. "Coach," he said as earnestly as possible, "as the others were giving their answers, I was trying to think as hard as I could what country Hitler came from."

Well, I teach them basketball, not history.

———

Two similar stories from other coaches: Bobby Crimmins, who used to coach and teach at Georgia Tech, told me that he had a player who was tired all the time. The kid said he wasn't getting enough sleep because his roommate studied late in the night and kept him up. "Coach," the kid said, "I don't understand it. He's an engineering student. Why does it take so long to learn to run a train?"

Another coach, whom I won't name, had his players get together for breakfast most mornings during the season. When a kid missed one morning, the coach called his house and his mother answered. She said she was sorry and he would be there in the afternoon. "Yesterday was his birthday," she explained, "and last night I told him for his birthday I would take him clubbing. And, coach, I'll be honest with you. We both got fucking blitzed."

Coaching is not my only basketball pursuit; I've also done some recruiting for Seton Hall. That started in the late 1970s. Bill Raftery, despite not appreciating me at Fairleigh Dickinson, had been hired to coach Seton Hall, a much bigger program. My brother Donald was an assistant coach for Raftery, and I asked Bill if I could help recruit around New Jersey. He gave me the names of three potential recruits and within a couple of days all three had committed to other schools.

But I had a great year in 1978 when I helped recruit Dan Calandrillo, a guard from Bergen County who had been courted by fifty schools, and Howard McNeil, who grew up in South Jersey but played for a high school in suburban Philadelphia. Calandrillo eventually made the Big East all-conference first team. McNeil, who was six foot nine inches, was a troubled young man and was eventually dismissed from the team for academic reasons. Both were drafted by the NBA, although neither made it, and both wound up playing overseas. McNeil's life later fell apart and he was convicted in 1999 of murdering a drug dealer who refused to give him drugs.

My recruiting days ended when the NCAA tightened restrictions for boosters and made what I was doing illegal. I still wear a huge sapphire ring from Seton Hall's appearance in the 1989 Final Four. It was a gift from then coach, P. J. Carlesimo, who said I deserved that ring "as much as a lot of our coaches."

I have one other NCAA championship memento. When I was governor, I got a call from George Blaney, an assistant coach of Connecticut. He told me his brother had been nominated to be a judge from Ocean County but one senator was holding up the confirmation. He asked if I could help him. I said I thought I could, but I wanted a favor in return. Connecticut had won the NCAA title in 2004 and I asked if he could get me a championship watch. He laughed and said, "I think it's doable." His brother got the judgeship and I got the watch. And time marches on.

I'm close enough to the Seton Hall basketball program that I helped former head coach Bobby Gonzalez negotiate some changes in his first contract in 2007. Gonzalez is a terrific coach, but the X's and O's of his life are not always in the right place.

Once I went to a high school game with him in Jersey City and the police escorted us into the gym. "Bobby," I whispered, "this isn't the first time you've been escorted by the police, is it?" He nodded. Another time, I set him up with my accountant to help straighten out his very confusing finances, and he started to complain about one of his supervisors in the athletic department. "He's got the fucking personality of an accountant," Bobby said. My accountant took no offense.

Gonzalez's team had nine technical fouls in 2007, his first season at Seton Hall, an outrageous number. Athletic director Quinlan even suspended him for a game after Bobby publicly ridiculed the officiating referee in the last game of the 2007–2008 season against Rutgers. The *Star-Ledger* ran a story shortly before that with the headline: "Gonzalez Fan Club Has Codey on Top, but Is That Enough." But I saw that game, and I was as upset at Gonzalez as any other Seton Hall fan.

In fact, the monsignor called me after that game and said if Bobby wanted to keep coaching at Seton Hall there were some changes he'd have to make. I told Bobby, and predictably his first reaction was to argue. "There is no debate," I said. "This is not debatable." Then I told him that within two seconds after we hang up—no, make that one second—call the monsignor and straighten things out. He did manage after that to cut down on his technicals, improve relations with some reporters, whom he cursed out every time they wrote anything negative about him or the team, and become less suspicious about the people he works with.

He was dismissed after the 2009–2010 season when Seton Hall lost an opening round game in the NIT and one of his players, Robert Mitchell, was charged on several serious counts in connection with a burglary. Mitchell had been kicked off the team days earlier for denigrating Gonzalez's coaching in the press.

I think Bobby was essentially gone before the NIT or the robbery when he angered Patrick Hobbs, dean of the law school, who was overseeing the athletic department, for lambasting the reporter who wrote the story about Mitchell criticizing his coaching. I told him from my own experience if a reporter gives an opinion you have to live with it, as long as there are no factual errors.

And despite his erratic behavior, he always stood up for his players publicly even when they were wrong. In private situations

I saw him act with great compassion and friendship that I will never forget.

His real problem may have been that he lived an hour away from the campus, which kept him from becoming part of the Seton Hall community. You can get away with that if you take the team to the Final Four in the NCAA tournament, but Bobby never even went to the tournament.

I also used to help represent a guy named Rod Baker, who was an assistant coach at Seton Hall from 1988 to 1991. From there, he went to the University of California–Irvine as head coach, and eventually to a head-coaching job for the Harlem Globetrotters. Two things about Baker: I never take money for representing a coach, but I'll take all the gear I can get my hands on. The Irvine school's nickname is the Anteaters, and I can assure you I was the only guy walking around Essex County with "Anteaters" on his back. And because the Globetrotters never lose, I used to brag that I once represented the most successful coach in the country. Really, though, that just helped to even things out. In 1996–1997, Baker's sixth and final season at Irvine, the Anteaters were 1–25.

Which reminds me of a football coach who had a bad run, but a great explanation. That would be Lou Holtz, who coached at six colleges, including Notre Dame, and he had a winning record at each one except his first, William and Mary. His explanation: "There were too many Marys on campus and not enough Williams."

————

Besides Bobby Gonzalez, another loose cannon I knew pretty well was Marge Schott, the late flamboyant owner of the Cincinnati Reds baseball team. Somehow, when I was a kid, I fell in love with the Reds of the 1950s with Ted Kluszewski and Frank Robinson, and I've rooted for them ever since. At some point, I wrote Marge Schott, an eccentric, angry woman who inherited the team from her husband, and told her I wanted to purchase some tickets. She sent me seats 2 and 3 in the front row behind the Reds dugout. Seat 1 was Marge's. She sat next to me after the first inning, and by the end of the second I realized she didn't know a damn thing about the game. But she had opinions about everything, most of them stunningly ill-informed.

Eventually, I'd go out there every summer and she and I would have dinner. She drank too much and I'd listen to her complain about nearly everything and everybody. I can tell you I positively, absolutely was not surprised when Major League Baseball made her give up daily control of the team in 1996 for making anti-Semitic remarks. Later, on August 18, 2005, I got to throw out the first pitch at a Reds game. It was a dead strike and I asked a coach what I registered on the speed gun. "Didn't register," he said.

I have a framed Reds jersey with my name on it from that day hanging in the conference room in my West Orange office. There's also a basketball signed by the Seton Hall Final Four team and a football from Rutgers head coach Greg Schiano.

As I said, they invented ESPN for guys like me.

7

Politics Gets Very Dirty

I learned in 1983 what Finley Peter Dunne, the Irish American humorist, had figured out more than a half century earlier. "Politics ain't beanbag." He could have added, "Especially in Essex County, New Jersey."

Until then, my assembly races and my election to the senate in 1981 had been pretty well greased. But in 1983, Joel Shain, the mayor of Orange, came after me in the Democratic state senate primary like a piranha that had missed a meal. The race was the most expensive legislative primary in state history to that point, and maybe the meanest.

How mean was it? as Johnny Carson might have asked. So mean that Mary Jo, who was new to politics and just hated to read anything negative about me, asked sincerely one day why I didn't get out of the race and "just let him have it." That was after Shain accused my dad and me of having Mafia connections because we had buried some wise guys from the Codey Funeral Home and because I once got caught in the middle of a police raid on Dippy DeVingo, a popular neighborhood bookmaker. Dippy was a former caddie, and my brother and I used to take him to golf matches with us.

This was in 1971 and I was driving a hearse back to the garage when I stopped at a deli for a sandwich. Dippy lived across the street, and when I saw his door open I went over to say hello. As soon as I got there, police who were already raiding the place came out of nowhere and started searching me. They found all of $5 in my pocket, and that was for the sandwich. It didn't take long before the police chief in Orange called my dad, trying to shake him down to keep quiet about my being there. He never paid a dime, and the incident turned out to be a small political gift.

Ray Durkin, who is married to my cousin Joan and was Essex County Democratic chairman in 1983, remembers that "the whole town loved the bookie so they all came out and voted for Dick. All the Italians voted for him."

Anyway, while I would do almost anything for Mary Jo, getting out of the race was not on my list of things to think about. What was on my mind was answering Shain's charges (new ones came flying in daily like Scud missiles), hurling back a few of my own, and raising enough money to stay competitive. Shain, an attorney, reported his assets at $1.9 million, compared to my $86,000. As I pointed out, "The only candidate in the State Senate primary election who got rich while serving in public office was Orange mayor Joel Shain." Unfortunately, he seemed prepared to spend most of that money beating me up. By election day he had spent $284,566 to my $154,771, a total of $439,337, which doesn't seem like that much these days. But then it was a few thousand more than had ever been spent on a State Senate general election, let alone a primary. Of course, in our district, the 27th, the Democratic primary was the same as winning the general election. To give you an idea, in 1992 Bill Clinton defeated President George H. W. Bush in Essex by 68,984 votes. His margin in the whole state was 79,341.

Shain and I, as the expression goes, had some history. We battled each other in the mid-1970s for Democratic Party leader in Orange. I won by a single vote. He challenged the outcome in court, saying the vice chairwoman had acted improperly somehow, and he won a revote. In the interim, he gave jobs to two of my supporters, which could have given him the victory. But he didn't know that an old Irish lawyer in a wheelchair (I forget his name) who voted for Shain the first time volunteered to switch. The way it worked out, that ensured my victory. For the second vote, the city Democratic committee met in a crowded uncomfortable room, with almost everyone smoking. The vice chairwoman, an ally, called the roll, and I asked her to call the Irish lawyer last. Shain would get a vote or two and then I'd match that. Then, I'd go ahead by a little and he would match me. There were forty-one votes, as I remember, and it was dead even, with the lawyer still to be called. Shain's people, thinking they had him, were shaking hands and congratulating one another. "How do you vote?" asked the vice chairwoman. "Codey," shouted the lawyer, and I burst out in laughter.

But that didn't prepare me for the senate primary in 1983. On one typical day, Shain charged me with sponsoring legislation to help an insurance company I was working for. "We are alleging," said Shain, "that he violated the conflict of interest law; it goes back to common law. When you are a public servant, you're obligated to serve the public and not yourself." A story in the *Star-Ledger* earlier that year said I tried to pressure the Division of Pensions into a ruling that would have helped an insurance agency for which I was a consultant. The attorney general's office found I did no wrong and I was cleared of all allegations.

Responding to Shain's assertion, I said: "There are two things Joel Shain has never done in his life: tell the truth, and run a clean campaign. I thought his kind of politics went out with McCarthy and Nixon." At another point, I compared him to Pinocchio. And I hit constantly at the high crime rate in Orange, charging that he was responsible when I really knew there were a lot of other factors. As I said, it wasn't beanbag.

This went on day after day for weeks, charges and countercharges in literature, newspaper ads, radio ads, and phone calls. It seemed to never stop and it was very depressing. Larry DeMarzo, my administrative assistant then and my good friend, still winces when anyone mentions the Shain race. Eventually, Governor Byrne, former governor Richard Hughes, and two dozen other leaders came out for me, saying, "We abhor Shain's constant malicious attempts to attack the integrity of Senator Codey and his family."

I thought things went well beyond the acceptable when we found someone from his campaign rummaging through our garbage and when he had people call my office, claiming to be state insurance agents investigating my business. There were always just a few more questions they wanted answered.

Not that I didn't cross the line myself once in a while. Like, when I sent a mailing to voters in African American neighborhoods with a photo of me and Kenneth Gibson, the black mayor of Newark. There was a suggestion there that I had his endorsement, when I had no such thing. But that's standard politics, like when some city council candidate sends out a picture of himself standing with the president. Not likely that the president ever endorsed him. Why things got so rough, I'm not sure. Could be that we were both young and ambitious comers in Essex County politics, and the winner of the State Senate race could confidently look forward to a successful public career. Despite her misgivings, Mary Jo campaigned door to door, often with John McKeon, now an assemblyman, but then a law school student who helped in my office. McKeon explains her effectiveness very simply: "She was a beautiful woman asking people to 'please vote for my husband.'"

In the end, I won big, 13,461 to 4,044, which surprised me, and probably Shain. People were so disgusted with the campaign he ran that I even carried his district.

Over the long run, though, I've owed a lot to Shain. Because of that race, I developed a system for low-key year-round campaigning that, as far as I know, is practiced by no other politician.

When I first learned that he was going to oppose me, which was about fourteen months before the primary, I started calling constituents who didn't know me personally, mostly African American and Jewish voters who weren't involved in politics. I didn't know them through the church and they weren't getting buried at my dad's funeral home. Larry DeMarzo and I dug into the election books at the county Hall of Records to see who voted in the last few primaries.

I believed candidates wasted time and money trying to appeal to everyone in a primary, when only about 20 percent voted. So I figured, let's concentrate on those 20 percent. And I wasn't interested in the people who cycled through the usual political events and fundraisers. They already knew me. We compiled lists by hand, and then I made all the calls personally. "Hi, this is Senator Codey. Are there any issues on your mind, anything you want to talk to me about?" If they didn't volunteer a topic, I'd throw out a few—taxes, crime, whatever. That usually broke the ice and they'd start talking. At the end, I asked for their support and thanked them for their time.

As we were talking, I addressed envelopes to them. Letters thanking them for talking to me were already inside. I cut it off at 9:30 P.M., drove to the post office and had those "thank you" notes in the mail that very night. Most people on the street never talk to their state senator and a pretty good percentage don't know his or her name. I thought the calls were a smart way to reach voters.

After that Shain race, I never stopped making the phone calls. I still go into the office on many Sundays, and sitting there alone I make my calls. Sundays are best because more people seem to be home. The more person-to-person contact you make outside the political season, the more effective it is. People don't see it as political then. Nobody ever hears from a politician when he isn't looking for a vote—or money. People remember it, and some have even framed my thank-you letters. And the truth is, I enjoy doing it.

Now, of course, people are thrilled that they're talking to a former governor. But it is hard to get them to believe it's me. I say. "Listen, look up my district office phone number and call and I'll wait for the call." And they do. I have no idea how many thousands of calls I've made over the years. But I do know that every time I call one constituent, he or she tells someone else in the supermarket or the beauty shop and it creates a buzz and a feeling that their state senator really cares. I've tried to interest some other senators in the system, but I don't know anyone who is as disciplined about it as I am. Another thing I do is study the obituary pages. Anytime a constituent dies, I get a senate resolution passed in his or her honor. Families don't forget it. But the phone calls more than anything have helped me to win some other tough races.

Like the one in 1993, a chaotic year even for Essex County. In retrospect, this was probably my most important victory, ensuring my independence and liberating me from boss control—not much easier in New Jersey than being liberated from Caesar in Rome. And there was no Cleopatra in the deal. It started when Tom D'Alessio, the former county sheriff who, in 1993, was both the county Democratic chairman and the county executive, came to my house for a little talk. D'Alessio, with a voice that most would call loud, said he—meaning the party organization—was not going to support the reelection of Cardell Cooper, the African American mayor of East Orange. "I'm getting rid of him," D'Alessio said. This had nothing to do with Cooper's qualifications. He had a master's degree in public administration from Rutgers and he was a successful mayor. Cooper's sin: arguing a year earlier that D'Alessio shouldn't govern the county and run the party at the same time. Too many conflicts of interest. "He is finished," Tom said. I should mention that D'Alessio at the time was under a federal indictment for extorting almost $60,000 from a garbage-hauling firm and laundering the money through his father's bank accounts.

"I'm sticking with Cardell," I said, adding as politely as possible that if necessary I would run my own line of candidates against the party organization. A quick lesson here in Jersey politics: county chairmen are elected by municipal chairmen who are elected by district chairmen. That gives them a large political army, and they control a lot of patronage and contracts, which means they can raise a lot of money, which means it can be politically perilous to run against the organization line. This race was also a microcosm of Essex County politics, where all the players are Irish, Italian, or black.

Our conversation then went something like this:

D'Alessio: If you don't run with the party, I'm going to run Bob Brown against you. He's a black guy and the blacks are going to vote against you because you're white.

Codey: That's life. I'm prepared to do what I think I need to do.

D'Alessio: All right, but we're going to kick your ass.

Codey: See you at the ballot box.

I was confident I'd win, although it wasn't a slam-dunk. But I believed I was doing the right thing and that was more than enough.

I had been in the legislature twenty years by 1993, and I figured I had enough support to pull it off. And in truth, to turn *The Godfather* saying around, this wasn't just business, it was also personal. D'Alessio didn't like me and he wanted me gone. He probably wanted to goad me into running off the line, figuring his organization, as he said, could kick my ass. And I didn't like D'Alessio's bullying style. I thought he was dishonest, and I was looking for an excuse to fight him. I also liked Cooper and respected what he had done with his life. He was one of eleven children, all boys, from a real poor family in a section of Newark nearly destroyed by the 1967 riots. Given where he started, he easily could have finished in jail instead of the East Orange mayor's office. I had mentored him along the way, and I thought he had a bright political future. In the end, he didn't have the fire in the belly for it and in 1998 he went to Washington as an assistant secretary of Housing and Urban Development in the Clinton Administration. But in 1993, people were talking about him as a possible governor some day.

Bob Brown was the mayor of Orange, the assemblyman from Orange, and the Orange Democratic chairman. He was not a minor force, especially in a district that was then 50 percent African American. In New Jersey, every legislative district has one senator and two members of the assembly, and I recruited two African Americans to run on my line for the assembly: Leroy Jones, an Essex County freeholder who had a contentious relationship with D'Alessio, and Nia Gill, an outspoken Montclair attorney. Our line became known as Line C.

But Cooper and I headed the ticket and we ran as ebony and ivory, salt and pepper, two good guys, both in their forties, running against the evil, crooked machine. Which the machine always is when you're against it. Tom Barrett, a political consultant who has since done a lot of work for me, worked for D'Alessio then. He warned D'Alessio that I would make him the issue, not Brown, and with D'Alessio under indictment I would win. He had it right. Our polls, and probably his too, showed that Democrats were ready to rally to an anti-boss campaign. Frank Baraff, my political consultant then and now, and Brad Lawrence, another consultant, devised an ad, the first of its kind as far as I know, that started with a picture of Brown, but by the end he had slowly morphed into D'Alessio. The concept was incredibly effective and would become a political advertising cliché in a few years.

Even though D'Alessio was the constant target, I did have fun pounding away at all of Brown's public jobs—five of them as I remember, enough that he made more than the president. Baroff concocted one piece of literature with President Clinton's face on the front with the question, "Who's the public official who makes more than the president of the United States?" On the inside was a picture of Brown. I had the idea of taking a photo of him at the Saint Patrick's Day parade wearing a big hat, and we put that on the front of a piece of literature asking, "How many hats does Bob Brown wear?" We then listed his jobs: mayor, assemblyman, county bond counsel, Passaic Valley Sewer Commission counsel, and counsel for something else. "In fact," it said, "he makes more money with your tax dollars than the

President of the United States." Once at a debate when he accused me of not doing enough to counter unemployment, I said unemployment would go down if he just shared a few of his jobs with others.

They put out literature castigating Cardell for supporting the white guy, me, against Brown and portraying me as another power-hungry pol. More than once Brown charged me with being a racist who didn't care about blacks in the district. At a debate in the packed basement at Saint Matthew's AME Church in Orange, he accused me, with more poetry than accuracy, of listening to "the songs of the suburbs," and failing "to stand up for our children."

"You are so full of hate," I responded as calmly as I could. "You can't go a minute without injecting race. Put race aside. Let's talk." Things got really tense that night when some of his supporters in the audience opened their jackets to make sure I saw their guns. We were both asked if we would retain D'Alessio as county chairman. I said "no," he said "yes."

Four days later, on June 2, a headline in the *Star-Ledger* pretty much solidified our victory: "United Black Clergy Group Endorses Codey, Cooper." The vote among the black ministers was unanimous; our opposition to D'Alessio was a big reason. Despite the ministers' support, New Jersey's National Organization for Women came out for Brown. Two women met with me and Larry DeMarzo to talk about abortion. As I recall, one had dyed orange hair and both were to the left of Che Guevara, and as belligerent. My position was that I favored parental consent for abortion if the girls were thirteen or fourteen, as opposed to sixteen or seventeen, when they are more mature. And even for the younger girls I said I would make an exception in cases of incest. That wasn't good enough for them.

But there were some great nights, like the time Cardell and I walked into an Italian restaurant and people cheered us for standing up to the bosses.

Our entire line won, and as I told Cardell, neither of us had to kiss the ass of the county bosses any longer. The election also helped me establish a reputation as a good government progressive who enlisted new blood into the party leadership.

D'Alessio, incidentally, was convicted on twelve counts in the extortion case and sentenced to forty-six months. I was not overly charitable in my remarks: "It's sad to see what happens, especially to a political career, when a person loses sight of certain values. It's time to move the county forward, because it's certainly been in reverse the last year and a half."

Funny thing, I always hated county politics. But you can't avoid it when they're trying to do you in.

The fighting continued the following year in the Democratic primary for county executive—the job D'Alessio had to forfeit after his conviction. This was an unusually tangled affair. The candidates were Cardell Cooper again and Tom Giblin, who had already succeeded D'Alessio as party chair. Giblin was practically born into Essex County politics. His father, John, had been head of Operating Engineers Local 68, the same union Tom would lead, just as Tom would also follow his father as an Essex County freeholder. It is the way of Irish political clans in Essex.

Cooper and I had become almost a team by then, and I signed on as his campaign manager. Interestingly, given how often race becomes a factor when a white is running against a black, I was a white guy running the black guy's campaign, and Giblin's campaign manager was State Senator Ron Rice, an African American. And more surprisingly, miraculously almost, the black candidate carried Livingston, which is virtually all white, but lost Newark, which is mainly African American. Cooper was like an early-day Barack Obama, appealing to the same educated, white suburbanites. Black opponents, like the then-mayor of Newark, Sharpe James, liked to say he was an Uncle Tom who knew nothing about the black street experience. James really was afraid that Cooper would compete for leadership among blacks.

We sought that year to win the support of Steve Adubato, the longtime boss of Newark's North Ward, one of those guys I don't get along with because they wield a lot of power but never really face the voters.

We met with Adubato and he said he had to think about it—he wasn't opposed to Cardell, he just wanted to be sure. I knew he was looking for something and I just couldn't help myself. "Steve," I said as diplomatically as possible, "you're a doublecrosser and everyone knows you're a doublecrosser. Today you are with me, tomorrow, you'll stab me in the back." He thought about that for a second or two and said, "Dick, you're right. My thing is deal by deal, and I'm going to support Cardell." Despite that, my relationship with Adubato deteriorated in later years. He runs a bunch of nonprofits in Newark and he maintains control by giving out a lot of jobs. He told me once that he's prepared to do anything to support his programs, that he'd cut an ally's throat in a heartbeat if he thought he needed him out of the way the next time. I told him once: "Your programs are good, but you are only interested in the power the programs give you." His reply: "So what, so long as the people are taken care of." Anyway, he's a very powerful operative in Newark and he hates that I'm independent.

Cardell and I settled on the same strategy against Giblin that we used against Brown. We tied him to D'Alessio and the disgraced Democratic old guard. And again we put together our own ticket, including incumbent sheriff Armando Fontoura, a buddy of mine. Armando, a big, boisterous Portuguese, was a little reluctant to buck the machine, and here's his memory of how I helped persuade him: "A few days before filing, Codey says, 'Come over for coffee.' I knew something was up. Codey doesn't drink coffee and neither do I. He says it will be me, him, and Cardell Cooper. He's got Dunkin' Donuts and juice and shit. Cardell has tea. Dick says, 'Here's what we're going to do. Cardell is going to run for county executive and we'll all be on the same team. We'll have a primary against those guys and we'll beat them.'"

I really wanted that one, and I bugged Cooper all the time to make the phone calls I made to voters and contributors. He hated to call strangers, and he hated to ask for money. He said he didn't want to bother people. Finally, I gave him a list of possible contributors and checked up every day to make sure he made the calls. He did it because he hated hearing from me more than he hated making the calls. We never raised the money that year that I thought we should, but we were well organized in the places we needed to be, like Livingston, Montclair, and West Orange.

Election night was a doozy. In fact, I have never seen one like it. At about 11 P.M., County Clerk Patricia McGarry Drake announced Giblin had won by 13 votes. By midnight, she said, oops, Cooper really won by 19 votes. At 1 A.M., she was back to Giblin by 13. By the time she got it right, after a review of all the voting machines, Cooper had won by 120 votes. Then, coincidental as this might sound, the absentee ballots favored Giblin by 120 votes. The result: a flat-out tie—22,907 votes each. Predictably, the election wound up in the courts. And it wasn't until August 18, more than two months after the primary, that a superior court judge broke the tie after agreeing to count 37 emergency ballots—ballots used when machines malfunction. They gave Cooper a 17-vote margin. The Essex County Board of Elections had a month earlier refused to count those votes, devising some story about them being improperly authorized. The real reason was the board wanted Giblin. But once the judge ruled, Giblin threw in the towel and conceded.

It was all for naught. The Republican, James Treffinger, the mayor of Verona, beat Cooper by a few thousand votes. Fontoura won, but with far less of a margin than a Democrat should get. But I told him to look at the bright side—he won and he no longer had to feel obligated to hire the people the organization tried to foist on him.

I ran one more race off the line, and again with an African American. This was only months after redistricting in the state—I led negotiations for the Democrats—and we had a major victory in that process. Essentially, we "unpacked" the districts with large black majorities, and created new districts with white majorities but significant numbers of blacks. The packed districts had been created to assure some black representation in the legislature—but not too much. We argued that such districts weren't necessary or fair. We said blacks could be elected from the majority white districts we were proposing, giving them more opportunities to win seats. The redistricting commission had eleven votes—five Republicans, five Democrats, and one neutral tiebreaker chosen by the state's chief justice. I'll explain later how we persuaded the tiebreaker.

One of those new districts was mine, the newly drawn 27th, which ran from west Newark to the western suburbs. Giblin, by now Essex Democratic chair for nine years, had been on the redistricting commission with me, and we both felt obligated to get an African American elected to the assembly. He wanted Mims Hackett, the African American mayor of Orange, and George Iverson, the white Democratic chair in South Orange, as the two assembly candidates.

Hackett was fine with me. Hackett is a soft-spoken Alabama native, the grandson of a sharecropper, the father of five boys and one girl, and a former schoolteacher. He moved to New Jersey in 1963 and became the first fully certified black teacher in Union City High School, and was once voted "teacher of the year." I met him in the early 1970s when he moved to Orange, a few blocks from me, and he worked as a legislative aide for my friend, Pat Dodd.

Mims first made it into the newspapers in 1975 in an unfortunate way. He was accused of pistol-whipping and beating the hell out of a guy named Larry Moss. Mims had come home from a walk with his wife, Bernice, found his home burglarized, was told by an acquaintance that Moss was the culprit, and, according to police, was trying to get Moss to confess. Moss filed a complaint and Hackett was charged with kidnapping. Hackett denied everything except that his house had been burglarized; police said he inadvertently admitted to the beating during questioning.

A grand jury declined to indict him after Moss recanted his story. But when Hackett announced his candidacy for Orange City Council in 1976, police pressed for another grand jury hearing and this time Hackett was indicted—one week before the council race. He believes to this day that the police pushed for the grand jury because they didn't want a black man on city council. But he was convicted and ludicrously sentenced to the mandatory thirty years for kidnapping. The story even made *60 Minutes*.

A few other Essex leaders and I appealed to Governor Byrne to commute his sentence, which he did, and Hackett was released after serving eight months. In 1980, a federal judge overturned the original conviction, citing serious errors by the trial judge. Hackett's record was expunged. Mims was also a big basketball fan; all his sons played basketball and football, and one, Marcus, played football professionally. By 1981, Hackett had served on the Orange City Council and then become mayor. And I was happy to have him on my ticket. It was Iverson I didn't want. I wanted John McKeon, who had been bitten by the political bug as a kid and just started hanging around my office and being useful. He posted signs and made phone calls when I first ran for the assembly, and when I won, as he says, he was deputy assistant in charge of setting up the chairs at the victory celebration. He was about fifteen at the time.

John, who looks a little like Erik Estrada, the very handsome if not very talented actor, eventually went to Seton Hall law school and did a lot of work on my first Senate campaign. By 1987, I named him my legislative counsel. In 1992, he was elected to the West Orange council. He then got beat for mayor in 1994, but was elected in 1998, and was extremely popular.

By 2001, he was itching to go to the assembly, he was my protégé, he had earned the shot, and I wanted him on the ticket. Giblin, asserting his role as county chair, objected and said he would pick the line, not me. I said, fine, I'll run against the line. Hackett, who had already committed to Giblin, was driving down to Alabama with his mother when I reached him and told him what I wanted to do. A little uneasily, he agreed to join the ticket with John and me. We called ourselves the "Essex Democrats." I warned them both that it could be a hell of a fight because we'd have an African American on our ticket and only about 15 percent of the district was black.

Giblin complained later that he tried hard to reach a compromise. "[Codey] wanted to pick all the candidates and there's not a senator in New Jersey who does that," he said. "My hands are clean. Dick Codey's are dirty." I'm sure he saw it that way, but I figured after all those years in the legislature I was entitled to run with the ticket I wanted. Besides, even though I expected a battle, I was confident that I had a good enough organization to win it.

McKeon and I had one meeting at the Star Tavern in Orange with Giblin and Tom Barrett. Giblin tried to persuade John to wait his turn and the organization would then support him. They said they thought they needed a Jew on the ticket in this new district. Neither John nor I bought any of it, and John said some less than respectful things to the chairman. John recruited Jewish leaders in the community to fax letters to Giblin supporting John. Giblin finally chose two white female freeholders to run for the assembly, one Jewish. But he never picked a candidate to run against me. I think he figured I wouldn't campaign if I were unopposed. But that was nuts. I went at it like it was my own race; my prestige—and my independence—was at stake. We really weren't sure how voters would respond to Hackett. He had never been in some of the white towns in the district, although a lot of people had read about his kids in the papers' sports sections.

We ended up losing almost every town, most by small margins, but we won so big in Orange, West Orange, and Newark that both Hackett and McKeon won. I always figured that getting Hackett elected—a black man in a white district who had been convicted of kidnapping—was my greatest electoral accomplishment.

Hackett even became chairman of my old committee on state government. But things turned badly on September 6, 2007, when I got an early morning call—never comforting—from John McKeon. One of Mims's sons had called to tell John that the FBI had arrested his father at seven in the morning. Even without John's call, September 6 was going to be a lousy day. I was scheduled to testify that morning before a federal grand jury investigating Senator Joe Coniglio of Bergen County.

Coniglio, a union plumber, is a good guy who I figured would never do anything wrong, and I still don't think he did. He wanted to retire as a plumber and was looking for something else. I said, "Geez, Joe, why don't you get a job as a union official?" But he said he didn't want to sit behind a desk. Some months later, in a brief conversation, he said he'd like to do something in government or public relations. I recommended he check out some institutions or corporations that often need knowledgeable people to handle political or community problems. He got himself hired as a $5,000-a-month consultant at the Hackensack University Medical Center—a job some argued that he wouldn't have gotten if he weren't a senator. Nonetheless, I thought he was unusually qualified to do public relations with the communities a hospital serves. The hospital was building a new cancer center, and it received $1.6 million in state money for the project. The feds concluded that Coniglio had no real job except to work in the legislature to get money for the hospital. Which is what that investigation was about. By September, the morning I got the call about Mims, we were two months from an election and our polls showed that the investigation was killing Coniglio. It looked like he would probably lose what is normally a safe Democratic district. So Joe Ferriero, the Bergen County chairman, and I sat down with him, explained the facts, and convinced him to drop his bid for reelection. He knew he had no choice, but he was concerned about his wife's keeping her job working for the Bergen County freeholders. But that was never an issue and Coniglio announced his withdrawal a few days after my testimony. Ultimately, Coniglio was convicted on five counts of fraud and one of extortion. After the verdict was announced, I said, "I have always known Joe Coniglio to be a caring and dedicated individual and this decision in no way changes my feelings about him." They say any prosecutor could indict a ham sandwich and I think the Coniglio case proved that in today's climate if you're a politician the jury will convict a BLT. I made sure to stay in touch with Coniglio even when he was in prison. (A couple of years later, in 2009, Ferriero was convicted of fraud in a federal case for secretly marketing a consulting firm he owned in towns where he had political influence. But the conviction was overturned and the charges were dropped a year later.)

In Hackett's case, he and ten other public officials at various levels of government throughout New Jersey were charged with accepting bribes from undercover agents and cooperating witnesses in return for awarding roofing and insurance contracts. Mims took $5,000 in cash from an undercover FBI agent outside the Orange City Hall in exchange for supporting an insurance contract with the city. While he was being taped, the agent slipped $5,000 in a brochure and handed it to Mims. Mims said he couldn't take it, but they pressed him and he relented. Then he used the money to pay for a picnic for kids in Orange. Every kid got a soda, a hamburger, a hot dog, and a backpack.

The next night Mims and his wife came over to talk. He said he had a lawyer who thought acquittal was possible. I said: "Mims, if what the government is saying is true and it's on tape, you're going to jail . . . and why in God's name you are meeting with three white strangers to talk about contracts is beyond me." I told him he had to resign from the legislature.

I had him sit at my desk, the same desk I used in the governor's office, handed him a piece of paper, and he wrote his resignation: "I, Mims Hackett, hereby resign as of September 7. . . ." I still have the original.

Bernice left my living room during the conversation and walked to the staircase leading to the second floor. She sat down and held her head in her hands. I'm not sure, but I think she was sobbing. I felt terribly, and also betrayed. Mims was my friend for thirty years. But I did recommend another attorney, whom he hired. Mims eventually pleaded guilty and avoided a trial.

I want to insert a few general thoughts here about corruption in New Jersey. A lot has been written so suggest that somehow this is a unique New Jersey problem. I don't think the citizens of New York or Illinois or Pennsylvania or Florida or a lot of other states would agree. We've had our share, no question about that. But I don't think we've had more than our share.

A couple of points to keep in mind:

- Many pundits believe that after Chris Christie was appointed U.S. attorney by President George W. Bush he quickly set his eye on the governor's mansion and devoted enormous resources to public corruption. You look hard enough, you'll find something, even if that something often amounts to almost nothing.
- With some exceptions, almost all corruption has been on the local level, rather than the state. New Jersey has local autonomy like nobody else—566 municipalities and 588 school districts for only 2,500 schools. That's just over 4 a district. They all have taxing power and they all award contracts. Which means there's a lot of opportunity for graft for a lot of poorly paid officials. The legislature does not award contracts, so there are a lot fewer temptations in Trenton.
- There's also a lot more scrutiny for public officials. And elected officials ought to be held to a higher standard. If a mayor has a city vendor pave his driveway with a value of $2,000, there's a news conference and an indictment. But if his neighbor embezzles $200,000 from his company, nobody outside the company ever hears about it. That's just a fact of life.

Taking bribes has been illegal since George Washington. We can pass all the laws in the world, but we will never change the evil that lurks in the hearts of some men and women.

I've been often asked how I avoided getting into any trouble after so many years in Jersey politics. It's easy really. The most important thing is that the day I'm buried, my wife and children can hold their heads up high. A lot of people have said I've made money in the insurance business because of political contacts. But the truth is that over three decades, I've turned down a lot of business opportunities that were both legal and ethical and worth a lot of money. I just wasn't comfortable with them. People would say, "Dick, why would you do that? At some point you're going to be out of office. And you've got a $30,000 pension to show for it." Which was true until I became governor. But that's who I am. And fortunately, my family is not starving.

———

Lord Palmerston, who served two terms as Britain's prime minister in the mid-nineteenth century, once observed that "nations have no permanent alliances, only permanent interests." In his own, somewhat less formal manner, Tom Giblin, the Essex County Democratic leader whom I defeated in 2001, says much the same about Essex County politics: "It's like square dancing. Sometimes you change partners." Giblin has been around almost forever and he knows what he's talking about. And the very next year, 2002, I supported him when he ran in the Democratic primary for county executive against Joe DiVincenzo.

It was another ugly Essex family brawl, with each candidate spending more than $1 million to slime the other. A million dollars to lead one county in one state! Sounds crazy. But the two most powerful people in Essex County are county executive and the mayor of Newark. There are a lot of jobs to give out and a lot of cachet. DiVincenzo won, badly disappointing Giblin, who thirsted for the job. DiVincenzo and I had been less than close for years. He's also real close to—some would say in the pocket of—Steve Adubato, the power broker who agreed with me when I called him a snake.

Three years later, though, when DiVincenzo kicked off his campaign for reelection on the steps of the Hall of Records in Newark, I was there to support him. And so was Giblin. Joe D, as everyone calls him, was going to be the Democratic nominee and it was time to square dance.

By then, I had become a leader in the senate and I would have no real opposition in my next election. That aside, in a world where memories are long and revenge revered there were more fights to come.

8

My Crusade on Behalf
of the Mentally Ill

When I was working for my dad, picking up dead bodies, I sometimes had to go to the morgue at the Greystone Park Psychiatric Hospital in Parsippany. Greystone was no ordinary psychiatric hospital. It was a campus of forty-three buildings and residential cottages on 130 acres surrounded by lush landscape and dominated by the historic Kirkbride Building, an imposing cathedral-like structure completed in 1896. From then until 1943, when the Pentagon opened, the Kirkbride Building was the largest structure in the country under one roof.

Greystone's original name could hardly have been more politically incorrect: the New Jersey State Lunatic Asylum. Still, it was considered a national model for progressive care, built and organized under the principles of Dr. Thomas Story Kirkbride, who believed mental patients could be treated best in buildings that provided privacy, comfort, a lot of sunlight, and individual attention. By the time I was picking up dead bodies, the facility, despite being expanded several times, was seriously overcrowded and most of Dr. Kirkbride's idealism could no longer be found at Greystone.

Any time I went to the morgue at Greystone, a patient was assigned to help me lift the body onto the stretcher, and I tipped him a couple of bucks. Once, I got a kid about nineteen, my age at the time, who was the first to tell me horror stories about the place—how carelessly older patients were treated, how female patients were sometimes sexually exploited, and how the buildings were falling apart. Coincidentally, the *Star-Ledger* did an exposé on Greystone a few months later, which stuck in my mind.

That's how I became interested in the mentally ill; that was the beginning of what would become a long-term effort to ensure humane treatment for them, and why I've become such a pain in the ass when the treatment falls short. Most people think I got into it because of Mary Jo's illness—and that certainly increased my interest—but it was Greystone and that nineteen-year-old patient that got me started.

If casino legislation was the hallmark of my assembly years, mental health has been the watchword of my senate years. When I became chairman of the health committee in the senate, I made the rounds of three large mental institutions, Greystone, Marlboro, and Trenton. I didn't have to be a psychiatrist to recognize that some of the employees I saw had no more idea of how to care for the patients than Nurse Ratched in *One Flew over the Cuckoo's Nest*. Some did fine, some tried hard but couldn't do it, and some just hung around and got paid. That's when I got the idea to check these people out. A friend in the Communications Workers of America got me the names, birthdates, and Social Security numbers of everyone employed at the three facilities, and a source in the state police ran background checks on them.

We learned that 326 of the 4,171 employees had been arrested and 177 of them had been convicted. And these were not mere victimless misdemeanors. There were people who had committed murder, manslaughter, sexual assault, and child abuse. Twenty had been convicted of assault and associated crimes and a quarter were convicted of drug-related crimes. One person had been hired a year earlier even though a murder indictment was pending, and another had been arrested ten times in a nine-year span for, among other behavioral shortcomings, sexual assault and kidnapping.

The Department of Human Services was failing to make basic background checks into those caring for some of the state's most vulnerable citizens. There was a lot of press coverage and some angry editorials when I made my findings public. The department correctly pointed out that state law forbids denying employment to rehabilitated convicts, but the commissioner still conceded the obvious: "Many undesirables have been hired in sensitive positions without the necessary precautions."

An internal department investigation came up with pretty much the same results. Several dozen people were fired or suspended. About

75 of the 326 had already quit, probably figuring they were going to be axed anyway. And human services officials pledged more thorough background and fingerprint checks in the future. But two years later I heard from a support group of patient relatives that proper checks were not being done.

That is why on February 5, 1987, I went underground for eighteen days to discover what was really happening to one of the state's most vulnerable populations. My investigation put me at the center of New Jersey's mental health system—and, in the process, made me perhaps the state's most recognized legislator.

I had started thinking about doing something like this about two months before the day I drove to Marlboro Psychiatric Hospital with my chief of staff at the time and good friend Larry DeMarzo. The plan was for me—using another name—to interview for a low-level job. Earlier, I tried for an attendant's job at Greystone using the name and birth date of James Kirkland, a convicted sex offender who was then dead. Kirkland's Social Security number was not in his police record, so I used the number of a Eugene Anderson, a convicted armed robber, also dead.

To get the Social Security card, Larry and I visited a hole-in-the-wall shop on Times Square—this when Times Square was still as seedy as Sodom—that openly sold fake documents, birth certificates, driver's licenses, Social Security cards, whatever. I gave the guy behind the desk the number I wanted on my new Social Security card, and presto, for a few bucks I was Eugene Anderson. With the name and number of two dead guys, I figured I was making it pretty easy for the hospital to reject my application, and Greystone, in fact, did. I then sent the same application to Marlboro in Monmouth County. There, I don't think it would have mattered had I used the name Charles Manson.

As requested, I gave the names and phone numbers of three people I said could vouch for my qualifications: two were senate aides and one a friend. None were called. Neither was the restaurant where I said I was working. The owner had agreed to cover for me if contacted. February 5 was my interview day.

According to the log I kept, I went to the appropriate office and was sent by a Mr. Magliaro to a supervisor in Cottage 16, one of a number of Tudor-style dorms housing patients. Without knowing me from anybody, and certainly not from James Kirkland, the supervisor, according to my log, volunteered that I would "see things that I have never seen before. She told me I would see sex between patients; girl to girl, boy to boy, and girl to boy."

Following this unexpected education I returned to Mr. Magliaro, who told me the supervisor liked what she had seen and the job was as good as mine. I just had to return in five days for a physical and "background check." The first part of the physical consisted of a urine test, during which I easily could have substituted someone else's; a blood test, administered so amateurishly that I had black and blue marks for a week; and a TB test. As for the background check, I handed over my fake Social Security card, and that was where I got nervous. It was not the best of forgeries, but the clerk just copied and returned it. I also gave them my fingerprints, which were never checked.

I was asked one question: Why did I want the job? "I want to work my way up," I said, and the clerk said I might run the place someday. Three days later, they examined my eyes, took my blood pressure, checked my weight, and said all was fine, but I still couldn't be cleared for work until my chest X-ray was read. I thought, "What a joke. Here I am, a sex offender and that's okay, but God forbid my chest X-ray isn't read."

Orientation was one forty-minute session the following week. The girl sitting next to me wondered why we had to be trained "to work with crazy people." At lunch, I sat next to a couple of attendants, one of whom worked an overnight shift and told me he got to play with "the pretty girls while they are sleeping."

This was followed by two days of a class for prospective aides. During the coffee break on the first day, an aide warned me that even if a patient becomes violent aides may be fired for striking back. The solution: take them into a closet where no one can see you. A classmate told me he had just served a jail term for failing to pay child support. The judge had offered him two options: sell his car and pay the support, or two weeks in jail. He chose the latter. Sitting next to this sensitive soul was a former drug addict. Overall, I felt half of my twenty classmates were too immature for the job and some were mentally unstable. The next day I was told to report to work at 11:30 that night. I guess my chest X-ray was okay. Job title: "Human Services aide."

Pay: $5.95 an hour—not exactly an incentive for top people, even in 1987.

I had already proved my point. People with no qualifications at all—even sex offenders—could get hired to care for mentally ill patients in New Jersey.

I then worked two shifts and saw things I found terribly trouble-some. In my cottage, with about twenty-seven patients ranging in age from twenty to fifty, rooms were barren and depressing, cell-like; clothes were torn, shabby, and ill-fitting; aides were supposed to make rounds every half hour, but they didn't; at 12:30 A.M., patients were awakened to urinate, too late in one case. Six sheets were put on the offender's bed to absorb any further problems that night, but I was told not to bother waking the patients again for the toilet.

The second night, an older aide, about sixty and more fit for the job than most I saw, told me that one of our patients had murdered a four-year-old boy with a two-by-four. He showed me the patient's medical log which said that the patient has strong hatred for two groups of people, neither of which I belong to, so I asked him to inform the patient of my Irish ancestry. One aide showed me where patient files were kept and we read some private material we had no right to see.

And one patient woke up during the night, screaming, frantically searching trash cans and licking ashtrays. My co-worker said he was looking for cigarettes and ashes—to eat. Being a nice guy he gave the patient a late-night snack—a discarded butt.

About 7:15 in the morning, one patient, unusually well groomed, asked if he could come into the kitchen for coffee, and one of the female attendants agreed. Turned out he was the murderer, but we had one of the more intelligent conversations I had at Marlboro. What I feared most during my tour never happened: that someone would recognize me and say, "Hey, you're a state senator; what are you doing here?" At 7:30, I left for good.

The whole experience was profoundly depressing, especially the patients who just lay in one corner or another, screaming or mumbling incoherently. I came away, as I said at the time, convinced that "these patients were probably treated with less care than the average prisoner. They are not dressed as well nor do they participate in as many activities as the average prisoner. The great irony, of course, is that most of these people have done nothing wrong." Of the daily routine, I said: "There is little, if any, activity for the chronic patients with whom I worked. They are housed in depressing cottages, stare at the walls all day and sleep all night." Some were simply put in front of a television from the time they got up to the time they went to sleep, sixteen hours later, with interruptions for meals only.

The story of my detective work exploded across the top of page one of the Sunday *Star-Ledger* on March 1. The reporter, Guy Sterling, was one of the few people I had alerted in advance about my sleuthing, and, by agreement, I called him every night to report what I had seen. In the end, Guy was disappointed that I worked only two days—he felt the story could have been meatier had I stayed longer and seen more. But as I said, I proved my point. And the reaction was swift.

Governor Thomas Kean, not one to be upstaged, was embarrassed by the headlines and referred to the investigation as an "escapade." Still, he ordered a speedy investigation of his own. What I had found, he acknowledged, "was totally unacceptable. Not even normal personnel procedures were followed." He ordered Human Services Commissioner Altman to report back within five days.

The following day, I held a news conference in the senate chamber, attracting more reporters—some from foreign countries—than some had ever seen in Trenton. The story had obviously angered and interested a lot of people. I also introduced legislation requiring criminal background checks for anyone working at a psychiatric institution, and a psychiatric evaluation for anyone working with patients. Kean said he would make no decision until receiving Altman's report. He said he wanted to be sure that what I had seen was not an "aberration."

One quick side note. A union official told me when my investigation became public that an African American woman with whom I had worked at the hospital called the union office and said she should have known something was suspicious. "White guys don't work the midnight shift," she said.

Altman within days recommended tighter hiring practices, including criminal background checks for institutional employees, and he assigned a management team to review Marlboro's procedures and patient care. Marlboro's director was reassigned. I was delighted.

Altman, by the way, was a bright, young public health official, but he didn't have the political street smarts needed in a job like his. But he was happy to have me around. His take: "There wasn't much political support for the institutions, so the giant stink was very helpful. Anything that focused attention on the institutions helped." Altman went on to become president of the Henry J. Kaiser Family Foundation, which does research into health care, and his is a major voice in the health care debate.

No matter what I learned firsthand at Marlboro, I was still shocked at hearings I held the following month. One witness testified that his thirty-two-year-old daughter had become pregnant twice during her three years at Marlboro. She had an abortion the first time; the second she had the baby and gave it up for adoption. "My wife and I tried to get her consent for an abortion," said the father, "but she was drugged to the point that you couldn't talk rationally to her."

Another witness, a one-time patient, said she was sometimes kept in seclusion for periods of one to three days, and once had been tied down, given an injection by aides, and raped.

The purpose of the hearing was the same as my purpose for working at Marlboro or checking the police records of workers in psychiatric institutions: raise public awareness and concern about mental illness. I think I succeeded. That I also became one of the state's most popular politicians was a nice side benefit.

In the next few months, the Kean administration instituted a $4 million emergency plan for Marlboro, which included hiring two hundred additional staff to care for patients and a new facility to screen patients. And finally, on June 28, 1988, Kean signed the bill I called for a year earlier for criminal background checks for all employees at psychiatric institutions and for all future applicants. It was a good day for New Jersey's mentally ill and their families. Another good day happened ten years later almost to the day, July 1, 1998, when Marlboro was closed.

But my battles with the mental health system weren't finished—by a long shot.

There was once a luxury hotel in East Orange called the Marlborough and owned by the Rockefeller Hotel Co. By August of 2004, it had become the Eden House, a state-licensed nursing home for the mentally ill, and I had heard the conditions were sickening. So on August 11, I paid a surprise visit with Robert Davison, the dedicated head of the Mental Health Association of Essex County. Coincidentally, it was the day before McGreevey announced his resignation. It was sweltering and we had to walk past weathered prostitutes asking for dates while being careful not to slip on the crack vials on the sidewalk outside Eden House. Seventy-one people who had been released from mental hospitals were living there like concentration camp victims. I found, as I said in a press conference my first day as governor, "dead mice, extreme heat, puddles of urine, cockroaches running all over the place." It smelled like a men's room in which the toilets hadn't been flushed for a week. There was no air conditioning. Three and four people were crowded into a room. Residents, many wandering aimlessly, complained that mice and roaches had the run of the place.

We were walking from the second to the third floors when two police officers, one a sergeant, showed up and said we were trespassing and had to leave. But the sergeant recognized me and told his companion, "I'm not throwing Senator Codey out." It was worse than what I had seen at Marlboro. Because I had invited a *Star-Ledger* reporter to tag along, the story got good play and the state health commissioner ordered inspections of all of New Jersey's 151 residential facilities for the mentally ill. Hal Katz, who owned Eden House, didn't even dispute my findings. He was receiving $595 a month per patient, which he said wasn't enough for him to do a better job. He was fined but he stayed in business. The state department of health closed the place a day after I left the governor's office; I said at the time, "I thought it was a great tribute to me."

Three years later, in August of 2007, I visited three nursing homes to check summer conditions. Here's how *Star-Ledger* reporter Mark Mueller described what we saw at a Newark nursing home: "Until she breathed, the woman on the fifth floor looked like a shrouded corpse. A sheet covered her body from head to toe. Uneaten dinner lay at the end of the bed, by her feet. No one at the Newark nursing home removed the sheet to check on her. In another room, Elizabeth Maxey tried desperately to feed herself, but she couldn't bring up her arm without shaking, losing bits of mashed potato and blobs of pudding with each attempt. No staff member came to her aid. The temperature in both rooms was close to 90 degrees, almost unbearable in the humidity.

"Neglect. Stifling heat. Broken televisions. Unsanitary bathrooms."

I called the state health commissioner to send inspectors immediately. The two other places I visited had no such problems. But one of them, a nursing home, was a client of my insurance company, and the owner called Rob Parisi, who ran the company for me, threatening to find another agent. Parisi called me and said the guy was irate. I said, "I'm not going to call them and I will never apologize, even if it means my family will be homeless. If they want to take their business somewhere with less integrity, let them." They did and it didn't matter.

When I became governor, I finally had the clout to bring a spotlight rather than a flashlight to mental health. I dedicated my first day as governor, November 16, 2004, to the issue. And I made clear that it would be a continuing priority. My first official act, at 7:50 A.M. on Day One, was a French toast and maple syrup breakfast-visit with fifty Greystone patients. My son Kevin came with me, which meant a lot. It was his first contact with the mentally ill and I wanted him to understand why I was so determined to be the governor for the most vulnerable. One patient chatted with me for a few minutes and then walked away muttering to herself: "They told you not to tire him out and you didn't. You did pretty good. I'm proud of you." As I told the press at Greystone: "This is where my heart is. We need to take a new direction in how we treat the mentally ill."

From Greystone, I returned to the State House in Trenton and started that new direction, signing my first executive order, which established a task force to reform the state's abysmal mental health system. I put Bob Davison, the guy who accompanied me to Eden House, in charge. I picked him because he was not a big player in the mental health bureaucracy. I knew if I wanted real change I couldn't rely on the same people who were screwing up the system—and benefiting. "I want your honest opinion and don't be afraid to piss people off," I told Davison. "As long as it's reasonable, I'll back you up." I stressed two other points: "I have fourteen months here and we need to get this done now. And don't give me bullshit." I set a tight deadline, March 31, four and a half months, for the report to be in. "This task force," I said in a brief speech before the signing, "is not to be perceived as an excuse for studying something to death, something we've done too often here in Trenton."

I concluded by pledging: "If there is anything that my administration will stand for, it is compassion and standing up for those who may not be able to stand up for themselves."

After the talk, I signed the executive order and took questions from the press. The task force, by the way, met my deadline with more than fifty specific suggestions, almost all which have been enacted. Many required legislation, but for many that I could implement on my own I signed an executive order. The order, I said, will "ensure the decades of neglect the mental health system has endured is a thing of the past."

Most important, I directed the appropriate state agencies to make sure their rules allowed for the 10,000 housing units for the mentally ill that I had proposed earlier in a State of the State address. That proposal became law in August of 2005, when I signed a bill allocating $200 million for the Special Needs Housing Trust Fund. There were more than 7,000 homeless mentally ill people in New Jersey, a horror about to end. I also established a governor's council on Mental Health Stigma to educate the public about mental disease and I got $250,000 in the budget for that.

Here's another good place to applaud my wife. A lot of what we accomplished was helped mightily by the speeches she made around the state talking about mental health and her own illness. She connected with people not as a politician, but as a New Jersey mother and schoolteacher and former patient. She was an invaluable partner.

Nor was I finished with my surprise inspections. In July 2005, when I was governor, I called Davison and told him, as he remembers it, "I'm hearing from my sources that there's no fucking air conditioning at Greystone. Will you confirm that for me." Bob found out that the Abell Building, which housed about two hundred people, was without air conditioning and the place was like a frying pan. I said I'm going up there to take a look. Larry DeMarzo, my point man on social issues like mental health, didn't want me to go, figuring it was like investigating myself. After all, I was governor. If something was wrong, I was responsible. But I went anyway, and Larry and Davison and a *Star-Ledger* reporter came along. On the way, we stopped at a hardware store and I gave money to the trooper driving us to buy a thermostat.

The front door was locked for security reasons, so we made our way around the back, plodding through some mud and high grass, which didn't make the trooper very happy, and we saw a guy peeling potatoes on a loading dock. "Hey, Governor Codey," he said, as though he was expecting me. "How you doing?" We found an open door and went straight to the dining room, where dinner was being served. Four of six fans were working there, so conditions weren't too horrible. But one staff member came up and whispered: "Go upstairs and see how hot it is." Upstairs was where the patients lived, and it was brutal. The temperature in rooms I visited was over 80 degrees, some windows couldn't be opened and fans or portable conditioners weren't working. In a day room where patients congregated, the thermostat recorded 89. The television was broken and showed just scrambled patterns. "How long has this show been on?" I asked.

The heat drained you and sweat dripped even when walking slowly. One patient told me he slept with his bedroom door open, sacrificing all privacy for a little ventilation. He said his roommate had slept a few nights earlier on a mattress in the hallway. Another patient told me about bed sheets sticking to his body when he slept. Patients in hospitals that treat physical ailments never have to put up with such outrageous conditions. That is the stigma of mental illness.

Janet Monroe, the hospital CEO, and other officials there, told me that an ancient, faltering electrical system couldn't tolerate more fans or portable air conditioners.

"Don't tell me you're not hot," I said.

"No," she said. "We're hot."

"This is just unacceptable," I said. "Get this situation fixed. Get bids on it tomorrow."

Within days maintenance and engineering crews were making improvements. Within less than two weeks, workers installed a temporary air cooling and ventilation system. Four massive commercial air conditioning units outside the facility pumped cool air into a series of yellow hoses, which, like elephantine straws, carried the air into wards of the Abell Building. It wasn't perfect, but it was a lot better. Had I gone through normal channels, even as governor, nothing would have been done until summer was over.

Once I did an inspection at Greystone and it was like going to a Potemkin village. Everything looked cleaner and more orderly than normal. I picked up one carpet and there was still a sales tag on the bottom. If I wanted the truth, I usually had to surprise them. Eventually, I knew the place so well, I referred to different areas as though they were rooms in my house.

March 15, 2005, was a great day. Demolition began on the 104-year-old dormitory building at Greystone so that construction could begin on a new $188 million hospital on the campus. I have never felt better than when I shouted at the guy operating the wrecking machine to "Go," and monster-like claws coming out of the machine's long arms started eating into the dilapidated building.

After Thanksgiving that year, I decided to do a sleepover at Greystone and bring a little Christmas spirit to the place. But I really wanted to surprise the patients. When I got there, Kevin Martone, whom I had appointed to head a state division of mental health services, and DeMarzo were waiting for me at the gate, but so were a bunch of other people. I was so angry—like a kid whose surprise has been ruined— I almost didn't get out of the car. I should have realized that when you're governor things get out. Anyway, I ate dinner and breakfast with the patients, and during the broccoli-and-cheese dinner, someone asked me what I thought of the food. "It tastes like shit," I said. The broccoli was tasteless, and the salad, served in a Styrofoam cup, was worse. And I can assure you we didn't have a choice of dressing. I just kept thinking, "Thank God, I brought pizza. I'll be a hungry guy after this."

If the food was bad at Greystone, it was probably bad in every institution. They all serve the same menus. Once Pete Cammarano, my chief of staff, was with me when I paid a surprise visit to Greystone and had lunch. It was the first institutional meal Pete had ever eaten, and he said it was the worst food he had ever had. All I could tell him was the patients eat like that every meal. Anyway, Martone was at my table when I offered my food review and he just blanched. A couple of patients nodded in agreement. But Martone did go out and meet with the appropriate people and told them that the food they serve patients should be food they want to eat themselves. And it has improved. Monroe, the hospital CEO, swears the broccoli and cheese dinner I had has never returned to the menu.

Otherwise that was just a terrific pre-Christmas visit. I brought pizza and soda to share with my ward mates. I handed out T-shirts with a basketball logo on the front and the words "Giving Recovery a Shot." On the back, it said Codey and the number 1. A chorus from James Caldwell High School sang Christmas songs. An African American woman named Peggy insisted on sitting in the second row behind me. The troopers got a little concerned, but I told them to relax. When there was a song about a couple going to Starbucks, she whispered in my ear: "You know we don't go to Starbucks. We go to Dunkin' Donuts." Peggy and I even got on the stage and joined in singing, "I Wish You a Merry Christmas." A staff member told me she had never before seen Peggy smile. Some of the patients hugged me and broke my heart with their personal stories about addictions, about living with bipolar and other diseases and coping with a mother's death. A few even urged me to run for president. As I was leaving after breakfast on the second day, one of the patients, Robert Romash, looked at my watch with the governor's seal and said how much he liked it. In the spirit of the evening, I gave it to him.

The following Christmas, Mary Jo and Chris came with me for another pizza party and we handed out small gifts. As we mixed with the patients, one woman, Barbara, hugged me and told us how mental illness and drug addiction had plagued her life. She hadn't seen her seven-year-old daughter in five years. "I want to get better," she pleaded. "I don't want to get high anymore."

Then she offered to trade some pearls for a Christmas brooch Mary Jo was wearing. Mary Jo really liked that pin, but she thought the trade was in a good cause. I don't know where Barbara is now. Maybe she and Robert have started a jewelry business.

One last Greystone story. In June of 2008, the new building seemed done and ready to open, but for one reason or another it never opened. In fact, a gala grand opening ceremony had been held seven months earlier. The contractors' excuse: they were still testing complicated high-tech systems. I wanted to see for myself and arranged with the Department of Human Services to sleep over on June 2. I was the first overnight resident and I had the place to myself. I toured the building, watched television, read a book, used the toilet, and went to sleep. And the next day I called the contractor and asked what the hell was going on. A day later, they announced their work would be done in a week and patients could begin moving in in a matter of weeks.

"You can't send all of the responsible officials over in their jammies for a group sleep-in," the *Star-Ledger* editorialized. "But is there anywhere else we need to send Codey in his?"

9

State Senate President

It was Christmas morning in 2000, the last Christmas of the twentieth century. The kids had opened their presents, we had gotten all the wrapping picked up and thrown away, and I drove to my office to call Leon Sokol.

Leon, a slim, street-smart lawyer who grew up in Brooklyn but made his career in New Jersey, had been counsel to the Democrats in the State Senate since 1976, and I've known him longer than that. The senate job is part time; in real life Leon is a senior partner in his Hackensack law firm, and I trust him to do a lot of my private legal work.

But it was the state legislature and its future that I had in mind when I called Leon on Christmas. Leon is Jewish so I knew I wasn't interrupting any family gathering. "Leon," I said, "I don't want to hear any shit. You've got nothing to do today." And we talked about redistricting.

It was a subject I had been thinking about a lot, maybe even obsessing over. It was how Democrats could retake control of the legislature; how I personally could become president of the State Senate—a job I coveted after all those years in Trenton. Republicans had held a majority in both houses since 1991, a reaction to huge tax increases—necessary, but unpopular—instituted by Democratic governor Jim Florio. But there was also the core reality that legislative districts were drawn to favor the Republicans. We made gains in every election after 1991, but realistically we could never overcome the GOP advantage in the assembly or the senate unless we reconfigured the state's forty legislative districts. (Each district elects one senator and two assembly members.) This was politics at the most basic level.

There was no way you could look at the old map and say it was fair. In 1997, the year I became minority leader in the senate, Republicans won 53 percent of the combined senate and assembly vote but 60 percent of the seats. They held a 24–16 margin in the senate. In the assembly races two years later, they won 52 percent of the votes but 56 percent of the seats. Their advantage in the assembly was 45–35, in the senate 24–15, with one independent. Our chance for a more favorable map was coming in April of 2001 during the redistricting ritual that overheats New Jersey's political climate every ten years when the new census is done. Anytime you redistrict, a couple of people are likely to lose their jobs. But if a new map helps swing control from one party to the other, a lot of people lose jobs and power. It's a big deal.

Every state has its own system for redistricting but, because of our election calendar, few, if any, are as intense as New Jersey's. We elect legislators in odd-numbered years, so our primaries in the first year of every decade are held only a few months after new census figures are reported. To get everything done on time, the formal redistricting process takes place within a few frantic weeks in the spring. New Jersey in 2001 was the first state in the nation to adopt its new map. There was no choice.

Each party names five members to a redistricting commission, and the fantasy is that they will deliberate and reach consensus. They never do, and when deadlock is obvious, as it always is, the state's chief justice names an eleventh member, a knowledgeable, neutral figure who, as George W. Bush would say, becomes the decider.

I was chairman of the Democratic commissioners and I named Steve DeMicco, one of the shrewdest behind-the-scenes Democrats in New Jersey, to work with me on strategy. We started well more than a year before the commission was to convene, and DeMicco was first to suggest the plan we ultimately adopted. The plan had great promise but also great risk because it interpreted the 1965 Voting Rights Act in a way that contradicted generally accepted reasoning.

In 1991, the eleventh member had voted for a Republican map that packed black voters into a few districts—a great decision for the Republicans. The theory was that whites wouldn't vote for blacks, so blacks had to be ghettoized to meet a section of the Voting Rights Act that said minorities must have an opportunity to elect representatives of their choice. In reality, a lot of Democratic votes were being wasted. A district we used to win by 70 percent, we now won by 85 percent. But districts we won by 4 percent we now lost by 4. The theory may have been true in some parts of the country, but in New Jersey since 1991, minority legislators could be, had been, elected in mostly white districts. We felt minorities could win in districts no more than 30 or 35 percent black, depending on how Democratic the white population was. Democrats, we felt, would vote for Democrats, regardless of race. If only we could get the minorities into those districts.

It was the law and the redistricting rules that I wanted to discuss when I called Leon Sokol on Christmas. He had been the Democratic counsel on the redistricting commission in 1981 and 1991 and he knew a hell of a lot about it. He was confident we could legally defend a plan that unpacked the largely black districts.

In addition to Sokol, other staff members included Donald Scarinci, a lawyer who had been counsel to the Democrats in the assembly; Kathy Crotty, executive director of the senate Democrats, and two Democratic redistricting experts from Washington—Sam Hirsch, an attorney, and Tom Bonier, a hall of fame numbers cruncher from the National Committee for an Effective Congress, which works on redistricting for the Democratic Party.

Bonier, working on a Dell laptop loaded with maps, voting statistics, ethnic breakdowns, and every other fact we might need, and DeMicco, who pretty much knows voter demographics for every street in New Jersey, decided which towns should go into which districts to make up our map.

Weeks before the commission met, Bonier presented the first version of our map to a meeting of Democratic commissioners, party leaders, and staff who would be working with us. He was nervous as hell. He didn't know most of those people and we were offering some pretty radical changes. Joe Doria, the assembly minority leader who was already upset because he was left off the commission, called it a "bullshit map." Others said it was pie in the sky and would never fly. And it did have some problems. We had put two members in the same district and several members had been moved out of their districts. So Bonier went back to his computer, and over the weeks he developed dozens of variations—all of which assumed unpacking. Every time he drew a new map, I'd ask the same question: "Will that get me to twenty?" meaning will we win twenty seats in the senate so we could at least share power with the Republicans. That was my big concern.

I personally explained the map to virtually every black and Hispanic Democrat in the legislature. I was the only white senator at the time from a majority black district and I had a good relationship with them. The maps dismayed some. Someone accustomed to winning with 85 percent of the vote gets a little paranoid when he knows it will go down to 70 percent, maybe even 65. My pitch was always the same. Without the unpacking, they would always be a minority within a minority. Which, I said, is what the Republicans wanted. With unpacking, they could become part of the majority and help run the place.

With the most reluctant minority legislators, I brought Bonier along to meet with them. Tom would break out his computer, show them a map of their districts, break down the voting patterns, and explain why they would be fine. Eventually, they all went along, which turned out to be crucial.

I also conferred individually with a number of commissioners, and we met as a full commission about a dozen times to agree on strategy. Once we all accepted the unpacking idea, we had one important tactic to work out. In our first presentation to the eleventh member, should we offer a map that was obviously favorable to the Democrats and bargain down from there, or one we thought had a realistic chance of being accepted. Sokol and I, old horse traders at heart, argued for the lopsided map. DeMicco and Bonier believed a realistic map from the start would create credibility. I gave up on that one and I'm glad I did.

Because time was so short, we agreed with the Republicans to declare a deadlock and ask for an eleventh member after meeting for just one hour at the State House. "We're as far apart as Sharon and Arafat," I said at the time. "The biggest problem is the clock is ticking and it's almost ticking away."

Within hours, Deborah Poritz, the state's chief justice, a Republican, appointed Larry Bartels, a forty-four-year-old Princeton University political science professor. Bartels was so scrupulously nonpartisan he wasn't even registered to vote. A day or so later, the redistricting contingent moved into the Doral Forrestal Hotel Conference Center in Princeton. There were our commissioners and staff, the Republican commissioners and staff, and Bartels and his small staff. For the most part, no one left for two weeks. I got home to sleep twice, and it was only about an hour's drive.

I read everything Bartels ever wrote, and I asked Scarinci and Tom Giblin, the state party chair and another commissioner, to do the same. The purpose, as Scarinci said, was "to get into his head." Scarinci even eavesdropped when Bartels was talking to someone else, just to see what he was thinking. And we were not above buttering him up. Bartels, who dressed in tweed jackets and sneakers, went to Yale and Berkeley. We got hats and T-shirts from both places, but we never wore them. In fact, I tried to stay as close as possible to Bartels, taking any opportunity to draw him into casual conversation. He enjoyed the NBA basketball playoffs and we could talk about that, and he had two daughters my sons' ages, so we talked about that. As I told our people, "When Bartels goes to the bathroom, let me know. I want to go in there and take a leak with him." It was important that he trust me.

The first night in the hotel, Scarinci noticed something that he thought was a positive sign. Everyone, Republicans and Democrats, ate dinner in the same dining room at the hotel. The Democrats sat at the same table, and as more came in we just pulled over another table and some chairs. The Republicans were sitting two at one table, two at another, having what looked like conspiratorial conversations. They didn't seem to be a team. And in fact they weren't. One commissioner, Chuck Haytaian, had just been dropped as state party chairman and his heart wasn't in the fight. Assembly Speaker Jack Collins, another commissioner, had announced he wasn't seeking re-election, so the process was less pressing to him. And Donald Di-Francesco, the then president of the senate, who had become acting governor when Governor Christie Todd Whitman went to Washington to head the Environmental Protection Agency for President George W. Bush, gave up his commission seat at the last minute to Senate Majority Leader John Bennett. That added confusion in their ranks.

The other difference was they had only white commissioners, four men and a woman. Our staff joked that they should be called the Blue

Ridge Mountain Boys. We had an African American assemblywoman, Bonnie Watson Coleman, and a Hispanic woman, Sonia Delgado, who once worked for me and had become a lobbyist. We also had two other white guys, Lou Greenwald, an assemblyman from South Jersey, and Giblin.

From a personal standpoint, Bennett and I really had the most at stake. Everyone knew the map would determine the state's political future for a decade—whether the Republicans would retain control of the legislature or the Democrats would get it back. And that meant one of us would probably become senate president. I also knew that if we lost the map fight, the political bosses in the state would have put enough pressure on legislators to overthrow me as minority leader. No question about that. Of course, we had no way of knowing at the time that McGreevey would be elected governor in 2001 and then resign so the senate president would become governor. But as things worked out, the governorship was also at stake.

It was clear from the first commission meeting that we were much better prepared. We had a strategy—unpacking—which they had not expected, and a plan for achieving it. As they admitted later, they just hadn't done their homework. They figured it would work as usual: they would submit a map they liked; we'd submit one we liked, and the eleventh member would look to compromise. But mostly they were overly cocky. They had the governorship, both houses of the legislature, and now a Republican chief justice picking the eleventh member. They figured in the best Jersey tradition that it was wired for the eleventh member to find a compromise a little to their side of the middle. We worked with experts from the national Democratic Party; they never contacted the national Republicans until late in the game. That cockiness would cost them.

From reading what Bartels had written we knew that he would demand statistical verification for everything we said, and that he would work on three principles:

> *Partisan fairness* (if a party gets 50 percent of the vote it should get 50 percent of the seats)
> *Responsiveness* (the plan needed a good number of competitive districts, so a swing in voter preference from one party to the other would show up in the legislature)

Accountability (to the largest extent possible, voters should be
able to vote yes or no on the incumbents already serving
them)

At the first meeting, Bonier did a ten-minute PowerPoint presentation that made the case for unpacking. Actually, we were now calling it "enhanced minority opportunity," a phrase proposed by Hirsch,
the Washington lawyer. We had kept our map secret until then—which
bugged the hell out of the Republicans—and before Bonier showed it,
he spoke for a few minutes about the importance of the fairness test.
(In fact, neither party really wanted fairness. Both wanted maps that
would give them 52 percent of the seats with just 50 percent of the
vote.) The Republicans started shouting "show us the map, show us
the map." And when Bonior did, it was a huge relief for us. Finally,
the idea was out on the table; it was no longer just theory. The
Republicans did a lackluster predigital presentation that essentially
offered the status quo. It was the difference between a silent movie
and a talkie. From then on, all the debate was about our plan.

That began two tense weeks. The Republicans went to their
suite, we went to ours, and Bartels and his staff to a third. We didn't
meet with the Republicans again until the end. Bartels and his two
chief aides, Ernest Reock, a Rutgers political scientist who also
worked for the eleventh member in 1981 and 1991, and former state
Supreme Court Justice Robert L. Clifford, moved from one delegation
to the other, asking for revisions of one kind or another in the proposed
maps, always striving to bring the sides closer. We would return to
the computer, move a district here, a district there—always mindful
that "one man, one vote," required all the districts to have about the
same population. This went on for ten to fifteen hours a day. People
slept only a few hours a night before going back to the maps, trying
to creatively reshape the districts to give Bartels what he wanted, but
never giving an inch on unpacking. Interestingly, the Bartels group had
no computers so they couldn't try out different maps on their own.
They depended on the two parties for that.

The Republicans wanted Bartels to reject unpacking altogether,
arguing, somewhat disingenuously I thought, that it reduced the
chance of minorities to be elected because they could never win in

majority white districts. Never had I heard Republicans so concerned about black voters. We argued that lumping minorities into a few districts automatically limited their prospects to elect more members. Near the end, the Republicans brought in Walter Fields, a former state official in the NAACP, to be a consultant. He had real concerns about unpacking, because it forced black legislators to forfeit some of their base. He told the *New York Times*, correctly I believe, that "if Republicans had tried the same tactics, they would have failed. No one would buy the fact that Republicans are trying to protect minority interests." But that was because Republicans had no track record of trying to protect minority interests.

Nonetheless, they never came off their position, even when it was obvious from the questions Bartels asked that it seemed he would accept unpacking.

And here's where their cockiness got them in trouble. As Reock later said of the Republicans: "They wanted to bully their way through" without being responsive to the eleventh member. We had decided early on that Bartels could not be bullied. As one member of our side said of the ultrastudious Bartels: "He's like a guy who got beat up every day in the fourth grade. He got past that and you can't intimidate him anymore." So any suggestions he and Reock made for map revisions, we tried to oblige.

Bartels called me into his suite once to say he was thinking of moving North Caldwell into my district and Cedar Grove out. I told him, "Listen, even the people who live in carriage houses in North Caldwell aren't Democrats." He said he was sure from the census that 15 percent of North Caldwell was black. "Who did the census," I asked, "the Black Panthers? I'm telling you, there are no blacks there." Turned out there is an annex of the Essex County Jail and the census takers counted the prison population. The trouble, of course, was the inmates couldn't vote. I told Bartels to make the change if he wanted. I'd win anyway.

By the end of two weeks, our suite, and I presume the others too, looked like high school students lived in it. Maps and papers and plastic cups everywhere; also, people were terribly tired.

Near the end, the Republicans called for one public hearing. They believed if they showed their map, and how it protected the seats minorities already held, they could get the black and Hispanic Democratic legislators to admit that unpacking unnerved them. But all the time spent talking to minority Democrats paid off and now one by one they said they had seen our map and were satisfied. That was it.

The next evening, April 11, about 6 P.M., Bartels came to our suite and said he was voting for our map. A very happy moment. Then he informed the Republicans. I'm told it was not a pretty scene. For two hours, in language they probably wouldn't want repeated, they yelled that he was being unfair, they questioned his timing and integrity, shouting that they thought their map was still in play. And they said they never expected him to pick one map over the other; they always expected him to reconcile the two.

Then, at about 10 P.M., there was a final public meeting where an official vote was taken. The Republicans objected to the meeting and only one of them, Bennett, showed up, although he had a lawyer and some staff with him. Bennett and I got to shouting at each other when he started throwing questions at Bartels, trying to delay—if not halt—the final vote. I wanted Bartels out of there before he could change his mind and yelled for a vote. But Bennett kept arguing and then DeMicco got into it with him, calling his concern about blacks and Hispanics "hypocritical."

This sent Bennett through the roof. The idea of a staffer getting in a debate among commissioners just infuriated him. Finally, at 10:31 P.M. the vote was taken: 6–1, with Bartels joining the five Democrats in favor of the map and the only Republican to show up to cast the one "no" vote was Bennett. Bartels was taking his own risk here. He didn't want to be overthrown by the courts, and that was seen as possible with our unpacking map. I learned later that he sought advice from Clifford and Reock, but the decision was his.

Bennett, whom I always considered a gentleman, was shaken. He felt he had failed the Republican Party and said immediately that the Republicans would appeal. I walked over to console him, told him even if everything broke our way the best I could see us getting was a 20–20 split, which would make us co-presidents of the senate.

They did appeal. A court comprised of three federal judges based in Essex County, a circuit judge and two district court judges, one

Nixon appointee and two Carter appointees, voted unanimously for the Democrats, saying the plan would "enhance and expand" opportunities for Hispanics and blacks.

The November election changed everything in Trenton, with almost all power moving from the Republicans to the Democrats. McGreevey was elected governor, and with the new map, Democrats won the assembly 44–36. In the senate, we won as many seats as I thought possible, and ended in a 20–20 tie with the Republicans. It was the first legislative tie since 1919; the assembly Speaker then was chosen by pulling his name out of a hat. Bennett and I had to figure out another way to make it work. Mims Hackett, the African American who ran off the line with me that year for the assembly, won, even though the district was now only 27 percent black.

"It's a brand-new district, and the most important victory to me was that we showed a minority candidate could win," I said at the time. "The people of this district reaffirmed my faith in them."

Some people have always been suspicious of my motives. Republicans, and even some Democrats, say I was only covering my own ass in fighting for the new map. The percentage of blacks in my district was cut from about 53 percent to 27.5. With Hispanics, the district became 35 percent minority. Most of the blacks I lost were put in a newly drawn 34th district that elected Nia Gill, a black attorney, to the senate for the first time. But my critics insisted I could not keep winning a district that was more than 50 percent black, and that was my primary reason for wanting to shed blacks from the district and put them in Gill's. I said then, and I say now, "Bullshit."

With the election over, we moved to the next interesting adventure: running the state senate with co-presidents.

This was never going to be easy, even though Bennett and I got along better than most Democrats and Republicans in what is a nasty political environment. There were even a couple of more twists to make the situation crazier. When Christie Whitman resigned as governor at the end of January 2001, to become head of the Environmental Protection Agency for the newly elected president, George W. Bush (I could have told her he didn't care about environmental protection), she was succeeded by the then president of the senate Donald DiFrancesco. (Like me a few years later, he held both posts.)

Donnie D, as everyone in Trenton called him, had been senate president for nine years and he was seeking the Republican gubernatorial nomination on his own in 2001 when questions about business dealings forced him from the race. He said he'd never run again for any office. Period. But he was going to keep his two offices until a new governor and legislature were elected in November and inaugurated in January. Which is where the first complication arose.

The old senate went out of business at noon on January 8, 2002, ending DiFrancesco's tenure as senator. And if he wasn't president of the senate he couldn't be acting governor. Jim McGreevey, the new governor, was not to be sworn in until January 15. So there was going to be a week when the senate president—that would now be Bennett and me—had to serve as acting governor. We came to a quick agreement: he would have the job for the first three and a half days, which allowed him to make the State of the State speech. That was important to him, and I said, "John, if you want it, it's fine with me." He still calls it the highlight of his political career. I would be governor for the next three and a half days. In return, I got the plusher office space first. As I said at the time, "I want to give my members a taste of the good life so they work harder." (One more little quirk: although the old senate expired at noon on January 8, the new one wasn't sworn in until 1 P.M., which could have meant an hour without an acting governor. Couldn't have that; what if New York attacked New Jersey? The void was filled by Attorney General John Farmer, meaning we had five governors in a week. Good experience if I ever wanted to take up politics in a banana republic.)

But this being Jersey, even before all that could happen, even before the election was a week old, there was preliminary maneuvering to get some senator to switch parties and create a majority. It would take only one senator captivated by the promise to head an important committee.

There was reason to consider it. The senate president in New Jersey has a lot of power—he or she names committee chairs, decides which bills come to the floor, dispenses little perks, and, of course, has a chance to become governor if something happens to the elected governor. (That has since been changed, with the state now electing a lieutenant governor.) With the governor and the assembly Speaker,

Phil Mickelson, me, Kevin, and Chris, as Mickelson wins the PGA tournament at Baltusrol Country Club. Very nice to my family and me, but he wouldn't give me a darn golf tip.

First pitch, Cincinnati Reds versus San Francisco Giants, August 2005. You're right; it was a strike.

James Gandolfini, Mary Jo, and I at the Governor's Mansion in Princeton. Tony Soprano didn't have anyone whacked but he did want to see McGreevey's bedroom.

There I am with the people I care about the most, patients at Greystone Park Psychiatric Hospital, abandoned by many, but still loved by a lot.

My Irish buddy President Barack Obama. Yes, he is part Irish; remember, it's O'bama.

There I am shaking hands with David Beckham, at the time the best soccer player in the world. I had no idea who he was.

Me, Jay Z, and Beyoncé—you tell me who she's standing closer to.

Here is the official first family photo.

That's right, I'm old school. You shoveled the snow and then you played basketball. I was about twelve years old.

My brother and I in our family apartment above the funeral home. Even though he is older, as you can see, I was the quarterback.

After many shekels, our son Kevin graduates from Drew University in Madison, New Jersey.

My friend former premier Mikhail Gorbechev, who was responsible for one of the largest changes in world history, and no, I didn't ask about his red spot.

Vijay Singh just congratulated me on my drive. It was right down the middle. A fun guy who was more than willing to help me and boy, did I need it.

Signing the agreement for the new Giants and Jets Stadium at the Meadowlands without using one cent of public money for construction of the stadium. And now we have the 2014 Super Bowl in New Jersey. Let's go, Giants and Jets!

he forms a triumvirate that pretty much runs state government. But I wasn't too concerned. The Democrats had just won the assembly and the governor's office and made major gains in the senate. "What are the Republicans going to offer?" I asked. "A first-class seat on the *Titanic*?" No one switched, although Bennett did say that while he didn't expect it, "I'm available if there's anyone from the Democratic side that wants to come over."

Bennett was like a kid who just caught a ball at Yankee Stadium when he was sworn in for his eighty-four-hour gubernatorial term. "Finally—whew," he said. "I am really overwhelmed. We really can't believe this day has come." He took it so seriously he got a trooper to drive his wife. His first act was to have DiFrancesco's gold-embossed name scratched from the door leading to the governor's office. Then he ran over to the assembly to make his State of the State speech. With no accomplishments as governor to brag about, he mostly recognized the people who were killed at the World Trade Center on September 11, 2001. He and his family ate dinner at Drumthwacket, the governor's mansion in Princeton, and they slept there. He even got DiFrancesco to let him throw a double engagement party for his two daughters at Drumthwacket two days before being sworn in.

I took the oath inside the governor's office (Bennett took his a few minutes later elsewhere in the State House). "If I can just ask one thing," I said, "can the state police lock the door so Bennett can't get in?" I started my short term the same way I started my term after McGreevey resigned: by visiting mental patients at Greystone. I was wearing a sweater that had "New Jersey Governor" embroidered on the front, which seems a little phony now. I returned to Trenton and signed my first bill, prohibiting nursing homes from pressuring patients into waiving their right to sue for inadequate care. Then I did what I always did: I went to coach Christopher's seventh-grade basketball team, and I made my first gubernatorial pronouncement: "Any ref who calls a foul on my son will not get a pardon."

I held a reception at Drumthwacket during my three days, but I made sure to invite local people who had worked for me and almost no one who might ordinarily be invited there. Mary Jo and the kids and I stayed there that first night and that had one obvious advantage:

it's a much shorter drive to Trenton from Princeton than from West Orange. The boys loved it there. When I left the first morning, Chris was taking a bubble bath in the Jacuzzi and Kevin was watching a Rodney Dangerfield movie in the master bedroom. There was also one serious disadvantage to Drumthwacket. I asked someone to go out and buy me a crumb bun, one of my favorite breakfast foods, but there were none to be found in any Princeton bakery. I'm sure there would have been no problem finding a croissant.

Both Bennett and I also made some appointments, which probably didn't make McGreevey very happy. I was sitting around with some aides and I asked Joe Fiordaliso, my assistant chief of staff, if he wanted to sit on the Essex County College Board of Education. "Why not?" he said. "Done," I said. My friend Kathy Crotty also got a seat on the New Jersey Governor's School Board of Overseers.

But Bennett did me one better. He pardoned an old buddy, Hugh Gallagher, who had been convicted of bookmaking.

Rutgers University asked for my papers after my three-and-a-half-day term. I told them to get the *Times*, the *Star-Ledger*, the *Daily News*, and the *Record* of Bergen County.

Harder was reaching agreement on how to run the senate with co-presidents. It took one hundred days of almost daily talks to work it out. We knew immediately that every committee would have co-chairmen. And we quickly agreed that Bennett would run the place for a few months, I'd run it for a few months and we'd switch off. The toughest question was who would decide what bills came to the floor. Bennett wanted us both to sign off before any bill reached the floor. I said that was unworkable. It would, in effect, give the Republicans veto power over McGreevey's program. Which would give them the leverage to negotiate for any changes they wanted. At one point, as the negotiations dragged on, I declined to have any hearings on legislation and Bennett refused any to move on McGreevey appointees. We finally compromised this way: in any Senate voting session, when usually thirty bills are brought up, I could post any nine I wanted and Bennett could do the same. In most cases, we supported one another's bills and there was no problem. If a tie vote seemed possible on some legislation, we had to lobby the other party to find a convert. Things then quieted down until late summer, when George

Norcross, the wealthy, powerful, and ruthless South Jersey boss with alliances around the state, including Essex County, tried to maneuver me out of the co-presidency. Norcross was a successful businessman—chief executive officer and chairman of Commerce Bank insurance services—who I know used his political clout to get insurance and banking business. And he was also a political bully who has been caught on tape—made by the state attorney general's office—bragging about crushing opponents' asses, teaching "jerk-offs" a lesson, and being so powerful that both McGreevey and Corzine had to deal with him. "Not because they like me," he said, "but because they have no choice."

On the same tape, he proudly told about reading the riot act to Herb Conaway, a talented African American assemblyman from Burlington County in South Jersey, and the only legislator to have both medical and law degrees.

Recalled Norcross: "I said, 'Herb, don't fuck with me on this one. Don't make nice with Joe Doria [a former assembly Speaker] because you don't want him pissed at you. 'Cause I'll tell you if you ever do that and I catch you one more time doing it, you're gonna get your fucking balls cut off.' He got the message."

If I had threatened an African American legislator like that in Essex County I could never run for office again. I'm not even sure I'd be allowed to live in the county.

Norcross and one of his allies, John Lynch, the former senate Democratic leader, had been after me since 1993 when they tried to finesse me out of the leadership. That was a good year for us. We went from thirteen seats in the forty-seat senate to sixteen. We were still the minority, but we were closing in quickly. Before that election, Lynch was minority leader and I was the assistant, and he and I agreed to the same arrangement after the election. But Norcross hatched a scheme with Lynch to overthrow me in favor of one of his handpicked people—John Adler of Cherry Hill, in the South. Adler, now a congressman, couldn't get the votes so they also enlisted Senator Bernard Kenny of northern Hudson County. The idea was for Adler and Kenny to become co-assistants and for me to be out. Not a plan I liked. I had the votes to stop them, but not enough to win outright, at least not without a secret ballot. So Lynch proposed that we go with three assistants. I said fine, as long as I was first among equals, which is how it ended up.

I ran into Norcross during the leadership fight at a meeting in Atlantic City. He asked me why I was struggling so hard over a meaningless crumb like assistant leader for the minority. "If it means nothing," I said, "why are you fighting me?" His eloquent response: "Why don't you go fuck yourself?" My retort: equally eloquent. We both knew he was trying to show his muscle by getting a South Jersey guy into the leadership. But he saw he couldn't control me, and relations, as they say, have been strained ever since.

Which is why he didn't want me to be president or co-president of the senate. And he figured he had the clout to do something about it. No question that he controlled South Jersey's Democratic votes, and he could get them to oppose me—even for Bennett, a Republican. Norcross usually worked in Democratic circles and Bennett didn't know him until a mutual friend, Republican state senator John Matheussen of Gloucester County in South Jersey, introduced them. Norcross invited Bennett and Matheussen to dine at an expensive French restaurant near Trenton called Rat's, appropriately named given what happened. According to Bennett, Norcross laid out a simple proposition. "I can make you president," Norcross told Bennett. If Bennett agreed, Norcross would get some South Jersey Democratic senators to vote for the Republican for senate president. Those Democrats, along with Bennett's twenty Republicans, would give him a majority and the presidency. I'd be minority leader at best, and probably not even that.

Bennett says he didn't answer that night, but on the phone a few days later he rejected Norcross's proposal. Here's his explanation: "I think at any given time I could have been removed if I didn't do what Norcross wanted. I knew Codey and had the ability to work with him. And I thought any change would undermine the senate as an institution. And it would not be a good idea for the state government to be in the hands of someone not elected. I figured I would take my chances with Codey."

Matheussen, even though a Republican, had an enticing incentive to cooperate with Norcross. Norcross had persuaded McGreevey to nominate Matheussen for executive director of the Delaware River

Port Authority—a joint New Jersey–Pennsylvania authority—and he took the job in May 2003. By 2010 his salary was $219,000 (plus the $16,000 car allowance), and he was in line for a sizable pension. Matheussen's resignation from the senate also helped Norcross, opening the way for him to get Fred Madden, a South Jersey Democrat, elected to the seat.

Bennett and Norcross had one more battle to wage a couple of weeks later, one that became a lot nastier. Norcross wanted Bennett's help with a bill the legislature was struggling over to provide funds for three sports arenas around the state, a large one in Newark and two smaller ones in Harrison and Pennsauken. Pennsauken is in Camden County, the heart of Norcross's South Jersey power base, and he really wanted that arena. First, he came from Pennsauken, but more urgently he had arranged for a hockey franchise there even though the funds had not been approved. For some reason that I never fully understood, but probably because of some business deal, he also pushed hard for the facility in Newark. McGreevey wanted the bill, but it was stalled in committee as we were coming to the end of the session.

Norcross, with John Lynch at his side, visited Bennett in Trenton at 11 P.M. as we were trying to get a budget passed and then adjourn the session. He had one request: get the bill out of committee and pass it on an emergency basis. Bennett says he told him there was no way he was going to press for an emergency vote on a multimillion-dollar bill on which there had been no hearings.

Bennett says Norcross started cursing and shouting and he responded with his own cursing and shouting. Bennett says here's what happened next: "I said, 'I think we're tired and we should just calm down and look at it another time.' That was not what George wanted at that moment. He wanted the bill moved. Eventually, I said 'I think it's time you leave.' He got up and then backed me into the wall and pushed me and, frankly, I pushed back. And then it got a little worse. I then told him to leave my office and he told me it wouldn't be my office for long." He was right.

The next year, the *Asbury Park Press* did a lot of reporting on the work Bennett's law firm had done for local governments and the size of the fees received. Norcross told me privately that he had his people do the research on Bennett. Ellen Karcher was planning to run for the State Senate that year as a Democratic candidate. When she refused to get out at Norcross's behest, she found herself in a primary against Norcross-backed Gordon Gemma. She won and then went on to defeat Bennett. As much as I liked Bennett, I made sure through my senate leadership PAC that Karcher had the money she needed to win. And while the election ended Bennett's twenty-four-year legislative career, Karcher's victory gave us a majority and I became the sole president of the senate.

Things would later go bad for Karcher, but for now I was very excited.

10

Governor,
Not *Acting* Governor

In truth, not much happened during my first months as senate president, and then, without warning, Governor McGreevey announced his resignation.

There was, however, one fracas even before I became governor worth mentioning. It says something about politics in New Jersey. I did something at McGreevey's urging that I hate to do. I broke my word. It cost me five of the six African Americans in the senate, all of whom were good friends.

John Adler, now a congressman, then a state senator from Camden County, was co-chairman of the judiciary committee when the senate was split 20–20. A couple of years earlier, hoping to replace me as minority leader, he on more than one occasion tried to spread stories to reporters about me. Peter Cammarano, my chief of staff, confronted him about the leaks. Adler denied them and Pete called him a liar to his face. Unfortunately for Adler, the press outed him to my staff when they found out the stories were untrue. Since 1993 we have made amends, and during his congressional run I raised $50,000 for him. When I became senate president I wanted to replace him as judiciary chairman, and I promised the promotion to Nia Gill, the African American senator I had recruited into politics in 1993. Mistake.

McGreevey called frantically insisting that the job go to Adler. His concern had nothing to do with affection for Adler, since he had none. Adler guaranteed McGreevey's animosity by referring to him as "an empty suit" when he first ran for governor. What McGreevey desperately wanted was a bill granting same-sex domestic partners many rights that married couples enjoy. This was before anyone knew for sure that McGreevey was gay. Everyone assumed his interest could be traced to Jamie Fox, his chief of staff, who didn't hide his homosexuality. George Norcross, who cares for nothing but power, squeezed the governor, threatening enough opposition from South Jersey legislators to kill the bill unless I appointed Adler. It was a threat he could carry out. I retreated for McGreevey's sake.

Gill was furious. She led four other African American senators to see Leonard Lance, who succeeded John Bennett as head of the senate Republicans, and offered to throw their support to him for president. That could have cost me the job, but Lance, an unusually polite and gentle man much influenced by precedent, turned them down. He believed the majority party deserved the senate presidency, and that was that.

But it didn't end there. A few days later, with the formal opening of the legislature, Gill's black colleagues nominated her for president. I had met with the black senators in the morning, trying to end the mini rebellion, but they insisted on pushing ahead. Gill, a statuesque woman with a flair for drama, said, "Issues have not been dealt with. Issues have not been heard . . . I don't want to do this. This is not a fight I want to have. But this is a fight I have to have, because my ancestors had it. Mr. Norcross can advance whomever he wants, but he can't foist it on the Senate. It's the Senate and the governor who have the say. We make these decisions." I must say I agreed with her on that. She got eight votes: the five African American Democrats and three Republicans. I got the rest and everyone, Gill included, stood and applauded.

In my remarks, I recalled bringing Gill into politics and said, "I haven't regretted it at all, and she's still my friend." She gave me the thumbs-up sign.

Eight months later, McGreevey was on television, revealing his relationship with Golan Cipel and telling the state he was going to resign, and I was on the phone with my son Kevin, saying, "McGreevey's gay, I'm the new governor."

And at 6:30 P.M. on November 14, the day before I was to take over, in the living room of my home in West Orange, I was sworn into office by Senator Lance. I thought that nicely symbolized that we would push through this state trauma not as Democrats and Republicans, but as New Jerseyans. The only other people there were Mary Jo, our sons, one pool reporter from the Associated Press, and Monsignor Michael Kelly of Seton Hall Prep, who began the ceremony with a prayer. "Coming out of the box," I promised the reporters standing outside my house, "you're going to see a different style, a different tone, and a different focus as well." I had been a legislative leader for a long time. I was confident I could be an effective governor.

———

After McGreevey 's announcement, but before I took over, all kinds of people—lobbyists, legislators, lawyers, financiers—started to treat me like some rich uncle about to die. They wanted a few minutes, they wanted meetings, they wanted to get my tea, and probably anything else I wanted. The *Star-Ledger* reported one day that I hooked a tee shot off the fairway at the Garden State Golf Classic and "a lobbyist ran down to fetch it." It was all kind of crazy. The governor of any state gets a certain amount of fawning attention, but Jersey is different because the governor here is more powerful than most of his peers. It's enough to make them jealous. When John Sununu was governor of New Hampshire, he saw Governor Kean at a meeting and greeted him as "Ayatollah Kean."

Here's why. In New Jersey, the governor was the only statewide elected official (we elected a lieutenant governor starting in 2009). Officials elected in most states—attorney general, treasurer, secretary of state—are gubernatorial appointees in New Jersey. So are the heads of the seventeen other departments and all the justices of the N.J. Supreme Court and superior courts. The governor also controls thousands of lesser positions. It takes a two-thirds vote in both houses to override his veto, and he also holds the unusual "conditional veto," enabling him to agree to sign a bill, but only if certain changes are made. Further, line-item veto authority allows him to eliminate specific budget appropriations while approving the rest. Basically, that makes his one vote more than equal to the entire legislature. (The U.S. Supreme Court has ruled that such power in the hands of the president would unconstitutionally give him too much authority over congressional legislation.) And besides all that, I was still president of the

State Senate, so I headed the executive branch and half of the legislative, elevating me to a whole different plateau on the influence meter. No surprise, then, that lobbyists were fetching my golf balls. And by the way, the Garden State Golf Classic, itself, was something of a Jersey classic. It is sponsored by lobbyists and the proceeds—about $45,000—go to a different legislative leader's political action committee. By chance, 2004 happened to be my turn.

One thing I couldn't do as governor was to perform weddings. That became a problem when Sal Cubeta, my barber in West Orange, asked me to officiate at his daughter's wedding. The solution: have John McKeon, my buddy and the mayor of West Orange, swear me in as a deputy mayor. Instead of taking any pay, I said I wanted to negotiate for lower property taxes. That didn't work, but Sal's daughter had a lovely wedding.

————

I caught a huge break on my first full day in office, November 16, when Josh Margolin of the *Star-Ledger* and Josh Gohlke of the *Record* of Bergen County asked to spend the day with me, from breakfast to bedtime. Despite being senate president, I wasn't a household name in the state until McGreevey resigned. One thing people learned early was Mary Jo and I would stay in West Orange and not move to Drumthwacket, the very elaborate governor's mansion in Princeton. Mary Jo, who also kept her job as an elementary school reading specialist, would have hated it there without her family and neighborhood pals. She did spend the occasional night there with some girlfriends—pajama parties for the more mature—which they enjoyed, but that was it. My kids didn't want to move for just fourteen months. As for me, as I said, "Where I come from, we were always trying to get out of public housing, not into it." I was just comfortable in my own place and saw no need for the pomp of Drumthwacket.

So the state knew already that I was a normal suburban Jersey guy with the same values as a lot of other folks in Jersey. I wasn't a patrician like Christie Whitman or a wound-too-tight workaholic like McGreevey. The stories in the *Ledger* and *Record* enhanced my image as an average guy you might meet in line at the movies, and people felt comfortable with that.

Some staff members advised me against doing those stories, but I knew that reporters cherish nothing more than access and they were unlikely to be very tough if I was going to be that open. Besides, some investigative reporters were practically in my bedroom anyway. Both papers reported that I ate Cheerios for breakfast, like I do about every morning, and Gohlke noted that I rinsed the bowl when I was done. I started at 6:30, a little earlier than usual, but as I said, "We have a big agenda." My priorities were clear: overhaul the mental health system, establish stricter ethics laws, increase money for stem-cell research, and balance the budget with no new taxes. And don't let it all go to my head. I didn't want people to be able say they remembered me before I became an asshole.

From home, I went to Greystone—underscoring immediately that mental health was an urgent priority—and joined about fifty patients for small talk and French toast—my second breakfast of the morning. My son Kevin came along because I wanted him to understand how vulnerable the mentally ill are and why I was so determined to be their governor. From there, it was back to Trenton, where my staff greeted me for the first time with "Good morning, Governor." There was a nice ring to it. I then held my first gubernatorial news conference to announce a mental health task force, saying: "If my administration stands for anything, it will be known for standing for compassion and standing up for those who may not be able to stand up for themselves."

I knew almost all the reporters pretty well I, but I was more nervous than I expected to be. My voice quavered a little and I was a little slower than usual with a quip. Most questions were run of the mill, but Michael Aron of New Jersey Public Television, a knowledgeable longtime capital reporter, pissed me off when he asked whether I was pursuing a personal agenda, rather than the state's, by seeking more help for the mentally ill and a new stadium for the Giants.

"Mental health for people who are poor is not a personal agenda at all," I said, "and I deeply resent that accusation. In terms of the Meadowlands, forget about me being a sports fan. We need obviously a new vision for the Meadowlands. We're losing the Nets, the Jets, and the Devils. What is the future of the Meadowlands; that's not a personal agenda." The *New York Times* said my "edgy response was a rarity," which was true. As I told the reporters, "It's a one-day honeymoon."

Somewhere during the day, I called Governor Ruth Ann Minner of Delaware, and when she wasn't there, I said, "Tell her Senator . . . uh, Governor Codey called from New Jersey." Several well-wishers in the State House greeted me as "Senator . . . I mean Governor." Hard to break old habits.

To emphasize the need for cooperation, I had an afternoon luncheon with Republican and Democratic leaders, something McGreevey never did. "I think it's a new day in New Jersey," Senator Lance said. Then, after a staff meeting I left about 4 P.M. for what I said was my most important date of the day: a parents' conference at Chris's high school. This was something I always did and I saw no reason to stop it. Chris was more nervous about that than I was about becoming governor. After that, I went home for Mary Jo's spaghetti and meatballs.

———

The state troopers who drive and provide security for the governor would never say so publicly, but McGreevey could be a pain in the ass for them. He maintained this frantic schedule, out all the time, attending one event after the other, always getting home late, meaning the troopers got home later. And while McGreevey was all business, I'd shoot the shit with them, talking about sports, about their families, whatever.

I'd also often get home at pretty normal hours during the week, so they could depend on a fairly regular schedule. When I expected to stay home on a Sunday I'd tell them not to show up. Even then, there was always at least one in the house next door, where they set up camp.

But they knew they'd be working Saturday nights because that's when Mary Jo and I usually went to dinner and a movie. Mary Jo and I both love movies, but she wasn't happy with me one night a few years before I became governor when we got to the theater and found the lobby packed and the film we wanted to see sold out. I bought two tickets for another film at the complex, but when we got past the ticket taker, I led Mary Jo into the theater with the movie we wanted to see.

They hadn't let anyone in there yet, so the theater was empty. "What are you doing?" Mary Jo asked.

"We're going to see the show," I said. She looked a little funny and said, "I thought it was sold out."

"It is," I said. "But don't worry about it. They don't really sell every seat." She said she didn't understand. "That's the difference between being born and raised in West Orange and being born and raised in Orange," I replied.

When I was governor, the troopers came to the movies and sat in the back. At the film, *Phantom of the Opera*, Mary Jo had to walk past the troopers to get the bathroom. When she got back to the seat she said, "The troopers think this movie sucks." I said, "It's all in the eye of the beholder, and besides, they're getting paid to watch it." The troopers also got to see more basketball than they ever dreamed of.

I really endeared myself to the troopers on a day we drove to Philadelphia to watch the Rutgers women's basketball team play an Elite Eight game against Tennessee in the NCAA championship. A victory, which they didn't get, would have put them in the Final Four. It started with me in my private office drinking Diet Coke and eating a hard pretzel, which can be difficult to digest, causing gas problems. Before leaving for Philadelphia, I was scheduled to take pictures in the governor's outer office with some people and then give a speech at a local Trenton hotel. As I walked from my inner office for the photos in the outer office I passed the troopers who, as was the custom, stood to show respect for the office of governor. Just then, the pretzels did their job and I let out a loud fart. The officers turned toward the wall and started giggling.

After finishing with the pictures, I called the officer who headed the security office, told him what happened, said I thought it was pretty funny but asked him to come upstairs and tell the troopers that I was angry.

Later, with some time to kill before the basketball game, I stopped at an Italian restaurant for dinner with the four troopers accompanying me. There, the chastised officers apologized for laughing.

"Okay," I said, smiling, "but from now on there's a new SOP. Whenever the governor farts, the trooper closest to the governor must say, 'excuse me, sir.'" They loved it.

Before troopers started driving me, there was Butch McManus. Butch used to be a deputy chief fireman in West Orange and, it turns out, his father and mine were first cousins. But we didn't know each other until after I was elected to the assembly in 1973 and he'd drop around my office every once in a while to shoot the shit.

Then in 1990, when he retired from the fire department after twenty-five years and didn't have anything to do, he started hanging around the office a lot and doing odd jobs here and there. He is about seven years older than I am and he talks in a gravelly voice with an accent that suggests he's never been out of Jersey. But he has a great sense of humor and he's fun to be around. Eventually, he started driving for me, and we had some funny incidents before he moved to the Jersey Shore about ten years later and wasn't available anymore.

Butch is not a very patient man, and traffic, which he defines as any car in front of him, drives him nuts. Once after dropping me off at an affair in Manhattan he couldn't find a place to park the car while waiting for me. He was half crazed when I got back. He started off like a mad man and I told him to slow down. "Slow down, nothing," he said. "I'm driving for three hours and you're in there having fun." I told him to get in the back and I took the wheel myself. It was too dangerous to have him trying to speed in and out of lanes to save an extra minute.

One night, he drove me and Mary Jo to a Governor's Ball in New Brunswick and traffic really was awful. Getting out of there after the ball was going to be hard, and Butch knew he'd probably explode.

Then, according to him, the following happened: "I parked behind a barricade and I see a local cop. I said, 'I just dropped Senator Codey off. When he comes out, if you move this barricade I can get out of here quickly.' To do this, I have to drive the wrong way on a one-way street for a block. But then I don't have to drive around. I said, 'You pull the barricades and I'll give you $15 to do it.' He said, 'No, problem,' and tells me where to park.

"When Codey got back in the car, I flipped my lights and the guy pulled the barricade. When we get to the highway, he asks, 'How much will this cost me?' I say '$40.' It was only $15, but I had to make some money."

This account was the first time I learned about being ripped off by my former friend, Butch McManus.

Then there was the night Butch took Mary Jo to Princeton to speak about postpartum depression and the car phone rang. The caller said he was Donald Trump and he wanted to talk to me. Butch essentially says "bullshit" and hangs up. And he told Mary Jo that it was my brother Bobby being a wise ass.

Well, of course it was Trump. He got me on another phone and he wanted me to know that it was the first time he had ever been hung up on by a chauffeur.

Before going to a Rutgers basketball game one night I had an appointment to meet someone for dinner. As soon as Butch saw the restaurant he said, "Oh, fuck it," and turned left to get into the lot. The fact that a sign about the size of the scoreboard at Yankee Stadium said "No Left Turns," didn't deter him for a moment. A cop, probably knowing from past experience that some jerk would make that left turn sometime during the evening, pulled him over in about a second. Butch took out the registration showing that car belonged to my company, the Olympic Insurance Agency, and Butch said, "I have Senator Codey here. I drive him."

"Sir," I interrupted. "That's incorrect; he used to drive me." Fortunately, the cop had a sense of humor and we got out of there with no further problems.

Butch drove me one night to do a radio call-in show at a small local station and Henry from Morristown called. "What's your question, Henry?" I asked. "I just want you to know that your position on guns is right on and you are great for standing up," and so forth and so on. After the show I got back in the car and Butch asked right away, "Hey, you remember that guy Henry from Morristown. That was me from the car."

I miss Butch.

———

I get along well with the reporters who cover Trenton, and they generally give me a good press. But I am always of two minds about the press. I think they are an essential part of the system, and I think any successful politician has to nurture them, something I try to do with access and humor. But I also think they sometimes have undue influence and their cynicism can be unhealthy.

When I like a story I call the reporter and say so. But I also call and tell them when I think they've made a factual error, which to the press means I have a slightly thin skin. And I always make the call myself—no asking a secretary to call and say, "Please hold for Governor Codey." I'd call and start every conversation the same way. "Hi, this is the guv calling." I know it's flattering to get called directly by the governor, and I think it might have given me a slight edge in the coverage. Besides, I don't like asking people to dial the phone for me. I also do virtually every interview requested, and Kelly Heck, my press secretary when I was governor, was instructed to return every phone call, even when she had nothing to say. Kelly was still in her twenties when she got the job; she worked for the Democrats in the senate and was assigned to me when McGreevey resigned. I kept her and she did fine, although she was sometimes intimidated by the reporters, and more than once I had to tell one of them to stop trying to take advantage of her.

Humor—especially slightly risqué humor—always helped with both the press and the public. There was a huge snowstorm on a Saturday morning in the first winter of my administration, and I spent a lot of time talking to reporters so they could keep the public informed about a difficult situation. Late in the afternoon, I went on the television and radio stations and announced a state of emergency, which meant no driving except for emergencies. I said I was declaring that Saturday night "stay at home with your family night in New Jersey."

The next morning I went to the Department of Transportation maintenance facility in Newark for a news conference and thanked everyone who remained home Saturday night, adding that I fully expected a statewide baby boom in nine months and a lot of newborns with the first name of Codey.

Another time, I was on my way to a Newark fire station to dedicate an official caisson to carry any fallen firefighter in the state, when I was told the press wanted to ask about reports of Viagra being given inadvertently to some sex offenders under a state prescription program. So I was ready with a response when they asked: "It's unfortunate that they got Viagra," I said. "They got an erection and the taxpayers got screwed."

Pete used to joke that Kelly should write a book called, *He SAID That!* but in truth I almost always knew what I was saying, and I knew that it improved the press coverage.

Once when Corrections Commissioner Devon Brown testified that he had been forced to keep fourteen patronage employees on the payroll, Republicans pretended to be so irate you would have thought they never got anyone a job. All fourteen had been hired during the McGreevey years, but instead of just rolling with it, Kelly made the mistake of saying the governor's office had no knowledge of "any so-called political patronage jobs." Which led the *Star-Ledger* editorial page to note that it was "hoping the tooth fairy stops by tonight." I called Fran Dauth, the paper's editorial page editor, and said, "This is the tooth fairy." We both had a good laugh. I had dinner with Fran and Jim Willse, the paper's top editor, before I was sworn in, just to create a relationship.

I got along very well with two *Star-Ledger* reporters, Josh Margolin and Jeff Whelan, and I filled them in sometimes on the political ins and outs of what was going on. The rest of the press corps complained that I was always leaking to them exclusively, which wasn't true. They found out a lot of stuff because they were aggressive and made a lot of phone calls. They also had more sources than a madam has johns (with apologies to former governor Eliot Spitzer). But the *Star-Ledger* was my local paper in West Orange, and I knew I'd have to deal with them when I was no longer governor. So, yes, I did occasionally give them a home court advantage. But when appropriate, I gave stories to other papers. And often, we had to make sure information didn't leak to anyone—and that became almost a full-time job.

But I have my problems with the press. Nobody elected them to anything and yet they have more power than most legislators. Every day, the papers decide what's important, what's wrong, what's right, what I should be upset about. Some stories should be on the back page but they think it's important and put it on the front. Automatically, that judgment becomes important, even when that judgment makes no real sense.

And they'll dig and dig to find anything negative, which is okay, but they won't spend ten minutes seeking out the positive. An example: I owned an insurance agency, and state insurance department officials said they were inundated with calls from reporters after McGreevey resigned asking if I had violated any insurance regulations. I was told they were even tempted to put a tape on the phone saying, "No, Senator Codey's insurance agency has no violations."

And then, about a month before I actually became governor, Ted Sherman, a *Star-Ledger* reporter, called friends of mine saying something like, "I hear Codey never drinks; I presume that means he's a recovering alcoholic." That really annoyed me. Irish jokes aside, I have never in my life had a sip of alcohol. Always seemed just dumb as hell to me. But Sherman was sure I was hiding something. Reporters also like to call professors for their opinions, knowing in advance that the professor will corroborate the point the reporters are trying to make. I call this the rent-a-quote.

When they do get on to what they consider a hot story, they'll report the smallest new detail and then, to make it seem weightier, they'll repeat everything they published before. This is known as "giving a story legs."

That's why I think it's hypocritical as hell for the papers to editorialize all the time against negative advertising by candidates when reporters spend all day trying to dig up anything at all that's negative. They'll say that negative advertising almost always distorts the truth, while their reporting is trying to discover the truth. I still think it's hypocritical.

That's because I remember there was no story when I mentioned to some reporters that Mary Jo and I turned down tens of thousands of dollars in honoraria every year for speaking engagements. In addition, we raised millions of dollars for charity speaking before groups that were honoring us. Elisa Ung of the *Philadelphia Inquirer* did write a story about an $8,369 check I received for unused vacation time after my gubernatorial term ended. I called the Treasury Department and said, "I was governor. There were no vacations." They said other outgoing governors took the money and recommended I do the same. I just quietly sent a personal check to Treasury to repay it. I never told Elisa about it; she found out when she checked my salary. But as I told her, even that decision was affected by the press. My original intent was to give it to charity, but I figured some reporter would find out and identify the charity. And they might not want the publicity.

Once, as I was leaving the State House through a basement exit, I saw two reporters waiting for the elevator. We got into a how-you-doing conversation, and one of them asked what I thought about some committee action. I figured that we're off the record but suddenly one of the troopers warned, "Governor, he just turned on a recorder."

The reporter said, "I'm sorry. I didn't know it was on." But the trooper wasn't buying it. "Governor," he insisted, "he just switched it on."

For the most part, some reporters just seem to assume that if you're a public official you're dishonest in some way. It's not true and I resent it. I've made mistakes—we all make mistakes, reporters, too—but that's not the same as being dishonest.

With that off my chest, let me say I also formed a new respect for a vast majority of reporters and editors, most of whom are decent and honest, and I came to like a lot of them as individuals. Two who come immediately to mind are Jim Willse, who retired as editor of the *Star-Ledger* in October 2009, after fifteen years in the job, and Frank Scandale, editor of the *Record* of Bergen County.

————

One of the more important events on the New Jersey political calendar occurs every year about the third week in November—the annual meeting of the League of Municipalities in Atlantic City, really a convention for Jersey politicians. In 2004, it came two days after I was inaugurated, and I regarded it as a wonderful opportunity to introduce myself to officials from throughout the state.

By the time of the meeting, the hottest question in Jersey politics was whether I intended to run for governor on my own in 2005, which meant a primary battle against Jon Corzine. I solemnly told the crowd I had done a lot of soul searching, that Mary Jo and I had had long talks together and with the boys, and we had arrived at our decision: "We are not getting another dog."

Eric Shuffler was my speechwriter. He was an adviser and speechwriter for McGreevey, and one of the McGreevey people I kept. He was smart, a talented writer and a soft-spoken, nice guy to have around. He also cared about sports. I called him almost as soon as McGreevey resigned, asked him to join me, and made him one pledge that sealed the deal: "I know you have a newborn, and I promise, you will be home at a reasonable hour every night to see him and your family."

I like short speeches and I told Eric I wanted to tell the League about myself, why I was in public service, and what I hoped to accomplish. I would give him an outline of what I wanted to touch upon, as I did for all my big speeches, and he would expand upon those ideas to develop the main speech. When he finished, I practiced the speech as though I was preparing for a Broadway opening, a routine I followed with all the big speeches, making sure I pronounced each word correctly, making sure the words worked for me and editing when they didn't. Usually, I practiced at Drumthwacket, the governor's mansion, where we set up a podium with a teleprompter, and I sometimes spent hours, with Eric, Pete Cammarano, and a few others, molding the speech to my style. I never did a lot of formal public speaking before I became governor, and I took a lot of pride in delivering the speeches well. In one speech, the State of the State, the teleprompter went down for a few minutes. Every time I was interrupted for applause, I turned to Ellen Davenport, the senate secretary, and whispered, "The teleprompter is not working." But from practice, I knew the speech well enough to keep going, and no one knew the difference. Which isn't to say I wasn't relieved when the teleprompter came back.

To the League, which was sort of my coming-out party, I said:

> My personal experiences, the values of my late mom and dad, have not only shaped the man I am, they define me as a public servant. The years I spent working in my father's funeral home—seeing the dignity he showed to grieving families instilled in me a sense of respect and compassion for our fellow citizens. . . .
>
> When people say we [in New Jersey] have problems, I ask which one? Is it the four-plus-billion-dollar deficit, the property tax crisis, the aura of scandal that hangs over the New Jersey political landscape?
>
> Let me tell you what *tough* is—watching your wife as she lies in a coma and having your children ask you whether their mom

is going to die . . . that's tough. If you want to talk about real problems, go to Greystone Psychiatric Hospital and try to answer the patient that asks when will I get out? Ask the father making the minimum wage about how hard it is to raise a family, or the single mom who can't help her kids with homework because she has to work a second shift. These are real problems being experienced by real people . . . and these are the problems that we in government must face.

I said I wanted safer schools, I wanted New Jersey to be a center of stem-cell research, and I wanted to build a bipartisan consensus. And I said I want to "serve my time with dignity and provide stability to our state government."

When I finished, I felt I had nailed the speech and the citizens of New Jersey knew where I would be coming from over the next fourteen months. I was particularly satisfied when a number of people told me that I was a lot better than Corzine, who spoke after me. I know I annoyed him a little when I left the stage immediately after my applause died down without waiting to hear him. But Lorenzo Langford, the mayor of Atlantic City, had alerted me that he badly needed to meet. Turned out he wanted to make sure about getting free tickets to shows or sporting events at the convention center. Which reminded me of the conversation I had with Bob Bowser shortly after he became mayor of East Orange in 1998. With a bit of disbelief in his voice, he told me that he had gotten a call from his superintendent of schools who said he had an emergency. Bowser invited him to city hall to talk about it. The emergency: the sons of bitches who ran the East Orange municipal golf course had started charging him to play. "They never charged me before," the superintendent said. "They will now," Bowser said he replied.

———

"Parts of New Jersey, as you know, are underwater," F. Scott Fitzgerald, who attended Princeton, once wrote. "And other parts are under constant surveillance by the authorities." Good line, no doubt about it, even though I have always believed that New Jersey's reputation for excessive corruption is more caricature than reality. Just look at Illinois. Still, it didn't take a saint, or even F. Scott Fitzgerald, to know that I had to do something as governor to reassure New Jersey citizens that their leaders were not just a bunch of villainous rascals. It was a political necessity and also the right thing to do. What a nice confluence.

The McGreevey administration had been stung by scandal almost from its beginning, and the end was so uncomfortably messy that I thought my first duty was to restore confidence that the state was being governed by honest adults.

My intention, I said two days after being sworn, was "to have a good sense of ethics for people who are employed by the taxpayers in the governor's office, and all the agencies and authorities throughout the state. . . . Whatever the price is to have good ethics, I'll pay it." And I started by reimbursing the state for using a police helicopter to attend a friend's funeral in northern Jersey and get back to Atlantic City for that speech before the League of Municipalities.

I made those "sense of ethics" comments as I appointed two people, Daniel J. O'Hern, a retired state supreme court justice who later died in 2009, and Paula Franzese, a Seton Hall law professor, as special counsels for ethics reform. I asked them to undertake an "ethics audit" of all executive branch agencies, including the governor's office, and report back with recommendations for reform in 120 days. I purposely named people divorced from the political establishment, people who could make the press and citizenry understand that I was serious. O'Hern had once worked for Governor Byrne, although that was many years earlier. I didn't even know what political party Franzese belonged to until a reporter asked at the press conference. She said Democrat.

I gave them staff help and only a few marching orders: let the chips fall where they may and be unstintingly candid. If they did that, I pledged to support them and to act. They came back with ten major recommendations, the most important being to create an independent ethics commission made up entirely of private citizens with sweeping powers to enforce standards, a uniform ethics code for all state employees, a ban on executive branch employees accepting gifts, ethics training for all state employees, and a meaningful ethics code for vendors and contractors doing business with the state. They also wanted a "plain language ethics guide" for all state employees.

We got all that and more. "Pay to Play" was an old tradition in New Jersey (as well as many other states) and I got regulations enacted (this was something that McGreevey started) prohibiting anyone contributing more than $3,000 to gubernatorial candidates or state and county political parties in the past eighteen months from getting government contracts worth more than $17,500. The bill failed on the first vote when all the Republicans abstained. Then, when it did pass, I noted that it had survived "some suspense, a few twists and turns. And even an argument or two. But some achievements are worth the struggle." In addition, I signed legislation freezing at $25,000 the amount that any individual or organization may contribute in a single year to state and county parties and political action committees, including the one I ran as senate leader.

I also signed an executive order forbidding trustees of state colleges and universities from doing business with their schools. That came after the *Star-Ledger* revealed some conflicts of interests on the board of the University of Medicine and Dentistry of New Jersey. I don't know how many trustees quit from around the state, but it was a bunch. Finally, I created the office of Inspector General with the power to investigate any state, county, or local agency.

If this sounds like bragging, it is. But I think I brought more ethical reform to New Jersey in just fourteen months than any governor before me. Leonard Lance, the Republican senate minority leader, said after my term: "He was like Ford after Nixon—saving a disgraced government." I appreciated that.

————

You can plot and plan with experts forever about winning public support and moving up in the polls, and then, like a quarterback looking left while some three-hundred-pound tackle is about to crush him from the right, you can be blindsided in an instant.

That's what happened to me, only in reverse, about two months after I was sworn in as governor. It started when a guy named Craig Carton, then co-host of a raunchy radio program, the "Jersey Guys," called Mary Jo "crazy" after she talked on television about her postpartum depression. Carton, with whom I'm now friendly, went on to host a New York sports talk show with the former NFL quarterback Boomer Esiason. But in Jersey, he was the kind of radio jock who thought it funny to ridicule the handicapped, and one afternoon he said I should approve marijuana for medical purposes "so women can relax and have a joint instead of putting their babies in a microwave. . . . Women who claim they suffer from this postpartum depression must be crazy in the first place."

I was about as angry as I can get when I learned about it the next day. Coincidentally, I was scheduled to appear that evening on the same radio station and take calls from listeners. I called the people who run the station and told them I was going to begin my show with a personal statement responding to Carton. After first objecting they relented when I told them that unless I could read my statement they'd have to find another governor to do my show. Okay, they said, three minutes. I said, "Fine, I'm not long-winded."

My show started at 7 P.M., right after the Jersey Guys finished, so I knew there was a pretty good chance I'd run into Carton at the station. I told my staff I didn't know for sure what I'd do if that happened, but it was possible I wouldn't be governor much longer.

Sure enough, I saw Carton in this narrow lobby as I was walking in. I approached him and said, as gentlemanly as I could, "You're despicable, disgraceful, and I wish I weren't governor. I'd take you outside now."

He asked if I was going to hit him, and I didn't say a word before a state trooper came between us and that was that. Except that the *Star-Ledger*, knowing I was going to be at the station, was smart enough to send a reporter there and it was a page-one story the next day.

After that, the press showed up en masse, and I told them I did what any husband would do if his wife were attacked. Papers all over the country picked up the story, including a wild charge from Carton that I was making terrorist threats and I thought I was a big man because I had troopers with me who had guns. He threatened to sue me, which, of course, he never did. And, gentleman that he was, he started referring to Kelly Heck, my press secretary, as my "spokesbitch."

My popularity zoomed. In a *Star-Ledger* poll, 81 percent said I had done the right thing. Michael Bloomberg, the mayor of New York City who had become a friend, called from Europe to congratulate me. He even sounded a little envious when he said people in politics don't often get the opportunity to do exactly the right thing at the right time. He mentioned Michael Dukakis's missed opportunity when he ran for president in 1988 against the first George Bush. Dukakis was asked at one of the debates if he would support capital punishment for someone who raped and murdered his wife. He said "No," and went into a long-winded explanation of his opposition to the death penalty. He was being real honest, but he came off as a wimp, and any chance he had of beating Bush was lost in that moment.

Speaking of missed opportunities, I always thought John Kerry would have been elected president in 2004 if he hadn't stood silently during a fund-raiser at Radio City Music Hall when Whoopi Goldberg lewdly, and at length, equated President Bush and his surname with a slang term sometimes used for a female body part.

It was in terrible taste. Kerry should have walked on the stage, interrupted her, and said in a nice way, "Miss Goldberg, while we disagree with the president, we will always respect the office. I can't allow that kind of dialogue to continue at my fund-raiser." Middle America was incredibly turned off by Goldberg's language and Kerry's failure to stop it. Had he done that, it would have been a great moment for him. But he showed no guts.

Bloomberg compared my response to Carton to Harry Truman's when his daughter, Margaret, an amateur singer, got a vicious review in the *Washington Post* for one of her recitals. I didn't know what he was talking about. "Mike, I'm not that old," I told him. And he explained that Truman wrote a letter to the critic, warning him: "Someday I hope to meet you. When that happens, you'll need a new nose, a lot of beefsteak for black eyes, and perhaps a supporter below."

I thought I was in good company.

And I better understood why Truman was elected president and Dukakis and Kerry weren't.

In the aftermath, a lot of reporters around the state were angry because they thought I had tipped off the *Star-Ledger* exclusively to be at the station. Not true. Several reporters called and asked if I was going to be there, and I said I was. Deborah Howlett, a *Star-Ledger* reporter who later went to work for Corzine, showed up. I wasn't going to kick her out. Tom Moran, a former *Star-Ledger* columnist, once wrote that I tipped off a reporter. I called him and said, "Totally false, ask the reporter." He did and he apologized. I would never do something like that in a situation affecting my wife. Not in a million years.

Happily, after that I remained the most popular politician in the state. My favorable gubernatorial ratings were always between 65 and 70 percent. Almost three years later, long after I was no longer governor, I was still the state's most popular politician, according to a Fairleigh Dickinson University poll. "If he could sing, he'd be a rock star," said Peter Woolley, the Fairleigh Dickinson pollster, after an earlier poll showed similar results. But I must say I like the accolades. Monica Yant Kinney, a *Philadelphia Inquirer* columnist, once wrote of me: "He adores being adored." Who doesn't?

———

After about a year, "acting governor" seemed to be a normal part of my name, like it was given to me at birth. I could imagine nurses at the hospital asking my mother: "What are you going to name him, Mrs. Codey?" And she replying, as though it was as common as Tom or Harry, "I was thinking of Acting Governor Dick." I had also grown more comfortable than I ever expected with the celebrity that came with the name. In fact, I enjoyed it most of the time, kind of like the frog who liked being the prince.

Two or three times a week, I'd go to political dinners in Paterson or Newark or Bayonne, the kind with pitchers of beer and beefsteak on rye bread for the main course (I loved the beefsteak), honoring different legislators. And I know it wasn't me, but the title of governor that was so alluring, but young women with big bundles of blond hair rushed to have their picture taken with me and get my autograph. I always made sure to have a few felt-tip pens. And there were standing ovations when I was introduced, and when I told my favorite joke people laughed like I was Rodney Dangerfield.

(The joke's short version: The pope is visiting New York, he's late for an appointment, and his driver isn't going fast enough to suit him. Finally, the pope says, "Look. You get in the back seat and I'll drive." He speeds across traffic lanes and past red lights until he's stopped by a cop. The officer takes one look inside the limousine and figures he ought to call his supervisor. "I was about to write a ticket," he explains, "but this is a real important guy." The supervisor asks, "How important—the governor?" "More important than that," he says. "The president?" asks the supervisor. The officer answers, "I really don't know who it is. But he's so important he has the pope driving him around.")

Sometimes at dinners like that someone, maybe a congressman, maybe a local lawyer, comes up and whispers in your ear, asking for this favor or that. Once someone suggested there was $1 million available for stem-cell research provided state inspectors somehow never notice when his client dumps some garbage where garbage isn't supposed to be dumped. "Sorry," I said.

Occasionally, I was embarrassed by the good wishes. More than once I walked into a restaurant in Essex County and some patrons stood and applauded. Once to cut it short, I told them, "Sit down. I might raise your taxes."

On Halloween, 2005, I took the state helicopter to Bridgeton in South Jersey for an outdoor ceremony along the Cohansey River to sign a bill increasing penalties on ships that pollute Jersey waters. It cost $176 million a year earlier to clean up after a tanker spilled oil in the Delaware River. We didn't come close to recouping that from the shipper. Obviously, I could have signed the bill in Trenton, but my visit helped get a nice mention in the local paper for the local Democratic assemblymen, who sponsored the bill and were running for reelection. I figured maybe they, and Steve Sweeney, the local state senator, who was also there, would repay the debt sometime. Especially since I was the first sitting governor in anyone's memory to touch foot in Bridgeton.

About fifty people watched the signing—it was a crisp, bright fall day—and I got off one good line in my little signing speech: "The bill means if you pollute, you give up the loot." When I was done, people rushed to shake my hand, or take pictures or say they wished I were running to be governor again. Then the assemblymen asked if I could make a quick stop with them at a Halloween fish fry in a local senior citizens center. You don't often get to eat a good fish lunch with old folks dressed as gorillas, cowboys, and the Cat in the Hat.

I like being around people and clowning with them, making them feel at ease. I knew that for most people, seeing a governor and interacting with him is a rare experience. One guy, an African American

I didn't know, hugged me and thanked me for what Mary Jo and I were doing on behalf of people with mental illness.

When we returned to Trenton, someone told me there was a lady picketing in front of the State House. Her name was Charlotte Riggs and she was carrying a sign that said, "Draft Codey for Governor. Power to the People Write in His Name on the Ballot on Nov. 8th and Remove Money from Politics."

I had had 3,000 Codey bobble-head dolls made with a face that almost resembled mine and a body that was a little slimmer. I gave them to visitors at the State House and I went out and signed one for her. "This makes my day," she said.

The bobble-heads became pretty popular souvenirs. When I was no longer governor, I spoke one night at the Monmouth County Mental Health Association dinner and auctioned one off. I started the bidding at $100, asked for more, and kept my spiel going for a few minutes, telling them I knew they were rich Republicans because they had tassels on their loafers, and certainly they could bid higher for the sake of mental health. I finally sold it for $3,900. I put my arm around the woman who won, and said, "Now that you've paid almost $4,000 for my bobble-head, we're going to put you in therapy right away."

Sometimes I had to laugh at malapropisms from people intending to offer a compliment. Once at the Meadowlands racetrack with my son Chris and a trooper, a man who looked like the Hollywood version of a $2 bettor stopped me and asked if I was Governor Codey.

I told him he had the right guy, and he said, very nicely: "My wife loves you. Can I take a picture with you?"

We took the picture, he looked at it for a second, and then said, not realizing how funny he sounded: "This will be great for me. My wife thinks only idiots and morons go to the track."

———

Many people believe that for the long term, my single most important gubernatorial accomplishment was to win a ban on smoking in all public places but one—the casino floors. I certainly know one person who believed that—Maureen Roehnelt, my longtime aide and confidante who was dying of cancer the day I signed the bill. She came at me nonstop and she was angry as hell when we compromised on the casinos. I hated that myself, but people had been introducing no-smoking bills for twelve years, and it wasn't going to happen unless the casino floors were left out. The casinos just had too much clout with South Jersey legislators. And 99 percent of the state was a lot better than nothing.

I knew I could get this done in New Jersey after having dinner one night with Mike Bloomberg in New York City. It was such a pleasure to dine without smoke wafting up into my sinuses, and I figured if New York restaurants, bars, and other public facilities could survive, so could those in New Jersey. I was so determined to get this done that I even had a Plan B. If we failed in the legislature, A. J. Sabath, then commissioner of labor and my former chief of staff, was ready to proclaim public smoking a hazard to workers in the state and I was going to sign an executive order banning it. When I relented on casinos, the assembly passed the bill on January 9, 2006, a little more than a week before Corzine was sworn in. "A family trying to enjoy a nice meal, or a worker trying to make a living, should not have to be put in harm's way," I said at the time. For good measure, we also got a bill increasing the minimum age for buying cigarettes from eighteen to nineteen. I signed the smoking ban bill at the Manor restaurant in West Orange. Maureen was in the audience, happy as could be. That day may not have come without her nagging. Also in the audience was someone holding a sign that said, "The lungs of N.J. thank you, Gov. Codey." That is what being governor was all about.

Maureen started working for me soon after I joined the assembly in 1974 when we were both in our twenties. I don't think I'll ever stop getting a little emotional when thinking about her death. She called on a Friday afternoon in early November 2006, when I was in Trenton. "The doctors can't do anything more," she said and she asked me to visit her hospital in Hackensack that evening, when everyone else was gone. I went to a Seton Hall game and then drove to see her. We talked for two hours. Neither of us ever cried. "Why can't I have breast cancer," she said. "Most people live with that." She also asked me to make sure her children were educated, which I have done. It was close to midnight when I left. She was surrounded by a white curtain, and when I reached the door I heard a small voice. "Dick."

"Maureen," I said. "Is that you?"

"Yes, come back." I walked back to her bed.

"You know I love you," she said.

I went home and told Mary Jo. And then I broke down and cried.

Maureen never took morphine; she almost never slept. She died a few weeks later, the day before Thanksgiving, on November 22. As I said at the time, "God gave me the greatest employee I could ever have asked for and she'll be deeply missed, not just by me but by the thousands of constituents she treated with dignity and class over the years."

She probably took some comfort in knowing it was the same date that John Kennedy died.

———

I pushed two other health-related measures as senator and governor; one made it because I signed an executive order; one didn't when it lost a statewide referendum after my term ended.

Under the executive order, New Jersey became the country's first state to conduct random drug tests on high school athletes who qualify for postseason play. The referendum that lost would have authorized a $450 million bond issue for stem-cell research in the state.

New Jersey has long been a center for pharmaceutical research, and I thought it was a no-brainer to invest in making it a leader in stem-cell research. Embryonic stem-cell research seems to have enormous potential to help those with spinal cord injury, Parkinson's disease, Alzheimer's, and an array of other maladies. But President Bush was against it, arguing that to destroy human embryos for the research was tantamount to abortion. For the same reason, the Catholic Church was also opposed—a great incentive for politicians to run for cover. Still, in 2002, two years before I became governor, the senate passed legislation I introduced declaring that New Jersey would encourage stem-cell research within its borders. This was a year before California voters approved $3 billion for stem-cell research.

"It is my hope that in ten years, the State of New Jersey will be the state where we have found a cure, where an Alzheimer's patient can once again remember his daughter's name," I said when the senate voted. It would have been good for the nation's health, good for the state's economy. But it sat in the assembly until near the end of

2003 before being passed there. More progress came the following year when McGreevey, much to his credit, signed an agreement with the Robert Wood Johnson University Hospital to allocate $6.5 million a year for five years to help get a stem-cell research facility built in New Brunswick. Opposition from the Catholic Church was so intense that McGreevey agreed not to take Holy Communion in public. Although he never had much of a sense of humor, he joked that he expected the Vatican to "expedite my ecclesiastic reprieve faster than Galileo's."

Once I became governor, I tried like hell to get more money, usually winning in the senate but getting nowhere in the assembly. Still, without much notice I did put $10 million into my one budget for stem-cell research, making New Jersey the first state in the country to appropriate money for such research. But I couldn't make real progress.

Under Corzine, the legislature did approve $270 million for five stem-cell research centers around the state. Politics being politics, legislators wanted a piece of the pie, even when the pie shouldn't have been divided. Corzine could get money for five centers, but not just one. Still, there was to be one main facility, costing $150 million and named for Christopher Reeve, the Princeton-born actor who became a spokesman for stem-cell research after a horseback riding accident paralyzed him. Ground was broken in October 2006, and even more money was expected when the legislature agreed to put a referendum on the 2007 ballot to borrow another $450 million for the research.

By then, though, the state was in a horrible budget mess, with a $3 billion budget gap, and the referendum lost despite polls showing great support. Voters wanted us to first get the economy in order. I was easily reelected that night and the Democrats gained one seat in the senate. We had a big celebration at a West Orange hotel, but losing the referendum, I said, was "more important than the [election] results for the future of mankind." I meant it. Construction on the research center was put on hold after that and a great opportunity was lost.

The drug testing started when Eric Shuffler read a story about a high school athlete in Texas who died from steroids, and he started to worry that someday his young son might have to choose between swallowing some green or blue pills or not making some team. He told me about the story and suggested I try to get something done to attack steroid use by high school athletes in New Jersey. As a basketball coach and the father of two boys who played high school ball, I liked the idea immediately and asked Larry DeMarzo, another sports junkie who worked on health issues in my administration, to come up with a plan.

We decided to name a task force, headed by my friend Monsignor Michael Kelly, the headmaster at Seton Hall Prep who lent me his Bible when I was sworn in as governor, to study the question and make recommendations. Among the other seventeen task force members were Peter King, the *Sports Illustrated* football writer and New Jersey resident, and a high-powered group of doctors, lawyers, educators, and high school and college athletic directors. DeMarzo was the senior policy adviser.

No one knew how common it was for high school athletes in the state to use steroids, but some reputable studies had found that nationwide about 3 to 4 percent of high school seniors were swallowing them. "This is an emergent public crisis," I said when I announced the task force. "New Jersey cannot and will not bury its head in the sand."

Taking my lead from the report's recommendations, I issued an executive order on December 20 that made New Jersey the country's first state to initiate random testing for high school athletes. The tests were to be limited to athletes whose team qualified for postseason play and we figured about five hundred kids would be tested the first year at a cost of about $50,000. "We don't have the luxury of putting it off or leaving it for someone else to deal with," I said in announcing the order. "This is a growing public health threat, one we can't leave up to individual parents, coaches, schools to handle." The next day, papers across the country carried the story and I even heard from a reporter at the *Guardian* in England, which carried a fairly lengthy account.

"Let's not exaggerate the problem of steroids among teenagers in New Jersey," King wrote in the foreword to the task-force report. "Steroid use is not an epidemic." The point was to keep it from becoming an epidemic. And I think we succeeded. When results came out after the first round of tests, only one kid in the 500 tested from 99 schools and 12 sports was found to be using drugs. "I don't think there's any way we could have been losers, regardless of what it shows," I said. "And the fact that one was positive means there's a heck of a lot more than one person doing steroids."

Within six months, Florida and Texas were also testing and other states were studying it.

———

Only once in my fourteen months as governor did the press really jump on me. And the press wasn't alone. Pretty much the entire faculty and student body at Ramapo College in northern New Jersey were angry. All of it in my opinion was because of knee-jerk skepticism toward public officials.

Ramapo, a small, state-supported undergraduate college, was seeking a new president. McGreevey supported State Senator Joseph Doria of Hudson County, and when I came in I agreed he would be great. Doria, a man of intense sympathy, was not just some hack we pulled out of the party organization. He had a Ph.D. in education from Columbia University, he had taught and directed the human resources department at Saint Peter's College for more than twenty-five years, he had taught at the Eagleton Institute of Politics at Rutgers, and he was the legislature's chief promoter of higher education. He had been in the assembly for twenty-four years before coming to the senate, and he been mayor of Bayonne since 1998. So he knew Trenton politics and how to get money out of the legislature—two important attributes for the president of a public college.

That was also part of the problem: too many jobs. Many saw Doria's bid for the $195,000-a-year Ramapo presidency as a way to fatten his pension, especially since he mistakenly wanted to retain his senate seat. McGreevey's support was partially out of guilt. Doria was Speaker of the assembly in 1990–1991, and when the Democrats regained control in 2001, many thought McGreevey would use his muscle to have him reelected. Instead, because of Hudson County politics, McGreevey chose Albio Sires, who was only a freshman. Ramapo was a way for McGreevey to make it up.

Shortly after I was sworn in, I called Gail Brady, chairman of the Ramapo trustees, and asked her to consider Doria. I didn't put any pressure on her, but she resented the call and issued a statement saying the process should be free of politics. I didn't call her again. Within a week or so, the search committee named five semifinalists, bypassing Doria. But before anyone was named, I had a chance to nominate two new trustees for the twelve-member board, meaning McGreevey and I together named seven of the members. One of my nominees was A. J. Sabath, a Ramapo graduate, my labor commissioner, who once worked for Doria. To the folks on campus, the fix seemed to be in.

Some 2,200 of the school's 5,600 students signed a petition complaining about political intrusion, and Clifford E. Peterson, a professor of international politics, spoke for the faculty, when he said in academese: "I basically feel we're fighting for the soul of the college and the principle of academic process and the integrity of the process."

A. J. came back from his first trustees' meeting saying that the place would blow up if Doria got the job. Pete Cammarano also met with some faculty member and they told him Doria would be entering a very hostile environment. By the end of December, Doria said he was no longer interested.

I still think he was the best choice they could have made. But he was a politician, making him automatically ineligible to many people. There was a lot of screaming about the good-old-boy network pushing one of the good old boys. I think it was bullshit and I was disappointed when he didn't get the job.

Two little additions to the story. The following March, I was at an annual formal Saint Patrick's Day dinner, attended by the archbishop of Newark and a lot of men in tuxedos. I was greeting people as they entered the ballroom, and one guy walked by me and said, "I didn't like what you tried to do at Ramapo College." He returned ten seconds later and repeated it. "Come here," I said, and then whispered in his ear: "Go fuck yourself."

Then I asked the troopers to keep an eye on him.

A couple of years later, I was at Ramapo with Bill Bradley to speak at a new sports and recreation complex named for him. The student-body president presented Bradley with a T-shirt with an outline of the arena and the words "The Bill," which is what the students were already calling it.

When I got up, I said, "It's good you didn't name the arena for me."

Two years after leaving the governor's office, 1 was also asked to speak at New York's annual Saint Patrick's Day Governor's Breakfast at the Waldorf-Astoria Hotel before the start of the parade.

Eliot Spitzer had resigned five days earlier as governor of New York amid revelations that he had frequented a high-end prostitution ring, so obviously he wouldn't be there, and David Patterson, his successor, was to be sworn in that morning in Albany. I received a call from a prominent Irish American attorney in New York who explained the situation and asked if I would fill in as host. "Sure," I said, "I've filled in for governors before."

"Let's be honest," I said when I got up to speak before about 2,000 people in the ballroom. "The only reason I was ever governor of the State of New Jersey was because of sex. And the only reason I'm speaking before you now once again is sex. Which goes to prove that you don't have to engage in the act to get enjoyment from it."

Sometimes as governor you meet and become friendly with people you never expect to meet and become friendly with. Take Jay-Z, the rapper and entrepreneur previously known as Shawn Corey Carter. In one of his many business ventures, Jay-Z is part of an investment group that owns the New Jersey Nets basketball team. I go to a lot of Nets games, and Jay-Z and I got to know each other talking hoops at courtside. I bragged once that I could name the college of every player on the court. He bet I couldn't. He learned better. Another time, I turned to him at halftime and said, "What's the difference between my posse and yours?" He looked at me quizzically and then smiled: "Your posse's guns are legal." In July of 2005, he asked me to attend the groundbreaking for the elaborate 40/40 sports theme bar he was building in Atlantic City, and I spoke at the press conference at Caesar's Palace. Beyoncé, a true class act, was there, and I decided to try a little hip-hop of my own. "If I were Jay-Z," I rapped, "Beyoncé would be my fiancée." He turned to his guys and said, "I told you this guy was cool." And I said, "Hey, can this white guy rap." (Jay-Z and Beyoncé were finally married three years later.)

All of which helped me impress a lot of fourth-grade kids in New Jersey. Under state law, all fourth graders have to learn about state government. As part of the curriculum in many schools, students take a class trip to Drumthwacket, the governor's mansion in Princeton. The folks who maintain the place like to hang pictures of the governor, and I gave them some of me with Mary Jo and the boys. They asked for anything different and I sent them one of me with Jay-Z and Beyoncé. I was told that nothing about the class trips that year excited the kids more.

———

I knew it before I became governor; it became more urgent for me after I became governor and studied the numbers. The State of New Jersey was in desperate financial shape.

In years when the stock market was high, business was good, and we collected more taxes than usual, we spent like we were rich. Which we were. When the stock market was down, business was bad, and we collected less in taxes than usual, we still spent like we were rich. Not a good policy. To pretend we could make it work we played every accounting game and used every gimmick known to politicians. That year, we were spending $3 billion in one-time-only revenue to balance the budget, so we were $3 billion in the hole before I started work on the new budget. The Garden State was in the economic mud and I felt I had to do something. It was, as Eric Shuffler says, "a real come to Jesus moment" for me.

I ordered the cabinet in my first week to prepare for administrative cuts, defer all unnecessary spending, and cancel all travel except for trips to Washington to lobby for more federal money. Then, in my budget address at the end of February I proposed spending $600 million less than that year's $28.3 billion, the first proposed year-to-year cut in fifty years. "The good news is, we're not bankrupt," I said in my address. "The bad news is, we're close."

As usual, I rehearsed the speech with Eric and Pete for hours, throwing out the words I was uncomfortable with, adding some stuff I wanted, and practicing until I was cocky about pulling it off. We did the early practices at Drumthwacket, and then the night before and the morning of the speech I did my final run-throughs in the assembly chamber, where I would give the speech.

I thought candor was critical, and one of the first things I did was take blame myself. "Each party has accused the other of recklessness and irresponsibility, of wasting taxpayer money and employing financial trickery," I said. "And I have made some of those partisan accusations myself. But the rhetoric has not solved the problem."

> And the political games have only made it worse. Fiscal gimmicks and borrowing have been a bipartisan budget addiction. Both parties have borrowed recklessly and spent well beyond the State's means. Both parties have placed political expediency over financial responsibility. Both parties have enhanced retirement benefits without thought to future costs. And both parties have been unwilling to address the skyrocketing cost of health care, whether it was for Medicaid, state workers, or retired teachers. The time has come for elected officials to put aside our partisan knives and work together to fix the budget problem.

I proposed some cuts and even a few increases for health-related programs. "The budget's now the subject of discussion and compromises all the way through for the next four months," I said after my speech. "Politics will play a role. How big remains to be seen."

It turned out to be huge. After some compromising, the budget that finally passed called for virtually the same level of spending as the previous budget, something that hadn't been done in a decade. By the time I signed the budget, though, Democrats in the senate and assembly had gotten into a vicious fight—close to a "civil war," the *Star-Ledger* said—that delayed passage until July 2, more than thirty hours past the legal deadline of midnight, June 30. The attorney general said we might even have to shut down the government, something I wasn't going to do.

The battle centered on my plan to sharply reduce promised property tax rebates for senior and disabled citizens from $1,200 to $800, and halve them for other homeowners, who were getting an average of $690. That alone would have saved $1.3 billion. The rebates were something of a gimmick by themselves. A lot of states allow you to write off some part of your property tax from state income tax; New

Jersey is one of the few in sending out a separate rebate check. The checks make the politicians seem benevolent, and the assembly, which has to run every two years, loved them. It didn't help my cause that assembly leaders first learned I was going to do this by accident. When I was rehearsing in the assembly chamber the night before the speech, Bill Castner, the chief lawyer for Assembly Majority Leader Joseph Roberts, was in his office doing some work. He could hear me through an internal audio system, and he alerted Roberts.

Roberts was not happy. Months later, as we were reaching June 30 and the budget debate was raging, Castner walked over to the senate and told one of my aides that the assembly would not take up another bill I cared about. As he was walking out, I beckoned him to the podium from which I was presiding, and whispered in his ear: "Hey Billy, next time you screw me, at least give me a kiss."

To ease the budget's path through the senate, I made an early agreement with Senator Wayne Bryant, of Camden County, chairman of the budget committee. Bryant, an African American, cared a lot about Camden city, an economic basket case across the Delaware River from Philadelphia, which was 53 percent black, 27 percent Latino, and almost 100 percent poor, with a median household income of $23,400.

Despite that, there had been some interesting developments there in the prior decade or so, and Bryant, for good reason, wanted that to continue. I pledged to work with him to save some Camden projects in the budget. On the day of my speech, he declared my budget "courageous," and he helped to move it smoothly through the senate. Unfortunately, Bryant, a talented legislator, was convicted in 2008 of bribery.

Roberts, the majority leader in the assembly who would go on to become Speaker, was also from Camden County, but he cared more about the political benefits of giving rebates than I did, and he started yelling about unfair rebate cuts almost before my speech was done.

There were other ways to bring in a balanced budget, all of which would hurt someone, and I thought hard about increasing the sales tax. But I opted for the rebates for a very practical reason. The Republicans had done the same thing a few years earlier and they paid no political price. I never took a poll on this; I just thought it would be accepted. And sure enough, members told me in the following days that negative feedback from constituents was negligible. So I decided to let Roberts yell, while I stuck to my plan. I was governor and could take the high road.

Roberts and I didn't have a tension-free relationship to begin with. He came out of the Norcross political machine and that alone made for some initial problems. But we worked it out over the years and by the time he retired in 2009 we were getting along very well. I always had a solid relationship with Albio Sires, the prior assembly Speaker. Sires, now a congressman, is a Cuban native whose family got out soon after Castro took over, when Albio was ten. He was also mayor of the New Jersey town of West New York, and once I drove to see him in his city hall office about another problem. I was probably the first governor to set foot in that building, and employees there rushed from their offices to see me. I handed out some miniature basketballs and took pictures with a lot of people. It was a little boost to Albio's prestige and we got the problem resolved in about forty minutes. He remembered that.

Albio essentially agreed with Roberts on the rebates, but he wasn't as inflexible, and sometime in May, when it was clear this fight was going down to the final buzzer, I met quietly with him at an Atlantic City hotel where we were both speaking. I said I needed his help and he said, "I'll tell you what, if the senior and disabled rebates are restored, I'll support you. But don't say anything until the end and I'll be with you."

At a meeting in my office in June, when tempers were already over the edge, assembly leaders suddenly proposed $600 million in tax increases to pay for rebates. Coincidentally, I guess, most of those taxes were to be paid by the two biggest employers in Newark and Essex County. "That's not going to happen," I said. Bernie Kenny, the senate majority leader, almost jumped out of his skin. "We reject your proposal," he yelled. "We reject your proposal." Sires and Kenny almost came to blows over that one.

There were no assembly-senate negotiations for two days and that's when reports started circulating about the government perhaps shutting down. I gave orders to the cabinet to keep working, no matter what. But I'm not sure how long I could have held to that position if a budget didn't get done.

On Thursday, June 30, deadline day, Albio was watching a report on New Jersey public television about disarray in state government and the possibility of a shutdown. He concluded that the assembly revolt had to end. He told Roberts he was going to call me and talk. We basically came back to our Atlantic City agreement. I preserved the rebates for seniors and the disabled. And everyone else was cut severely. I also gave up some spending that I wanted.

Deal done.

I should mention that I had given Albio something else he wanted earlier in the year. He was a vehement advocate for having a state lieutenant governor, someone to become governor in case, as with McGreevey, the governor resigned or couldn't carry on. He yelled that no one should have the power I had running both the executive branch and half of the legislative. But really he thought it might be another slot for getting minority members into the leadership. The legislature had to put it before the voters as a constitutional amendment. I wasn't thrilled about it. After all I never would have been governor if we had had a lieutenant governor. But I told him if he could get the necessary support in the assembly and senate, I'd put it up for a vote. He did and I did. And the voters approved it in November.

After the budget passed with no increase in spending and no gimmicks (almost), I told John McCormac, the treasurer, I wanted to call the three companies that rate the credit-worthiness of government bonds—Moody's, Standard & Poor's, and Fitch—and lobby for a higher rating. Higher ratings mean lower interest rates.

He said governors don't do that; treasurers meet with rating agencies. No, I said, I'll do it, and he gave me a quick tutorial on the questions they might ask. I spoke to a few officials at each agency and made sure to ask each one where he lived. As I expected, about half said New Jersey. I gave them all a speech about how we held the line and how good it would be for the home state if they could honestly raise our rating, which had declined over the past fifteen years. One of them, Standard & Poor's, gave us an uptick from AA− to AA on one kind of borrowing and from A+ to AA− on another. Whatever that means.

One confession here: I wasn't an expert about budgeting when I became governor. I had been in the legislature thirty years, but never on a budget committee where I had to burrow into the numbers.

So I told McCormac: "I need help and if you can help me out of this situation, I'll kiss your rear end on State Street." He was a big guy and he offered a pretty big target, but it was one promise I never kept.

———

It's funny how things catch on. The state's great search for a new state slogan started with a spur-of-the-moment decision and probably created more interest and greater response than anything I did as governor. Plus, it was fun and it didn't cost anything.

A New York company named Lippincott Mercer, which gets a lot of money for figuring out how to promote brands so that consumers will buy Brand A rather than Brand B even when there's no difference, was hired by the Commerce Department before I became governor to come up with a new, sexy, tourist-luring slogan for New Jersey. About two months before I left office, they came back with "New Jersey: We'll win you over." For that, we paid $260,000.

I almost barfed when I saw it. Then I really got sick when I saw the price. As I said at the time: "It reminded me of when I was single and I'd ask somebody out and she'd turn me down and I'd say, 'Give me one date for a chance to win you over.'" In other words, it felt like a slogan for lonely losers.

This was more important than it may sound. Tourism, particularly in Atlantic City and other beach towns, is a big deal for New Jersey, bringing in about $32 billion a year and accounting for more than 400,000 jobs. I ordered a very unhappy tourism department to junk a planned advertising campaign built around the slogan and announced a statewide contest—let New Jersey residents write a New Jersey slogan. We unexpectedly got so many entries in the first few days that we had to establish a special phone number and Web site to handle the ideas. Newspapers wrote about it; talk show hosts talked about it. People stopped me at ballgames or restaurants to give me their ideas. My favorite was "New Jersey: Love at first sight." Some of the other ideas that came in:

"New Jersey: We Love You Baby!"
"We Don't Need No Stinkin' Slogan"
"New Jersey: Expect Delays"

"Come to New Jersey: We'll Tax the #&!@ Out of You"
"If We Can't Fix It, It's Not an Election"
"New Jersey: A State of Confusion"

In the end, we got more than 11,000 proposals. The Commerce Department cut that to one hundred, a list I carried around for a few days, asking everyone I knew for an opinion. Then, with my staff, we came up with five finalists and asked the state to vote.

The winner, with 3,373 votes: "New Jersey: Come See for Yourself." Other finalists: "The Real Deal," "Expect the Unexpected," "Love at First Sight" (my favorite), and "The Best Kept Secret." When I heard that last one, I said that had been true until August 12, 2004, the day McGreevey announced his resignation.

I haven't been governor for a while now, but people I meet still mention the slogan contest. Go figure.

———

Then there was the time I had to make clear I was ready to take New Jersey to war against Delaware to protect our sovereign prerogatives in the Delaware River. We wanted to help British Petroleum build a liquefied natural gas receiving station on the Delaware. The pier would have extended 2,000 feet into the water and some Delaware warmongers said that would cut across their state line. They based that provocative opinion on a pact drawn up by William Penn in the 1600s. Wayne Smith, the Republican majority leader in the Delaware House of Representatives, and the chief aggressor, introduced legislation authorizing Delaware's National Guard to defend "against encroachments on the territory" by New Jersey.

My response: "In a war, we'll kick their ass. We have the Battleship *New Jersey* trained on them right now." Assemblyman John Burzichelli of Gloucester County, on the Jersey side of the river, did point out one problem. We'd have to find the key to the *New Jersey* before we could deploy it for action.

Even without that, Representative Smith should have checked the comparative size of the two states. We have 8.6 million people; they have one-tenth of that, 853,000. We'd kick their ass anyway.

Jersey Boys, a musical about Frankie Valli and the Four Seasons, premiered in the August Wilson Theater on Broadway on November 6, 2005, and Rocco Landesman, who owned the theater, invited me and Mary Jo. Rocco, by the way, was his middle name, but he never used his actual first name, Fredric, even though that seems to go better with Landesman. Rocco, who produced such plays as *The Producers* and *Angels in America*, was later named by President Obama to head the National Endowment for the Arts. We sat a row in front of Rocco and his wife and he kept leaning over to tell Mary Jo that he'd give me $2 million if I ran for the U.S. Senate to replace Corzine. Corzine was going to have to appoint someone when he became governor, but there would be an election two years later. At intermission, we chatted with the actors Joe Pesci, whom I am friendly with, and Robert De Niro, who insisted that the state slogan should be "New Jersey: You got a problem with that?" I liked it. I just wasn't sure I had the balls to do it. After the play, which went on to win a Tony Award, we went to a reception a few blocks away, where they were serving White Castle hamburgers, an old Jersey delicacy. I was in line to get a couple of Cokes for myself and Mary Jo, and Tony Sirico, who played Paulie Walnuts on *The Sopranos*, was behind me.

Sirico tapped me on the shoulder and said, "You see this fucking broad behind me. If I don't get served in three minutes, I'm going to turn around and say, 'Can I fuck you?'" He didn't get served, and damned if he didn't make his pitch. She just laughed.

The thing about Sirico was that Paulie Walnuts was not exactly a fictional character for him. He had served time for armed robbery and was reputed to be a member of the Colombo crime family.

Tony Soprano, by the way, lived in my district in Essex County, which was no accident. The show was created by David Chase, who grew up David De Cesare in an Italian household in Essex. So when I was governor, we honored Chase at a reception at Drumthwacket. You learn a little about people at such an event. James Gandolfini, who played Tony, told me almost as soon as he walked in that he wanted to pose then and there for whatever photos had to be taken and get it over with. After that, if anyone asked for a picture, he said, "Wait until I'm drunk," his code for "I don't want to be bothered." Dominic Chianese, who played Uncle Junior, was the nicest of all. He would chat with anyone, even the statues. And my buddy James Gandolfini had just one request: he wanted to see the bedroom "where McGreevey had fun with that guy."

―――

I haven't been to the White House often, but two funny things have happened because of visits there.

Bill Clinton was president the first time. I don't remember the event, but I was with two black ministers from New Jersey, my friend Reginald Jackson, president of the Black Ministers Council in the state, and William D. Watley, of Saint James AME Church in Newark. When we left, Watley made sure to take a few of the monogrammed towels. I called him a few weeks later, pretending to be a Secret Service agent. He was away, but I told his secretary we were investigating the matter of some stolen towels at the White House and asked that the minister call back. But I left a fake number. I called him again a few weeks later and asked the Reverend Watley if he had received the same call I had about stolen towels. He said he had, but when he called back the number had been disconnected. He sounded a little nervous. "You have been had," I said, laughing. I don't think he agrees, but I thought it was funny as hell.

When I was governor, President Bush and his wife, Laura, hosted a dinner for governors and spouses attending the National Governors Conference. I'm not big on formal dinners; in fact, I hate them. But I told my wife we'd probably never get another chance to have dinner with the president of the United States. Governor or not, you still must pass through a metal detector to get in the White House. I walked through and set off the alarm, scaring everyone, me most of all. The guy behind me must have thought I was carrying a Kalashnikov. Security people quickly escorted me to another room, and left me there. I had no idea what set off the alarms. When the agents returned, one said he knew I was governor of New Jersey, but they couldn't figure out why the machine went off. They asked if I had a doctor's certificate saying I had a metal plate screwed in somewhere. "No metal plates," I said. Then they asked if I had had any recent medical procedures. I said I had had a stress test. And that was that. They figured I still had some of the radioactive dye circulating in me.

There was a cocktail hour (I was one of the few governors drinking Coke) and then every couple, one at a time, was escorted into a small room for a brief chat with the Bushes and the requisite photograph, which I really treasure. I may not have agreed with him much, but he was president of the United States. I know it's old school, but that's the way I feel. Then it was into the dining room, with marines acting as ushers, and the rule was that you couldn't sit with your spouse. Karl Rove's wife was next to me, explaining how much she hated Washington, and Governors Ed Rendell of Pennsylvania and Ruth Ann Minner of Delaware were at the table. I reminded Minner that I once contributed $1,000 to her campaign and suggested it was time to give it back. There were Sharpie pens on the table and everyone was asked to autograph each menu. I still have mine.

At one point, Rendell said: "Dick, do you know right now who is the twenty-third person in the order to succeed the president?"

"Eddie," I said, "I don't have a flying idea."

"You, Dick."

He then went through this litany of people, starting with the vice president and down though the House Speaker and the cabinet. Eventually, he said, it gets to the governors, and because New Jersey was the third state to join the Union I was the third in line once it got down to governors.

"I assume you're ahead of me," I said.

"You're right, and so is she," he said pointing to Minner, whose state was first. "This is an important table," I said. "We got three of the first twenty-three." For national security reasons, it probably should have been illegal for the three of us to fly on the same plane. You wouldn't want to lose numbers 21–23 in one crash. (Actually, I'm not sure Ed knew what he was talking about. I saw nothing about governors when I read the constitutional amendments about succession.)

After dinner, the Marine Corps Band played, and then we heard a concert by Marvin Hamlisch, who wrote the music for *A Chorus Line*. When Hamlisch finished we went into a lobby for more drinks, and Mary Jo and I found ourselves talking to Mitt Romney and his wife.

When we walked away, I told Mary Jo: "The guy is never going to be president. Too stiff." I felt confirmed during the 2008 primary season when all the Republican candidates were asked their opinions of the others. Romney was the most disliked. And speaking of Romney, I spoke during that primary period at a Morris County Chamber of Commerce luncheon. I said I knew that most of them were Republicans and told them that I was confused about their candidates: "The Mormon [Romney] has only one wife, but the Catholic [Rudy Giuliani] has had three."

Back at the White House, Mary Jo and I somehow wandered into a room where the Bushes were chatting with another couple. The president looked at me and asked one question: "Why didn't you run?"

———

I think I have less of a need to show off or look important than a lot of politicians, especially politicians who become governors. But one thing I hated was the title "acting governor." When Gerald Ford succeeded Richard Nixon, no one called him "acting president." I thought I deserved no less, and everyone knew it. So in the final days of my term, as something of a favor, both houses of the legislature voted unanimously to bestow the title "Governor" on anyone who serves six months or more. "One of the major pieces of legislation during my administration," I said as I signed the bill. "I feel great."

And then I took a razor blade and dramatically scraped the word "acting" off the glass of my office door. "I've got a future in building management," I joked.

A year later, there was a ceremony in the senate chambers to unveil my official gubernatorial portrait. I noted that I had chosen a New Jersey artist, Paul Jennis, but that I had warned him in advance that if the painting made me look too heavy "there might be two hangings— the portrait and you."

I pointed out how surprised my parents would have been had they still been alive. The only government building where they expected to see my picture was the post office. Then I said I was proud of what we had accomplished, especially in restoring normalcy to government, and added: "I consider myself a pretty lucky Irishman."

And that was no blarney.

In my State of the State speech five days before Corzine was inaugurated, I said with utter sincerity: "I'm sad that it's over, but I'm glad that it happened."

As I had said in some other speeches: "We set a record for New Jersey governors. No tax hikes; no scandals."

11

Keeping NFL Football
in New Jersey

Near the end of September 2005, the 27th to be exact, I pushed my gubernatorial authority as far as it could be pushed—into New York and under the Hudson River. That's when I managed to have traffic stopped in one lane of the Lincoln Tunnel so Jersey State troopers could escort Paul Tagliabue, then commissioner of the National Football League, from Manhattan to my Newark office as though he were the king of England. Tagliabue was key to achieving one of my top goals as governor: an agreement with the New York Giants and New York Jets football teams to jointly build a new stadium in New Jersey. I wanted him to feel loved and to know that I thought he was one of the world's important people.

Never had two American franchises in a major sport constructed a joint home field, and the Jets and Giants were not making it easy to get this done. Already, after arduous negotiations, we had a deal with the Giants to build—and pay for—an 80,000-seat stadium they would operate and control. The estimated cost was $750 million. We now wanted the Giants to accept the Jets as equal partners, and we wanted the Jets to sign on. Unfortunately for us, the teams and the men who ran them had been rivals for so long they had become the Hatfields and McCoys of the Upper East Side. They didn't like one another; they didn't trust one another; they had different cultures; they didn't like making concessions to one another.

They already shared a home field, Giants Stadium, which the New Jersey Sports and Entertainment Complex owned and leased out. But as the name reflects, the stadium, which opened in 1976, was built for the Giants. The Jets, like some poor relative scrounging for shelter, moved there in 1984 after decamping from the New York Mets' Shea Stadium. But they were never comfortable playing in a place named for the competing suitor for the affection of New York–area football fans. In fact, New York City was where they really wanted to be, and that was dragging out our negotiations. We were trying to force them into a corner—and a quick decision. But by September 27, the talks were close to collapsing.

The deal was not only important for New Jersey; it also had great meaning for the NFL. A joint stadium in the New York–New Jersey market could be the league's shrine—football's Yankee Stadium—and perhaps the most iconic sports facility in the country. Tagliabue wanted it as much as I did. For the others, there was a lot of money and many big egos at stake. The Giants were owned by John Mara and Bob Tisch, the chairman of Loew's Corp., the hotel and financial conglomerate, who bought 50 percent of the team from the Maras in 1991. The Mara family was as much a part of the National Football League's history as pigskin. Tim Mara, a New York bookmaker, bought the Giants in 1925 for $500, observing that "an exclusive contract for anything in New York is worth $500." Tim's son, Wellington Mara, was named co-president when he was fourteen, and he ran the team for decades—an owner who counted some of the players as his best friends. John was Wellington's son. (Wellington Mara and Bob Tisch were both fatally ill at the time; Mara died in October and Tisch three weeks later. Once, before he became so ill, Tisch put his arm around me and said, "Dick, why don't you come when we play in Philadelphia?" "Bob," I replied, "if you really want to bribe me, take me to the San Diego game.") The Jets are owned by Woody Johnson, the billionaire and very private scion of the Johnson & Johnson pharmaceutical empire. Others involved were Jay Cross, the Jets president, a sophisticated developer and financier whom I mocked for wearing suede shoes and ran the team for Johnson; Tagliabue, who played college basketball at Georgetown and was the NFL's attorney before succeeding Pete Rozelle as commissioner; and a bunch of high-powered lawyers. New York City's mayor Michael Bloomberg was also in there, angling to lure the Jets back to New York.

And now Tagliabue was coming to save the deal for the stadium, and the NFL. That alone put pressure on the Jets. As he said, "I'm from Jersey City, and I learned one thing: Where you have a meeting is sometimes as important as if you have a meeting. And that's why I came to you and let the Jets know that I'm coming to you."

Long before I was sworn in, I said that a new stadium in the Meadowlands was part of my game plan. In addition to the Giants and Jets, three other teams played in the sports complex at the Meadowlands, and all, like the Jets, were planning or ready to split. The Nets of the NBA hoped to move from the Izod Center in the Sports Complex to Brooklyn, the Devils of the NHL were on their way to a new arena in Newark, and the MetroStars, a Major League Soccer team, was moving to a new stadium in Harrison, with a new name, the Red Bulls. The Meadowlands also housed a racetrack and Xanadu, a 5-million-square foot, multibillion-dollar entertainment and shopping center, which was under construction. Xanadu turned out to be a major factor in our negotiations because the Giants, particularly Mara, worried that its traffic would disrupt ingress, egress, and parking on Sunday game days.

The Meadowlands brought New Jersey into the big-time sports market, and I thought we had to keep it a big-time sports center. "If we don't do anything," I said a few days before being sworn in, "what does the place become? Is it just a dying football stadium, a racetrack, and a place for shopping? I don't think that's right." Also, keeping two teams in Jersey for the long term, both named New York, was a sweet idea. Alliterative names like Jersey Giants and Jersey Jets might sound better, but you take what's possible.

Talks with the Giants to build a new stadium started shortly after I became governor, and they were contentious on their own, especially given the dissension on our side. George Zoffinger, appointed by McGreevey to be executive director of the New Jersey Sports and Entertainment Authority, was a hugely successful financier, but he thought a new stadium for the Giants made no business sense for the state. He was an amazingly stubborn advocate, not the type to discreetly voice objections privately; a man who essentially believes that anyone who disagrees with him is, by definition, wrong. He drove Mara crazy, and he didn't like me at all. He said once that I wanted a stadium because I was "a jock wanting to hang out with other jocks." I finally barred him from the talks and named two chief negotiators: Paul Fader, counsel to the governor whom I kept from the McGreevey administration, and Carl Goldberg, chairman of the Sports Authority. Fader was a talented and thorough lawyer; Goldberg a seasoned negotiator and an expert on complex real estate deals.

To me, people like Zoffinger didn't understand the psychological value of the Giants and Jets; that they had become, like Springsteen and the Shore, part of the morale and sociological fabric of the state. Over time, no one would care if the Sports Authority made a million dollars more or a million less; they would care that the Jets and Giants remained in New Jersey and the sports complex was economically successful.

That's why even before I became governor I called the Wilpons, Fred and his son, Jeff, who own the Mets, and offered to build them a stadium if they moved the franchise across the river. As expected they turned me down, but I told them that maybe the publicity could get them a better deal in New York, where they were playing second fiddle to the Yankees.

Bloomberg said he thought the whole thing was pretty stupid. "I can't imagine why any sports team would ever want to move out of New York," he said.

To which I said: "He should realize the Jets, Giants, and Nets all moved from New York. Clearly, he knows as much about sports as I do about synchronized swimming."

One quick story about Zoffinger and Bloomberg. Bloomberg always seemed to me to be arrogant and self-important and I decided, before meeting him, that I didn't like him. Pretty stupid, but that was the street kid in me reacting to a billionaire. We finally met at a parade after I became governor and he told me that Zoffinger had forbidden him from landing his helicopter at the Meadowlands when he went to Jets' games. I called Zoffinger and said, "You may not like him and I may not like him, but he's the mayor of New York and he can land his helicopter at the Meadowlands whenever he wants." Fifteen minutes later, Bloomberg called to say, "Thank you," and added: "The executive director of your Sports Authority is a jerk-off." "Mr. Mayor," I said, "you're not telling me anything I don't know." Then he invited Mary Jo and me to have dinner with him and his girlfriend. I accepted reluctantly, but he couldn't have been more delightful. After that, we spoke many times on the phone and at events in New York City. I consider him a friend and I give him an A for his job as mayor.

Zoffinger and I got into another fight after I told the *New York Times* that I had problems with the Xanadu development. One of those problems was the potential of traffic delays getting in and out of the complex. When he saw the headline, he called and scolded me a little condescendingly, saying, "Do you know what you've done to the Mills stock?" Mills Corp. is one of the developers. But to rectify the situation, he had drawn up a clarification statement for me to release. I told him not to bother sending it to me. "George," I said, "I don't own the stock. I could care less. It's not my job to worry about it." In the end I concluded he was just a two-faced guy. He'd leak stuff to the press and lie about it and he kept vital information from the commissioners. He really wanted to run the Sports Authority like an all-powerful czar.

Meanwhile, the Giants, in exchange for paying for a new stadium, asked for seventy-five acres of land for the stadium, a training facility, and related retail and restaurant development. They would pay rent on the property. The state would also have to spend tens of millions to retire the debt on Giants Stadium. Even if I agreed with Zoffinger, the Giants had a lot of leverage. Their lease, which ran to 2028, obligated the state to maintain the stadium at "state-of-the-art" levels. Giants Stadium was thirty years old and little had been done to modernize it. By the Giants' estimate, $300 million was needed to make it "state of the art." And for sure, they'd be back ten years later for another $300 million or so.

The seventy-five-acre request gave me a chance at one meeting to demonstrate that I may not be a Tisch or a Mara, but I wasn't going to be pushed around. Accompanying the Giants' owners to various meetings was a guy from the Hammes Co., which builds and redevelops stadiums. At one meeting he said, as though it was already stipulated, that the Giants needed one hundred acres. "Last time, you said seventy-five acres," I said, and he denied it.

"You're a damned liar," I said, and I'm sure my face was as red as a Jersey tomato. The young snob was trying to get one over on me and I was not going to take it. Fader pulled a piece of paper from his briefcase proving that they had asked for seventy-five acres. I said I wanted the guy from Hammes out of the meeting, I couldn't trust him, and I didn't want to deal with him again. He never returned.

By design, two major parties were missing from the table: the Jets and Xanadu's developers, Mills Corp. and Mack-Cali Realty. Both they and the Giants, according to their leases, had the right to sign off on anything major the others wanted to do. But we decided to operate like jugglers with three balls in the air. Don't try to catch them all at once; you're sure to drop at least one. We figured if we signed the Giants, we could go after Xanadu, take care of its problems, and then go for the Jets.

At that point, the Jets didn't want to speak to us, anyway. They had bet on a stadium on the West Side of Manhattan to be built if New York got the 2012 Olympics. It was unlikely; New York was competing against London, Paris, and Moscow, and we didn't think it would happen. But we couldn't say it. What could be more unpatriotic after 9/11 than to wish anything negative for New York? But we let the Jets know if the stadium didn't get built we'd like them to be 50–50 partners in the Meadowlands. This was not necessarily something the Giants wanted. To them, the Meadowlands was their home and if the Jets came, they should come again as tenants in the Giants home. I was confident the deal would be attractive enough to overcome any Giants qualms.

Although, it sure didn't look like it on March 9, a day when the shit hit the fan. The Giants said the deal was off and then called a press conference to announce it. I followed with an impromptu news conference of my own in the Meadowlands' icy parking lot, where I said I believed an agreement would yet be signed. This was the Giants' home. I had no idea if I had any right to be so confident, but I knew I had to say something to demonstrate that I wanted to preserve the marriage.

Besides Xanadu, the Giants' big concern on March 9 was my refusal to sign a deal prohibiting future governments from imposing a tax on luxury suites, ticket sales, or other revenue producers unless it was deducted from their rent. As I told the *New York Times* in an interview, "If a future legislature approved a tax, don't you think the team would pass it on to their customers?" I, in fact, had included a luxury-suite tax in my budget, and from their reaction you would have thought I was trying to hold up a mom- and-pop store. I agreed to drop the proposal, but I couldn't commit future governments.

It took a few weeks, but when I thought everyone had cooled down, I called the Giants and got talks started again. I hated to, but I caved in on the tax issue, agreeing that any additional tax would be offset by reduction in rent up to the total annual rent of $6.2 million. The Giants also got the right to negotiate further with Xanadu. We gave them forty-five days, which turned out to be not nearly enough. We finally signed off on April 13, after Fader and Goldberg negotiated for four frantic hours in the Giants' lush wood-paneled offices with dramatic black-and-white photos of Giant greats on the wall.

At a press conference the next day, I said this was the best deal for the taxpayers of any stadium deal in the NFL. Later, some people said New England's was better, but ours was damn good. In any case, the Giants were signed up.

Now for the Jets.

A big break came in June, a month before the Olympic Committee was to vote, when the West Side Stadium faded away for lack of political support. "It's full-blast now on negotiations with the Jets," I said, probably a little too triumphantly. "It's bad news for New York, but it's good news for New Jersey, and hopefully, we can keep the Jets here for as long as possible."

Mara slowly came around to the idea of sharing a stadium with the Jets. The savings in construction costs if two teams shared the burden was too great to pass up, plus it seemed stupid to have two new stadiums a few miles apart. And with the wonders of modern digital lighting and signing, the stadium could be lit in Giants blue when they played and Jets green when they played. And they would sell the naming rights, so the stadium would be named for some company instead of either team. (Even this created unexpected political pyrotechnics. At one point Allianz, a German insurance company that had had ties to Nazi Germany, was the frontrunner. Talks ended with them after a violent reaction in New Jersey and New York. "Shaming Rights," shouted a New York Daily News headline.)

Things got quiet for a while and I told Laura Mansnerus of the *New York Times* that both the Jets and Giants want to be partners, but "like in any dating adventure, there are always disagreements. But I'm sure they'll eventually go to the altar." Also, the Giants and Xanadu had still not reached agreement.

When the two teams got into serious talks, the Jets had one objection above all others. They could not bear to have the Giants' training field virtually adjacent to the new stadium. It would re-create the humiliating sense that they were tenants on Giants' property. Nor did it help that when the Giants revealed their version of a new stadium a "Giants" logo dominated the façade.

By September, the Giants-Xanadu impasse was a big problem and I said if they didn't reach an accord by the 16th the Sports Authority would vote to abrogate our deal with the Giants. As with all these things, talks stretched to meet the time available, and finally, at 11:05 A.M. on the 16th, a deal was struck. Xanadu developed a plan that satisfied the Giants worries about game-day logistics, and it agreed to give the team $15 million to cover any disruptions caused by construction. It was, as Mara said, a real hurdle to get over. Meanwhile, the teams kept talking but were getting nowhere, and tempers kept getting meaner. After one disagreement between Tisch and Goldberg, Tisch wrote this e-mail to Fader: "I really tried to have a positive conversation with Goldberg. I cannot listen anymore to him insulting me and John Mara, being unbearably self-serving. And I am too old and too secure to listen to any more of his rantings. I honestly called him with the sincere goal of having a constructive discussion. Sorry, I'm done eating shit. Steve Tisch."

Eventually, I felt it necessary to set another deadline, September 29, for the Jets to sign on to the deal. As I told Woody Johnson, "the time for dating is over." And then, in a surprise to us, the Jets informed the NFL that they were still discussing plans in New York for a $1.35 billion stadium in Queens. They obviously figured they could get the two states into a bidding war. Fader and I both went ballistic and he called Charles Bagli, who covered the story for the *New York Times*, and unloaded. "Jay Cross flat out told us after the West Side stadium fell through that he was intent on bringing the Jets to a new stadium in New Jersey, with the Giants as full partners," he said. "He was not at all interested in Queens. It would appear that he was less than completely truthful with us. It would appear he now wants to go to Queens." Fader said the Jets could build in Queens, if they wanted, "but don't prevent New Jersey from getting a world-class stadium. Be honest and truthful."

One of our advantages was that Bloomberg, who supported a Queens stadium, was up for reelection in November and he didn't want to tell New Yorkers that he might spend millions of dollars to help the Jets return to the city. That was another reason we were determined to get a deal done quickly—before election day. I like Bloomberg, but competition is competition. Another plus for us was that neither Jon Corzine nor Republican Doug Forrester, the two gubernatorial candidates, were big fans of the stadium. Either one might kill it, so everyone knew it was better to work with me as governor. I asked the Sports Authority to meet on the 29th and unilaterally rescind the lease agreement that said the Jets had the right to sign off on anything that was developed at the Meadowlands. That would return us to a Giants-only stadium. What was the harm? The Giants would have the stadium and the Jets, if they got nothing better, would have to play there. But they would be tenants only, which would torment them. I wasn't sure I had the votes, but I thought it was worth the shot. I was gambling that the Jets wouldn't gamble on losing both New Jersey and Queens. To make the Jets gulp a little when they thought about the stakes of that gamble, Goldberg told them once that without an agreement they were out after 2012, when their lease expired and "you can play in a high school stadium in Staten Island."

And a couple of days before I set the deadline, I spoke to Woody Johnson and bluffed a little. "If you don't do a deal with the Giants by deadline," I said, "I'll get the votes to do a deal with the Giants. If you don't get Queens you'll never be more than a tenant. You'll have no input. And even though you have the right to prevent a new stadium and can try to prevent it, I will take you to court on that issue. And I will do everything possible to make you lose." That was a little less brazen than it seemed. NFL bylaws said no owner could prevent a fellow owner from doing their own business, so I thought I was pretty safe.

Then on the 27th, Tagliabue called to say he wanted to meet with us and he wanted to do it in New Jersey. And I arranged for his private lane in the Lincoln Tunnel.

——

After we talked some, I told him I was going to call Mara, Tisch, and Johnson and arrange a 5 P.M. meeting at Goldberg's office. (Tisch lives in California and he'd be on a speaker phone.) We'd either make real progress or, as we say in Jersey, fuhgetaboutit. The Jets would be in the cold. I thought this would be a terrific deal for everyone and I told Mara and Tisch and Johnson, "If this doesn't work out, I'm nominating all of you for president of the lucky sperm club," born rich, but not smart. In addition to the owners, the others there that night included Joe Shenker, the Giants lawyer, Jay Cross, Fader, Goldberg, and Roger Goodell, the NFL attorney and now commissioner.

Tagliabue set down the one condition that may have gotten everyone in a negotiating mood when he said he would not permit the Jets to keep the Giants from a new stadium. And he threw in a sweetener when he said because league rules provide $150 million for any team building a new stadium, he thought we could get $300 million for a facility housing two teams. Still, the training facility continued to be an issue, and I finally broke the bottleneck by agreeing to give each team twenty acres for their own complex—the Giants behind the racetrack, and the Jets within twenty miles of the stadium. That was the compromise that delivered the Jets; the Giants agreed after they became certain that it was the last real problem. The land for the Jets would be valued at between $10 million and $15 million, but it was a money-making investment for the state. The Jets then trained on Long Island, so they worked in New Jersey and paid state income tax only on game days—about ten a year, counting pre-season. With them practicing in Jersey, we could collect the tax for every day they and everyone else from the team worked. Given the salaries paid quarterbacks and offensive tackles, not to mention head coaches, we thought this was very good business for New Jersey.

Overall, Fader calculated in an op-ed column he wrote for the *Record* of Bergen County in June 2010 that the state stands to realize

$31.3 million from the stadium annually in taxes, rent, and operating-expense savings that the teams will now pay. That's $15.3 million more than the $16 million in rent the Giants paid on the old stadium. Stadium design was another obstacle. Cross, a trained architect, considered himself a design maven, and this was important to him. In the end we decided the teams could work that out between themselves, and they agreed ultimately on 82,500 seats, with two hundred suites. (The cost ended up being about $1.6 billion.) When we finished at 11:30 that night, we decided to hold another meeting the next day. We were close to the goal line, but it wasn't easy getting there. Fader had noticed that Tagliabue during the night had scribbled on a piece of paper: "train wreck."

I wasn't at the meeting on the 28th, but both Fader and Goldberg told me there was still a lot of ill will in the room with everyone dancing around the outstanding disagreements. It was Goldberg's birthday, and the mood was suddenly lightened when his assistant, Cynthia Pasaoane, brought in a birthday cake she bought at Baskin-Robbins that was half green for the Jets and half blue for the Giants. Little figures of a Jet and a Giant were on the appropriate colors. She cut a green piece and gave it to Mara and a blue piece and gave it to Johnson, and told everyone they had to be in good cheer because it was Carl's birthday. I'm told from then on, as though they had gone through a bonding ritual, things moved more smoothly and they pretty much resolved every outstanding concern.

On the 29th, the deadline I had imposed, the Sports Authority met, and by 11 A.M. they figured to take up the question of whether to unilaterally rescind the Jets' right to approve whatever the Giants did at the Meadowlands. The Jets and Giants had decided to meet before then so the last lawyerly phrases could be written. Tisch took the red-eye from L.A. to be there for the deal signing, and John Mara came from Sloan-Kettering Hospital, where his father was dying. Fader called someone and asked what Cross, a serious dresser, was wearing. When told it was a dark, pin-striped suit he figured the deal was in the bag. "That sounded like a press conference suit," he said. But it wasn't until 2:34 P.M. that Joe Shenker sent Goldberg and Fader the revised Memorandum of Understanding with the note that said simply, "As Promised."

At a news conference at Giants Stadium later that afternoon, I added my signature to the agreement and said almost giddily, "The deal is now sealed. . . . Our grandkids and our great-grandkids can root for the Big Blue and the Gang Green right here in their own backyard." You could tell that Johnson was still a little disappointed that he didn't get his own stadium in New York. Mara enthusiastically told the press he was confident the two teams would "create the premier football and entertainment complex in the NFL." Johnson, more subdued, said, "This hopefully will be a great partnership."

Even then, the Giants and Jets had a few issues to iron out between them. And so it was that finally at 11:44 that night, Shenker sent his last e-mail to Goldberg and Fader: "john [Mara] just signed and jay [Cross] and steve [Tisch] signed by fax from their homes so we r all done and I'm going home to sleep for first time since tues!"

Clyde Haberman, a *New York Times* columnist, called to ask if New York could have its name back. I told him anytime; that it rankled me whenever I went to a game and saw *NY* painted on the field instead of *NJ*. But I gave him fair warning that "I wouldn't put it past myself late at night to go onto the field and do away with the *Y* and paint a *J*. I'm capable of that."

Wouldn't that be fun some Halloween night?

Three years later, the Jets held a ceremony to open the new training facility. By then, much to the aggravation of their fans, the teams decreed that anyone buying season tickets must first purchase a personal seat license. When I spoke at the ceremony, I couldn't resist asking Johnson whether he had to pay for his seat on the dais. I couldn't tell if he smiled. It was a pleasure to get to know the Maras, Tisches, and Johnsons throughout the stadium negotiation process. They are all classy, intelligent, and down-to-earth good people.

One last important detail: During the negotiations, former commissioner Tagliabue and Roger Goodell, then league attorney, now commissioner, committed to supporting a Super Bowl at the new stadium if it got built.

That game will be played in 2014. It will be the first Super Bowl ever played outdoors in a cold weather region.

12

Bowing Out as Governor

A couple of weeks before the gubernatorial election in 2005, the *New York Times* ran a story with the headline: "If Codey Had Run, He Might Have Won in a Walk." That's true. Both private and public polls were showing I was the most popular politician in the state, well ahead of both Jon Corzine and Doug Forrester, the Republican gubernatorial candidate who lost by nine points

"Democrats and Republicans, pundits and professors, and just ordinary residents are gushing over a longtime member of the entrenched Trenton elite, a man widely viewed as an antipolitician of sorts, a bona fide Jersey guy, complete with rumpled suits, comb over and spaghetti-and-meatballs belly," is how Jeffrey Gettleman put it in that *Times* story. I frankly resented the belly blow, and I understand Gettleman studied philosophy at Oxford, so I'm not sure what he knows about bona fide Jersey guys.

So if I was so popular, how come Jon Corzine became the governor of New Jersey and I went back to full-time work in the State Senate? Simple answer: Jon Corzine is very rich, worth hundreds of millions of dollars, and I am not. If that sounds like I'm a little bitter at Jon, I'm not. I get along with Jon. I don't think he's a bad human being.

But did I think it was fair? No. I had been in government thirty years. I worked my way up, I got an unexpected chance to show my skills at being governor, the people liked the job I was doing, the McGreevey scandal was starting to fade into the background, and then this Wall Street financier comes along and says, "Step aside, young man." I was being dislodged by Corzine's money, not his superior ability or standing with voters. So while I wasn't bitter at Jon, I was at my party. When he announced his candidacy just three weeks after I was inaugurated, I thought party leaders should be saying, "Hey, wait a minute. We just got through a scandal. Let's give Codey some breathing room instead of slapping him with a candidate for his job right away. Let's give this thing more time. It looks like he's doing a good job and the public likes him. Maybe you, Jon, should stay in Washington and Codey should run for governor." But we were in New Jersey and that's not the way it worked. The county bosses, who have a lot of power, could only see dollar signs going from Corzine to their organizations, just as they did in 2000 when he first ran for the U.S. Senate. I don't think there's another state in which I would have been denied the nomination.

The calendar didn't help either. Because the New Jersey primary is in June, I had to decide by late January or early February 2005 whether to battle him for the nomination. I had been governor only a few months then and I wasn't yet as popular as I would later become, or as well known.

Corzine's life had really been across the Hudson River, on Wall Street, where he gained fame and fortune as the CEO of Goldman Sachs, the investment company. His U.S. Senate campaign in 2000 was his maiden venture into electoral politics, and quite a venture it was. He spent about $60 million of his own dollars to win the office. God knows what he was willing to spend to become governor, a job he wanted even more. His money could buy enough negative advertising to make Mother Teresa look bad. And I am no Mother Teresa. During three decades in the legislature I had cast more than enough votes, when put in the hands of a skilled ad agency, to make me look pretty stupid. Also, questions had been raised about whether my brother Robert, an assistant attorney general at the time who had tried some of the state's more complex cases, had been given undue consideration for a special assignment so his pension could be increased. In truth, the pension had nothing to do with the assignment. And I had nothing to do with his salary or pension, but the issue was out there. Over five or six months, the ads would have pounded at my popularity. It would have been unpleasant for me; the boys, especially Chris, would have hated it; and Mary Jo would have suffered. She takes any criticism aimed at me very personally.

Still, I thought real hard about running. I loved being governor, I loved the way it allowed me to highlight the issues I cared about and I was damn good at it. Besides, the challenge of running as the underdog against a mega-millionaire had gotten my political juices surging. Corzine was concerned enough to initiate a preemptive strike and announce his candidacy unusually early, on December 2, 2004, before I had enough time to find the toilet paper in the governor's bathroom. He had also begun quietly rounding up support from the twenty-one county Democratic leaders, who have tremendous influence over party business in New Jersey. No surprise there. Over the years, he had donated millions to their political operations. Plus, he could pay for his own campaign, so they didn't have to spend time raising money for him. Without organization support and with no chance to raise anywhere near the money Corzine had, I figured he'd clobber me.

That's New Jersey politics.

Anyway, here's how it all played out, beginning with Corzine visiting my home on August 17, 2004, five days after McGreevey disclosed his homosexual affair with Golan Cipel and announced that he would resign on November 15. Corzine was clear he wanted to run for governor, and his morning visit was really the first little scrimmage to feel me out about my intentions. There would be others. When Corzine arrived, Mary Jo, who cares little about politics and less about gossip, asked how his wife was. "I don't have a wife," he said. "I'm divorced."

"Oh, I'm sorry, I didn't know that," she said. "Who was the woman I saw you with when I met you?"

"Mary Jo, that was my girlfriend at the time," he said, a little smile poking through his beard (making him eventually the second consecutive elected New Jersey governor with a beard, so to speak). "She wanted to be my wife. And that's why she's no longer my girlfriend."

That girlfriend was Carla Katz, who turned out to be something of an embarrassment when he actually did run for governor the following November. Katz was president of the Local 1034 of the Communications Workers of America, which represents thousands of government employees in New Jersey. She and Corzine had had a two-year romance, and it was revealed during his gubernatorial campaign that he had given her a $470,000 loan, allowing her to buy her former husband out of a home they owned. He then forgave the loan. Not surprisingly, Local 1034 endorsed Corzine, and people then wondered how tough he would be when he had to negotiate new union contracts.

Later, it was learned, the package he gave her totaled about $6 million and included enough cash for her to buy a $1.1 million condominium in the same Hoboken building in which Corzine lived. There was also a trust to pay for her children to attend college and a sport utility vehicle that cost about $30,000. I'm not sure why he was so generous. His explanation to the State Ethics Board: "It is not easy to disengage from a relationship that is both personal and political."

Anyway, once he and Mary Jo cleared up his marital status, Corzine got down to business. He said he wanted to run for governor if the opening occurred. Under state law, there would have been a special election had McGreevey's resignation taken effect before September 3. I didn't have the resources or the name recognition to compete in a special election, and I wasn't even sure I wanted to. "Jon, that's fine," I said. "I have no problem with it."

Then he said he was getting a lot of criticism for being the candidate of the bosses. I said, "Jon, that's going to happen because that's what they want and you're their candidate." The next day, on August 18, Corzine said publicly that he told McGreevey he was prepared to run for governor, but McGreevey "made it clear in our conversation his absolute intent to serve until November 15, 2004. I accept the decision as final." And final it was, assuring that I would definitely become governor on that day.

Presuming that would be the case, I told Corzine in our meeting that I was inclined to serve my fourteen months as acting governor, until January 2006, and not seek my own four-year term. That was an error.

It was all thrust upon me so quickly. There was an avalanche of pressure, and I couldn't think about being governor and campaigning at the same time. Running for governor in a tough primary is murderous work. I'd have to sprint around the state day and night for six months, sacrificing home life, my movie dates with Mary Jo, the teams I coached, and everything else important to me. All while working to be a successful governor. Plus, running is very costly. There are no New Jersey–based commercial television stations, so candidates must buy time in New York and Philadelphia, the first and fifth most expensive markets in the country. I'd be spending countless hours on the phone, pleading for campaign contributions, often from reluctant donors. After all, Corzine would be expected to win, so why make an enemy of the next governor by giving to his opponent.

I was so set against running that I was ready to say so publicly in September 2004, until I was persuaded that I'd be making myself an ineffectual lame duck before I started. Some friends even recommended that I ask the county leaders to stay neutral in case I changed my mind. That really set me off. "I'm announcing," I said with uncharacteristic anger, "and don't tell me not to again." The whole idea of being governor was obviously getting to me. I should have taken their advice and gone to the leaders. By the time I was ready to fight for the job, it was too late. Corzine had them lined up.

Corzine and I didn't talk much after that until October, a month before I actually took over. He came to the house again and this time the conversation was a little different. I said I had grown more comfortable with the notion of being governor, I was confident I could do it well, and seeking my own four-year term was a possibility. "Jon, I'm still inclined to think that I wouldn't run, but I'm not going to tell you that I'm not," I said.

My thinking (really my pipe dream) was I would perform so well that people, including party leaders, would say, "Hey, why get rid of the guy? Let's keep him, and keep Corzine in the Senate and don't put his seat into play." That way I could have gotten the nomination without a bloody primary and without sacrificing the rest of my life for six months. But in this life, in New Jersey, that ain't the way things happen.

Corzine and I had no more sit-downs until I decided definitely not to run. But like a good defensive coach, he figured out my strategy and countered with his early December announcement before I could establish myself. Polling then showed me 40 points behind him in a Democratic primary. By January, I was only 10 points down, which was a pretty phenomenal gain.

One poll, though, was a severe disappointment. The poll done by Fairleigh Dickinson University, my alma mater, was fine; it was the accompanying press release that hurt. The poll came out on January

10, one day before the State of the State. It showed that about 65 percent of voters knew who I was, as opposed to about 25 percent two months earlier. Forty-eight percent who knew of me had a favorable opinion and only 7 percent gave me an unfavorable rating. In a head-to-head match, I was 14 points behind Corzine among Democrats who had voted in previous primaries. Among all voters, I was even. Without campaigning for one minute, I was gaining ground quickly.

But the headline on the press release was "Richard Who?" because 35 percent still didn't know who I was. That took a lot of wind from my sails. I called the polling people and said I was embarrassed to be an FDU alum.

Still, every time I met with the press, someone would ask whether I was going to run against Corzine. Usually I would say I was still weighing my options. Once, I said, "Listen, I'm not going there. You want to, ask me about the election. But I'm not going to talk about Wall Street versus Main Street." I heard the Wall Street comment pissed off Corzine, but didn't he understand where I was coming from? I felt that after three decades in government I was being cast aside for some privileged Johnny-come-lately who hadn't paid his dues. So I enjoyed sticking it to him.

I held two meetings with my top advisers before coming to a definite decision, the first at Drumthwacket, immediately after my State of the State, the second a few days later at my home. Participants included Harold Hodes, my lobbyist buddy who has been around state politics for decades and was once Brendan Byrne's chief of staff; Pete Cammarano, my chief of staff; A. J. Sabath, labor commissioner and political adviser; Bill Maer, a lobbyist and political consultant; Larry DeMarzo, an old friend and aide who rejoined my staff when I became governor; John McKeon, an assemblyman from my district, mayor of West Orange, and longtime ally; Maureen, my longtime aide; and a few others. Not there were Steve DeMicco and Brad Lawrence, probably the most talented Democratic consultants in New Jersey who run a firm called Message & Media. I had done a lot of work with them. DeMicco was instrumental in the redistricting fight, but they had signed on with Corzine. I was not happy when he told me.

The meetings lasted about ninety minutes each, and there was a lot of disagreement, sometimes even anger. Pete and Harold strongly urged against running, arguing that I would be buried by the money Corzine could put into TV ads and by his political support. Maureen and McKeon were the leading advocates for running. A. J. and Bill were with the antis. Larry leaned toward my running, but he had been away from politics for a long time and didn't argue strenuously. The way it worked out, the people who had been with me from my early West Orange days wanted me to run; the people I met in Trenton argued against it. Everyone was kind of astonished when Hodes, who is usually content with five-word statements, made what was for him an impassioned speech against running.

McKeon, fuming, thought that was no accident. He suspected that Hodes, the leading Democratic lobbyist in the state, wanted to be able to tell a Governor Corzine that he had talked me out of running. I don't think that was his motive at all, but as I said, there was a lot of animosity.

Those who wanted me to run said Corzine's money advantage was offset by my performance as governor and the fact that people liked the way I governed. I thought that was a little naïve. And Corzine wasn't twiddling his thumbs. On the day of the State of the State, an anonymous Democratic source told the *Star-Ledger* that Corzine was just waiting for that speech before buying ads and organizing public commitments from the leaders who had committed privately.

Maureen and Pete remained semiestranged for a long time after that. Once, after the decision had been made, Maureen saw Pete coming in to see me, and asked sarcastically, "Coming to wave the white flag?" I think if she had a knife in her hand she would have stabbed somebody. A year later, she still referred to Pete as "the other side."

At the second meeting at my house, which was larger than the first, we decided if we could get support from just one important leader from outside Essex, my home county, we might give it a shot. We chose Joe Ferriero of Bergen County, a short, scrappy street guy who almost single-handedly had moved Bergen from Republican to Democrat. Larry DeMarzo thought it a mistake to essentially give Ferriero a veto over our decision, but there was no real choice. I needed some base outside of Essex. Pete drove up to meet with Joe, and they talked for two hours over a few beers in a tavern in Old Tappan. Joe never budged.

He had committed to Corzine and was going stay committed. Joe, like me, coaches youth sports, and he had to leave for a game. Pete, trying everything he could think of, followed him home and said he would sit in the stands so they could resume the conversation after the game. Joe told him not to bother. Pete called me and reported the bad news. When I called Joe later, he said, "Dick, you've done everything great. My people love you. And if I asked my people who's the best choice, they would probably vote for you. But for me, Corzine is a natural choice." I said, "Joe, I think for your people it's a mistake, but do what you have to do."

By now, things were getting ugly. I was angry at Corzine for getting in the race before I had a chance to show my stuff. Jon was mad at me because he mistakenly thought I was planting rumors about him. He knew I had relations with the press and the Trenton political world that he couldn't match, and it worried him. The political class could talk about nothing else: Will Codey do it or won't he? On a Friday night in January as I was trying to rethink all the options, I went to watch Chris's Montclair-Kimberley team play against a high school in Newark. I looked up and there was Josh Margolin of the *Star-Ledger*. A lot of reporters were trying to find me, and he had figured out where I would be. I didn't talk to him during the game, but afterward I shook some hands and we spoke for five minutes. I didn't tell him what I was going to do, but I did say the process was "agonizing."

In another oddity of timing, it was three days earlier, on January 25, that I had had my confrontation with Craig Cartin, the shock jock, and received rave reviews for standing up to him. But I knew the race had become impossible.

That weekend, in an annual Jersey tradition—one the good-government people just hate—the state's Chamber of Commerce hired a private train with eighteen or so cars to take elected officials, lobbyists, and assorted other political types to Washington, ostensibly to meet with the congressional delegation. In reality, it's more of a party than a business trip. I flew down rather than take the train.

On the way back, Pete got a call from Steve DeMicco, who wanted to put me and Corzine together so I could get out of the race. I had already put out signals that I was ready to throw in the towel, and this was to make things formal. Corzine chose a little Italian restaurant he frequented near the Holland Tunnel in the Tribeca section of Lower Manhattan. He was a regular there. Pete and I drove without the troopers. DeMicco drove Corzine, and he said later that Jon was buoyant, although because of my popularity he still wasn't 100 percent convinced I would get out.

We met in a large, private backroom that Corzine had arranged for with tables lined up in the middle. It was like the two bosses with their two consiglieres. It turned out to be relatively pleasant. We swapped stories and I agreed to announce my support for him. I reminded him that I told him months ago I wouldn't run, but he had forgotten. He said, "Dick, you never told me you weren't running. This is the first time I ever knew that." I figured he just never believed it. At the end, we looked each other in the eye and we shook hands. And that was that.

All the while, given the setting, DeMicco said later he was thinking of a similar meeting scene in *The Godfather* when Michael Corleone goes to the men's room, comes out with a gun that had been planted earlier, and shoots the two men he's been talking to. "I was trying to figure out where the gunman was coming from," DeMicco said.

The ride home was gloomy. Pete didn't say a word and neither did I.

I made the announcement on January 31 in the governor's office. "In life," I said, "each of us is hopefully given our moment in the sun, but a moment is worth only what you do with it. I have tried to the best of my ability to use my moment wisely, to lead our state through this difficult time."

I said I planned to spend the rest of my time as governor working for increased financing for the mentally ill and stem-cell research. Period.

Once elected, Corzine had to name someone to fill his seat in the U.S. Senate. Polls showed I was far and away the top choice of New Jersey voters. Bill Bradley was urging me to talk to Corzine about the job and so were Democratic leaders in the U.S. Senate. But I really didn't want it. I'd be in Washington three or four nights a week and Mary Jo would be in New Jersey. That was not a life either of us wanted. I never asked Corzine to consider me and he never asked me about it. Even though I didn't want the job, I thought I deserved to be asked. I felt like Rodney Dangerfield getting no respect. To end all the speculation, I eventually announced that I didn't want to be considered. I said in talking to the press that I told Mary Jo "it was an early anniversary present. And she told me I was cheap." Corzine named Robert Menendez, a congressman from Hudson County who coveted the office.

I think I could have beaten Forrester by 15 points, instead of the 9 that Corzine won by. Hell, more than 10,000 voters wrote in my name, unprecedented in New Jersey, even though I sincerely urged people not to waste their vote that way. But I'm not sure I could have beaten Corzine in the primary. And had I lost the primary I couldn't have gotten anything done in the last half of my governorship. I would have been a lame duck with a lot of people gunning for me.

So maybe it all worked out for the best.

13

The Past . . .
and the Future?

The headline in the *Star-Ledger* of October 1, 2009, shouted out that my senate presidency was coming to an end, and not by choice: "Codey's Control Crumbling."

The first paragraph of the story by my friend Josh Margolin was a straightforward summary of what had happened: "Richard Codey's hold over the Senate presidency and all its attendant power collapsed yesterday when a dozen members of his own party turned their backs on him."

After plotting for years, the bosses, led by George Norcross, had finally corralled a majority of senate Democrats to unseat me and install Steve Sweeney from Gloucester County in South Jersey. And by late September, at Senator Ray Lesniak's home in Elizabeth, they came together to formalize the deal.

There, in a meeting attended by six white men and no minorities and led by Norcross, agreements were made to determine the Democratic leadership in the senate, the assembly, the important legislative committees, and even the state Democratic Party. Participants besides Norcross and Lesniak were Sweeney, Senator Bob Smith from Middlesex County, Essex County executive Joe DiVincenzo, and State Democratic Party chairman Joseph Cryan, an assemblyman from Union County, where he was also an undersheriff. Norcross had never been elected to anything and wasn't even a party leader, and DiVincenzo had never been elected to the legislature. And yet there they were, helping to dictate the legislative leadership. That was just plain wrong.

After settling on Sweeney, which by then was a formality, they shook hands on Sheila Oliver of Essex County to become the first female African American assembly Speaker, succeeding Joe Roberts, a Norcross man from Camden County in South Jersey who wasn't seeking reelection. Oliver, a friend of mine, first ran for the assembly in 1993 on a reform ticket in Essex County, but she wasn't elected for another decade. Her promotion to Speaker would reverse the previous geographic alignment by putting a South Jerseyan in charge of the senate and a North Jerseyan in charge of assembly.

But as pundits and others pointed out, Norcross, with his influence over Sweeney and the five other South Jersey Democrats, was sure to have a lot of sway in the senate, and DiVincenzo would have a lot of say in the assembly. Oliver, after all, was on DiVincenzo's payroll as assistant county administrator. She wasn't even invited to the meeting in Lesniak's living room, although Cryan, who would leave the meeting as her majority leader, was. But she was the prize given to DiVincenzo in exchange for my Essex County scalp.

He told the *Star-Ledger* that his goal was to make sure that Essex held on to one of the leadership spots. "If Senator Codey had the votes, we would be with Codey," he said. "He did not have the votes. That's it." Of course, I may have had the votes had two of the other three senate Democrats from Essex County, Nia Gill and Theresa Ruiz, voted for me. But Ruiz, who was DiVincenzo's deputy chief of staff, and Gill, who was the attorney for the Essex County Improvement Authority, voted for Sweeney. Both are talented legislators, but DiVincenzo had made clear they were voting his way on any decision he made regarding the senate leadership. But DiVincenzo's real goal was just to knock me out.

There has long been a myth that there is a tradition in the legislature of sensible power sharing between the North and the South, but Norcross has skillfully exploited that tradition over the years to the South's great benefit, something he could do because he so tightly controlled the southern votes in both houses. Roberts's departure gave him a chance to argue yet again that power ought to be split evenly. But in truth, South Jersey has about 23 percent of the state's population and its influence is way out of proportion. At one point, for instance, the Speaker and Budget Committee chairman in the assembly and majority leader in the senate all came from South Jersey. I believe in diversity in the leadership, but we had geography trumping ability. Crazy.

I should say the following about Norcross's control over the southern legislators, some of whom are quite talented. He does not by any means control every vote, and he doesn't want to. I'd say that 98 percent of the time he doesn't really care how the legislators vote, and they are free to do what they believe is right. It is in the leadership caucus votes and the 2 percent of votes that may affect business or things of interest to him where he asserts his influence. On these votes, legislators who are part of his machine, and want to remain so, rarely have an option. They vote as Norcross wishes or they are pushed into political oblivion.

The deal to force me out was two years in the making. And looking back I think I started to become vulnerable on a dreary political morning in late October 2007, when we received new polls on a state senate race in Monmouth County—and they weren't good. Ellen Karcher, a Democrat and an ally, was seeking a second term in a tough, dirty, but very winnable election when scandal erupted. Instead of paying normal residential property taxes on the 8.7-acre parcel she and her husband owned, which would have amounted to about $39,000, the couple was paying the much lower farmland assessment, about $24,000. The farming consisted of raising and selling about a half dozen Christmas trees each year.

Once the story hit the papers, Karcher's poll numbers against her Republican opponent, Assemblywoman Jennifer Beck, collapsed faster than a botched soufflé. On the morning of October 24, Frank Baraff, my main political adviser, was on the phone. He and I had been studying the same polls. "Other than her saving someone's life, how do we save her ass?" I asked.

"I shouldn't say this to you because you'll fire me," Frank replied. "But she's a corpse. I think it's irretrievable." I agreed. When she had run her first race four years earlier and defeated John Bennett, my old senate co-president, she represented herself as Miss Clean. Ethics was her issue and now she had broken the trust—if not, technically, the law. And you couldn't very well say, "Well, look, she paid $24,000."

That would only show that she was a very rich lady trying to game the system.

I sunk $2 million of senate majority PAC (Political Action Committee) money, which I raised for senate Democrats, into that race and we lost. I might have won another Democrat seat elsewhere by reallocating that money. And he would have owed me. But Karcher was an incumbent and I was committed to her, and I followed through on that commitment. Two South Jersey candidates, Jim Whelan and Jeff Van Drew, received about $2 million of senate majority PAC money between them and won, and both voted for Sweeney. Knowing full well they wouldn't vote for me in a leadership fight, my job was still to get Democrats elected, not secure my leadership post for the future, and that's what I did. I was also a little blindsided by two senators with whom I had met individually early in the process. Both of them looked me in the eye, shook my hand, and promised I could count on them. And then voted against me.

How, you may be asking, did I have all those millions to dispense in the first place? There is something called the Senate Leadership political action committee, which is controlled by one person: the senate president. The PAC gets contributions from lawyers, lobbyists, doctors' groups, teachers' groups, and just about any other group with an interest in legislation. I targeted the senate races that Democrats could win and distributed the money to candidates who needed the help. It's a lot of power and just one of the reasons people will do a lot to get the job.

Anyway, losing Karcher's vote opened the way for the beginning of Sweeney's offensive, which started immediately after the 2007 elections. Bernie Kenny from Hudson County was my majority leader, but he decided not to seek reelection that year. Several senators expressed interest in the job, but in the end Paul Sarlo of Bergen County was the only publicly announced candidate, and I supported him. Behind the scenes, though, Sweeney was quietly building on his southern base and lining up votes.

Sweeney kept telling me and Sarlo that he wanted to be budget committee chairman. As late as an hour before the Democratic caucus was to vote for majority leader, he came to my office to play out a calculated charade to buy time to corral votes in caucus. He complained that Norcross was pressuring him to run and then phoned Norcross and told him he was in my office telling me that he wasn't really interested in being majority leader. What nonsense! He returned a half hour later to say he was running and confident he had a majority in the caucus.

He and Norcross had picked up two votes in the south when Van Drew and Whelan defeated Republican incumbents. So they had the six South Jersey votes and he smartly lobbied other new senators—some even before they were elected.

The important votes against Sarlo were Lesniak, a senior senator and sophisticated power broker, and two from Middlesex County, Barbara Buono and Smith. The Middlesex people had never before partnered with Norcross in senate leadership fights, and that was kind of unexpected.

When the caucus met, I was unanimously reelected as senate president, then, looking for more time to lobby for Sarlo, I made a motion to delay the vote for majority leader. The vote on the motion was deadlocked 11–11, with one senator still to vote, Loretta Weinberg from Bergen County. Weinberg cast the decisive twelfth vote against the motion. Sarlo had told me before the vote that he was assured that Weinberg would do nothing to hurt him. Such is politics.

Sweeney came to my office after the vote, almost apologetically, and said, "I'm going to work to earn your trust back."

"Does that mean you'll support me until the end of the term?" I asked. He said, "Absolutely." The term would end after the 2011 senate elections, so he had to support me in 2009, when senate leaders were elected for the following two years. I asked him to sign a letter to that effect, which he did. "I, Stephen Sweeney, will support Dick Codey for senate president in 2009."

Sweeney told PolitickerNJ.com two years later when he was gathering support for the senate presidency that he said to me, "You want a letter? Come on. What is this? This is a joke." He never said anything of the kind. He just wrote the letter.

Then he said two other things that were laughable. One was that by dating the letter he meant that his pledge was good only for that day. The other that I insisted on the letter because of my "paranoia."

What paranoia? I had real enemies and they were gunning for me. And 2009 was their year.

There were twenty-three Democrats in the senate, so twelve votes were needed for victory. Theoretically, the Republicans could have taken sides and altered the balance, but that would have been contrary to accepted tradition.

The group at Lesniak's had at least eleven votes when they sat down to meet, although outside the South only one had publicly committed—Brian Stack, a senator from Hudson County and the popular mayor of Union City. Stack was particularly important because he was the first northerner to announce for Sweeney. Because it is unusual for local candidates at one end of the state to receive money from the other end, the *Star-Ledger* noted at the time that the money stirred "speculation that South Jersey Democratic boss George Norcross already is trying to line up allies for post-election skirmishes over the leadership of the next Legislature." Pretty prescient.

In addition to Stack and the southern six, there were Lesniak, Buono of Middlesex, who, they agreed, would become majority leader, Smith from Middlesex, and Nicholas Scutari from Lesniak's Union County. He committed to me up until it looked like I didn't have the votes anymore. He stayed with me as long as he could and took a considerable amount of pressure from high-ranking Union County officials who threatened to throw him off the party ticket.

DiVincenzo had said he would be happy to supply the thirteenth and fourteenth votes, but not the twelfth and decisive vote. Ultimately, though, they persuaded him to commit, making it easier to convince others who could have gone either way that Sweeney was the future and I was the past.

Lesniak had said for a long time that he was neutral in the race and hadn't made up his mind. I knew he was full of shit, and I told him so. I knew he had tried to recruit Senator Sandra Cunningham of Hudson County during the summer, and when she spurned him he asked that she at least not commit. But she stuck with me and I have a lot of respect for her. Others, including some I still consider friends, were under intense pressure and forced to switch their votes to Sweeney. Those who resisted and stayed committed to me were

Nick Sacco, Joe Vitale, John Girgenti, Bob Gordon, Shirley Turner, and Ron Rice. I say thank you for that support and friendship.

When Norcross left the Lesniak meeting he said he was driving to see Sarlo to tell him Sweeney had the votes and it was time to sign up. He was ready to offer him the Budget Committee chairmanship and a spot on the 2011 committee to redistrict the state—the same committee I headed ten years earlier, which led to Democrats taking over the legislature. Sarlo called me the next day and said, "Dick, you know I have to look out for myself." Sarlo got his chairmanship, which is what he wanted, and his vote made twelve even without DiVincenzo's two. While the Lesniak meeting was at it, they also decided that Assemblyman John Wisniewski of Middlesex should become state party chair, which he did. They decided this without anyone even representing Governor Jon Corzine.

Once the bleeding started I couldn't find a tourniquet to stop it. I felt like Chuck Wepner, the old heavyweight fighter from New Jersey who was known as the Bayonne Bleeder. I tried to hold senators in line, and I asked the Essex County mayors to publicly endorse me and put pressure on DiVincenzo, which they all agreed to do. The mayors stayed with me all the way—except for the most important, Cory Booker of Newark, who caved in. I considered Booker a friend, but he bolted as soon as he became convinced that Sweeney would get the needed votes. We've seen each other since, we say hello, and I'm always civil. But was I deeply disappointed in him? Yes. As I told him, "If ever there's a war and we're in the same foxhole, I'm running the hell out of it."

How did I lose DiVincenzo and the two Essex Democratic senators? First, you have to know that the Serbs and the Croats have nothing on Essex when it comes to holding a grudge. This went back to 2002, when I supported Tom Giblin over DiVincenzo for county executive. "The thing about Essex politics," former Democratic U.S. senator Robert Torricelli told the *Star-Ledger* after Sweeney had put together his coalition, "is that no slight is so small or insignificant that twenty years later it would not make all the difference. That's what happened here. . . . These are people who have been waiting for the moment for more than a decade. And the only thing that mattered was the final game."

DiVincenzo kept telling people that he was angry because he had renamed the South Mountain sports arena in Essex County, which houses a skating rink, after me and I never showed the proper appreciation. He even complained at the Lesniak meeting, "I named an arena for the guy and he fucked me." I thought that was childish talk. But at one rally where we both spoke, I said: "He names an arena for me. Now, he looks like he wants to put me on ice. You just never know in politics."

It was really Stack and DiVincenzo who made the difference. Had I held them, I would have won.

In the months before the final vote, the effort to unseat me really reached bizarre proportions. Someone started a Web site called CodeyComeClean, which posted links to any newspaper stories that hinted at anything negative about me. Someone eventually connected the site to a Web site operator in Missouri named Steve Israel. Call me cynical, but somehow I had trouble believing that someone in Missouri spent his nights worrying about the senate leadership in New Jersey. Eventually, a connection was found between Israel and Steve Ayscue. Ayscue, Norcross's leading political consultant, ran a blog whose name told you everything you needed to know about him: "The NJ Hired Gun Blog."

Then Mark Sheridan, a New Jersey attorney with expertise in insurance and a former council to the Republican State Committee, started sending out OPRA (Open Public Records Act) requests about the agency I had sold. Sheridan's father just happens to be the chief executive officer of Cooper Hospital in Camden, where Norcross is chairman of the board of trustees. Sheridan said his client had nothing to do with Norcross or his father. I don't believe him.

And then there was an anonymous whistleblower who likened himself to "Deep Throat" and started calling me in July 2009. Someone, he said, was working overtime to discredit me. Anytime anyone named Codey was identified in any financial transaction—mortgage, credit report, anything—it was flagged and sent to these people. It addition, the caller said they were investigating rumors about my sister, a nun, and my two brothers. The caller mentioned a "George" from the South, but never named Norcross.

He spoke to my aide, Justin Davis, and Justin said, "We're talking about the same person from South Jersey, George?"

"Oh, yeah," said the caller.

"George Norcross?" Justin asked. And the caller replied: "I didn't say any names, but you know who it is." I let Tom Moran, a *Star-Ledger* columnist, listen, and he wrote: "For anyone with affection for Codey, this was a painful moment. He was swinging at Norcross and missing." That was because Norcross was never named, and who knew who made the calls anyway. But I thought the caller's answer to Justin's question was proof enough about Norcross.

I had lived with this for months, and before I went to Moran I asked two former heads of the criminal justice department in New Jersey and an individual who had been head of the Secret Service in New Jersey to listen. Based on the caller's apparent intelligence and the facts that he was obviously not scripted and didn't ask for anything, they concluded my "Deep Throat" was legitimate.

Funny thing, before I lost the senate presidency there was a moment in July of 2009 when, hype aside, what really may have been the biggest Jersey scandal of all time seemed to give me a chance to run for governor. Corzine was running for reelection, but he was faltering in the polls, and then this crazy scandal hit that involved some of the usual players—mayors, assemblymen, city housing authority members—and some very unexpected players: five rabbis. Talk about incongruous perp walks! The *New York Times* published a photo of four guys, all with their hands cuffed behind their backs, being led to a police van. Two were in short-sleeved shirts and jeans or slacks; the other two in long dark coats, black hats, and beards as fluffy as cotton candy. In all, there were forty-four people charged, twenty-nine from New Jersey. Many of the rest were from Brooklyn.

Actually, there were two separate scandals, one involving politicians taking kickbacks, the other rabbis laundering money. The connection was the informant, Solomon Dwek, a one-time developer and the son of a rabbi, who had been indicted a few years earlier on a $50 million bank fraud.

To help investigators (and himself), Dwek secretly taped meetings with the rabbis, who allegedly agreed to launder money for him when he told them he was trying to hide assets. The case moved to public corruption when one of the alleged money launderers—not a rabbi—introduced Dwek to a politically connected building inspector in Jersey City. Things accelerated from there.

The case was brought by the U.S. Attorney's office in New Jersey, which had been headed by Chris Christie until he resigned to run against Corzine for governor. But Christie still received priceless publicity from the story. Despite the millions Corzine would spend on the campaign, he knew his chances were grim. And he apparently called the White House to see if officials there could provide a graceful exit from New Jersey.

About the same time, Newark's Mayor Booker commissioned a poll that, I am told, showed me defeating Christie by about eighteen points. I never saw the poll, but Booker told me, "Obviously, you're the choice." I then received two calls from high-level national Democratic operatives. In the first, I was told that Corzine had indicated he wanted out of New Jersey; in the second I was asked if I might run if Corzine got out. I said I might. But when I spoke to Corzine he said he wanted to run for reelection and I assured him of my support if he stayed in. That was the end of it until Christie trounced Corzine in November.

———

In the end, here's the summary. I did the legislative map, which allowed the Democrats to win the assembly and senate. Without that map nothing would have been possible. Then in the midst of the McGreevey scandal I became governor when it looked like the party was dead. As I said before, we never raised taxes and we never had a scandal. I raised more money than any presiding officer in the history of the state to keep the party in power. After fourteen months in office, we gained seats in the legislature, and a Democrat, Corzine, was elected to succeed me. I made life better for the state's mentally ill and I tried like hell to get money for stem-cell research that potentially could make life better for many more. I also wrote a casino bill that has served the state well for decades. I don't think there's any more I could have done for the party or New Jersey.

I sought reelection for senate president even though I knew it would be an ugly, disgusting fight, and a lot of friends and reporters advised me not to do it. I stayed in for one main reason: I wanted the senate to remain an independent body controlled by its members and not outside forces. I don't regret it. Somebody had to make the statement.

Do I think my career is over? No. Will I run for reelection to the state senate? I don't know. Would I run for governor? I don't know. Would I run for the U.S. Senate? I don't know. Any of those possibilities could happen. I just don't know.

But until I make those decisions, I can still look back in wonder that a kid who grew up in a small apartment above a funeral home in Orange and went to three high schools before he could graduate had an opportunity to sleep with the first lady of New Jersey; to have dinner at the White House with President George W. Bush, Mrs. Bush, and all the other governors and their spouses; to meet with the former Soviet president Mikhail Gorbachev; to negotiate successfully with people named Tisch, Mara, and Johnson for a great football stadium in New Jersey that will host the 2014 Super Bowl; to play golf, have dinner, and laugh with Tom Coughlin, the Giants' Super Bowl–winning coach; to throw out the first pitch at a game for my favorite team, the Cincinnati Reds; to exchange phone numbers with super stars like Jay-Z, Beyoncé, and Brooke Shields.

And most important, that I had a chance to bring about positive change for the people of New Jersey, my home state. I am forever in their debt.

Index

About the Authors

Richard Codey, who has been in the New Jersey legislature for thirty-eight years, served as the minority leader of the state senate for four years, co-president for two, and president for six. He was governor of New Jersey for fourteen months from November 20, 2004, to January 20, 2006.

Stephen Seplow is a former reporter and editor for the *Philadelphia Inquirer* and was a Pulitzer Prize finalist in 1995.